The Library of International Relations
Series ISBN 1 86064 080 X

Series Editor: Professor Alex Danchev
Department of International Relations, University of Keele

The Library of International Relations (LIR) brings together the work of leading scholars in international relations, politics and history, from the English-speaking world and beyond. It constitutes a forum for original scholarship from the United Kingdom, continental Europe, the USA, the Commonwealth and the Developing World. The books are the fruit of original research and thinking and they contribute to the most advanced debate in both political theory and practice and are exhaustively assessed by the authors' academic peers. The Library consists of a numbered series and provides a unique and authoritative resource for libraries, academics, diplomats, government officials, journalists and students.

The Library of International Relations

THE STRUGGLE FOR LEBANON

A Modern History of Lebanese–Egyptian Relations

NASSER M. KALAWOUN

I.B.Tauris *Publishers*
LONDON ● NEW YORK

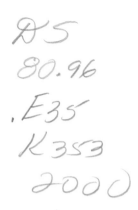

Published in 2000 by I.B.Tauris & Co Ltd
Victoria House, Bloomsbury Square, London WC1B 4DZ
175 Fifth Avenue, New York NY 10010
Website: http://www.ibtauris.com

In the United States and Canada distributed by St. Martin's Press
175 Fifth Avenue, New York NY 10010

ISBN 1-86064-423-6

A full CIP record for this book is available from the British Library
A full CIP record for this book is available from the Library of
Congress

Library of Congress catalog card: available

Typeset in Garamond by A. & D. Worthington, Newmarket
Printed and bound in Great Britain

Contents

Acronyms

AU	Arab Union
CENTO	Central Treaty Organization
CIA	Central Intelligence Agency
LL	Lebanese Lira
MECAS	Middle East Centre for Arabic Studies
MEDO	Middle East Defence Organization
MENA	Middle East News Agency
NATO	North Atlantic Treaty Organization
PLO	Palestine Liberation Organization
PRO	Public Record Office (Kew, London)
SSNP	Syrian Socialist Nationalist Party
UAC	United Arab Command
UAR	United Arab Republic
UN	United Nations
US	United States

For my parents, Mounif and 'Aisha

Acknowledgements

I am grateful to a large number of people and many institutions that helped me in this project. First, I would like to thank the Hariri Foundation for granting me a scholarship to further part of my research. His Excellency Dr Ghazi al-Ghosaibi was a great source of encouragement and inspiration. I am indebted to Professor Tim Niblock for his patience and valuable comments when he supervised the original work at Exeter University.

I am thankful for the help offered by the following institutions. In London: the Public Record Office at Kew, *al-Hayat* newspaper, the British Library, the Senate House and School of Oriental and African Studies' libraries. In Paris: the Sorbonne library. In Cairo: the al-Ahram Centre, AUC and Cairo University libraries. In Oxford: the Centre for Lebanese Studies and St Antony's College library. I am grateful to the many people who granted me interviews, in particular the late Mahmud Riad, Raymond Eddy, Dr Boutros Boutros-Ghali, Munah al-Sulh, Anwar al-Jamal, Salim Nassar, Hamdi al-Tahiri, Sulaiman al-Firzili, Nadim Dimashqieh and Amin Huwaidi. I would also like to mention some of those who provided me with informal advice, in particular Dr Charles Tripp, the late Nazih Ayubi, Abdul Majid Farid, Dr Ali al-Dine Hillal, al-Sayyid Yassin, Peter Colvin, Nadim Shehadi, Muhammad 'Awdeh, Professor Tony Allen, Dr Beverley Milton-Edwards, Dr Imad Bashir and Nada Itani. Jill Devey was generous in helping to produce the original manuscript. I wish to extend my gratitude, too, to Dr Lester Crook for his precious help in editing this book. Finally, my thanks go to Soraya, Mounif and Nabila for their patience and understanding in allowing this book to come to light.

NMK
London

Preface

Inter-Arab relations are rarely the subjects of serious books due to the explosive and sensitive nature of Middle East politics in the modern era. Official archives of newly created states, if they exist, are not open to researchers, and memoirs reveal little beyond self-justification. Economic realities are lost under a heap of political rhetoric, and former security and political officials are tight-lipped. But the challenge proved worthwhile. This book concerns the evolution of relations between Egypt and Lebanon during the last 50 years. It relies essentially on a Ph.D. thesis covering the 1952–70 period. It focuses on the attempt of President Jamal 'Abdul Nasser to impose Egyptian hegemony on successive Lebanese governments, as a part of his drive to control the Arab political system. This attempt enabled Nasser to create a power base among Lebanese Muslims, in order to check the Lebanese regime's traditional inclination towards the West.

Although President Sham'un's administration was able to manipulate the Iraqi–Egyptian rivalry between 1952 and 1955, it proved impossible to do so after President Nasser opposed the Baghdad Pact. This development placed the Lebanese regime, as well as other undecided Arab states, on the defensive in their relations with Egypt.

The Suez War of November 1956 ushered the start of political conflict between the Lebanese and Egyptian governments over the nature of relations with the West. President Sham'un viewed his acceptance of the Eisenhower Doctrine as an expression of his will to conduct relations with the West free from Egyptian dictate. As a result, Nasser held an informal political alliance with the Lebanese opposition, and they worked together to undermine Sham'un's foreign policy drive.

The union of Syria and Egypt in February 1958, forming the United Arab Republic (UAR), accentuated the internal divisions between the government and opposition in Lebanon, and led subsequently to the outbreak of the Lebanese civil war of 1958. The Lebanese–UAR conflict was taken to regional and international arenas, culminating in the US military intervention of 15 July 1958 – to protect the Lebanese regime.

The period of co-existence between the Lebanese and the UAR governments began after Fu'ad Shihab succeeded Sham'un as president of Lebanon in September 1958. This process continued well after Syria's cessation from the UAR in October 1961, and proved to be beneficial for both Egypt and Lebanon. For Lebanon, Egypt provided a shield from the Arab radical forces of Syria, Iraq and Palestinian guerrillas. For Egypt, Lebanon became a favourable ground to launch political and media campaigns against rival regimes in the Arab east.

The Cairo Accord of 1969 saw the culmination of Egypt's active role in Lebanese politics. Sadat's different national and regional agenda contributed to Cairo's retreat from the affairs of the Arab east, and Lebanon in particular. The Camp David Accords led to a political and diplomatic boycott between Beirut and Cairo, which lasted for over a decade. Since the early 1990s, Egypt has returned to play a calculated role in Lebanese foreign policy – but always in conjunction with Damascus.

Introduction

The analysis of the foreign policies of developing countries has been dominated by three approaches. First, the psychological approach views foreign policy as a function of the impulses and idiosyncrasies of a single leader. Kings, presidents and prime ministers are the source of foreign policy; war and peace become a matter of personal taste and individual choice. But the main drawback of this approach is that it ignores the internal, regional and international contexts within which foreign policy is formulated and implemented. Secondly, the Great Powers approach views foreign policy as a function of East–West conflict. The foreign policies of developing countries are seen as lacking autonomy and as reacting only to external initiatives created by foreign forces. The weakness of this approach is that it neglects the role of domestic factors and implies that developing countries lack a genuine foreign policy. Thirdly, the reductionist or model-builder's approach views the foreign policies of developing states as determined by the same processes and calculations that shape the foreign policies of developed countries. But this approach does not account for such factors as modernization and dependency status in the global system.[1]

The Third World countries are, in fact, an integral part of a world system in which they are affected by global stratification and inequality. Therefore it is important to see how external constraints affect the foreign policy-making process and the international behaviour of states in a given region. According to Ali E. Hillal and Bahgat Korany, developing countries are faced with three essential issues in the field of foreign policy. The first issue is the aid/independence dilemma, which may lead to a trade-off between the need for foreign aid and the maintenance of national independence. Thus, while President Nasser was more concerned with independence, Sham'un was more interested in extracting foreign aid (via his acceptance of the Eisenhower Doctrine). The second issue is the resources/objectives dilemma, which refers to the ability of leaders to pursue objectives falling within their country's capabilities. Nasser, for example, followed an unfeasible goal in his campaign in the Yemen in the 1960s, which led to the draining of his country's resources. The third issue is the security/development dilemma, which refers to the difficult choice faced by most developing countries on whether to feed the population or defend the nation. In this scenario, the main objective of foreign policy can become the acquisition of external resources for the sake of societal development. A case in point was Nasser's acceptance of 'unconditional aid' from East and West to help improve Egypt's infrastructure, but at the same time freeing domestic resources for the purchase of arms.[2]

Despite some common socio-economic features and interests, the Third World is not a unified bloc. The Arab world, for instance, possesses several characteristics, which predominate over inter-Arab variations and make it a distinct group in many respects from other developing countries. These shared characteristics include an Islamic component, cultural homogeneity, Arabic language and the concentration of a vital economic resource in certain Arab countries – oil.[3]

The Arab regional system, which was created at the end of the Second World War, represented the will of the newly independent Arab states to co-ordinate their efforts in the various fields. The Alexandria Conference of Arab States, held on 25 September 1944, ignored calls for the creation of a unitary state with central political authority, and opted instead for a loose confederation among independent and sovereign states. Lebanese Maronite Christians were wary of any drive toward Arab unity under whatever guise. A special resolution was attached to the Alexandria Protocol by which other Arab states undertook to respect Lebanese sovereignty. This resolution stated that:

> The Arab states represented on the Preliminary Committee emphasize their respect of the independence and sovereignty of Lebanon in its present frontiers, which the governments of the above states have already recognized in consequence of Lebanon's adoption of an independent policy, which the Government of that country announced in its programme of October 7, 1943 [the National Pact], unanimously approved by the Lebanese Chamber of Deputies.[4]

The adhesion of Lebanon to the Arab League Pact placed this country in the Arab orbit, specified the conditions of co-operation with other Arab states, and consolidated the national and geographic entity of Lebanon. This, in effect, set limits on the Arab nationalists' drive towards seeking political unity with Syria, in particular. But the compromise created a link between the internal politics of Lebanon and Arab regional politics, putting Lebanese stability at risk whenever Arab relations passed through crises.[5] Moreover, competition between Lebanese sects for a bigger stake in the state rendered the latter irrelevant not only during the civil war but also at any difficult juncture. This could blur the distinction between the president (a Christian Maronite), the prime minister (a Sunni Muslim), the speaker of parliament (a Shi'a Muslim) or any other official or communal leader, as each would claim to 'speak on behalf of Lebanon'. Therefore political legitimacy of the state is accepted only if it is built on a religious and sectarian tolerance.

The Lebanese regime adopted a sort of self-defined neutrality characterized by solidarity with the Arab world, conciliation and mediation between Arab countries in time of conflict, and a pro-Western tendency in international politics, which nevertheless steered clear of violating the spirit of non-alignment.[6] This was designed to ensure internal stability between the two major communities of Lebanon, i.e. Muslims and Christians. Moreover, it aimed at making possible the survival of a country with limited resources, which relied extensively on commerce with the Arab hinterland, banking services and tourism.

Egypt's leading position in the Arab system was underscored by the establishment of the Arab League headquarters in Cairo under an Egyptian Secretary General. Egypt's position was further enhanced through the maintenance of an informal alliance with the Saudi dynasty to oppose the attempts of the Hashemites in Iraq and Jordan to influence regional politics. To this end, the Egyptian government opposed in the early 1950s the creation of a Middle East Defence Organization (MEDO), sponsored by Britain and France in particular. The Lebanese government played no major part in inter-Arab quarrels during this period, despite being seen by Egypt as a soft target for foreign penetration into Arab ranks.[7]

THE STRUGGLE FOR LEBANON

The main feature of the global system during the 1950s and the 1980s, was the polarization between two blocks headed by the two superpowers, the Soviet Union and the USA. Arab states possessed modest military and economic capabilities creating a state of dependency on the global system in order to achieve structural development. This restricted the ability of any state, including Egypt, to manipulate inter-Arab economic relations since inter-Arab trade was limited in scope. Moreover, none of the Arab states were affluent enough to offer financial aid to the rest in order to develop influential relationships.[8] Arab states tended to quarrel, not so much over *whether* or *not* to accept foreign aid but *when* and *from which* side. A case in point was the Egyptian objection to Lebanon receiving US aid under the Eisenhower Doctrine, due to the America's earlier withdrawal of its offer to help build the Aswan Dam in Egypt. It was clear, also, that the USA succeeded gradually in substituting France as the protector of the Lebanese state, created in 1920 – and by implication the protector of Lebanese Christians. Egypt, on the other hand, took up the banner of protecting Muslim interests under Arab nationalist ideology.

The instruments of political warfare were used extensively by all Arab states, though with varying skills, to achieve their objectives. These instruments included diplomacy, propaganda, cross-frontier alliances, subversion, cultural activities and the threat of the use of force. The conditions were ripe for the use of these methods in the Arab states due to internal cleavages, political instability and the extensive permeability of Arab societies. Both strong and weak states used these political instruments to defend their interests or attack their rivals. Egypt, for instance, employed its political instruments to the full in the 1950s and 1960s in order to compensate for its limited military and economic capabilities. The Egyptian government's domestic strength and the appeal which Nasser's policies attracted in other Arab states facilitated the use of these instruments. This allowed Cairo to apply real pressure on other governments and to achieve considerable hegemony in the Arab system.[9]

The reaction of other Arab states to the attempted imposition of Egyptian hegemony on the Arab system increased the levels and sources of conflict among the various regimes. This inter-Arab conflict was fuelled by political ideologies, held by emerging political forces (the Ba'thists, communists and Syrian nationalists etc) which campaigned against the artificial nature of the state and territorial framework. This in turn gave rise to numerous merger schemes such as Greater Syria, the UAR and the Arab Union of Jordan and Iraq. The concentration of geopolitical and ideological capabilities encouraged the Egyptian regime to believe that Egypt was entitled to lead the Arab system. Egyptian governments pursued various methods at their disposal aggressively to destabilize the region and change the status quo. For instance, the use of affirmative diplomacy was aimed at cowing other governments. But when this failed the Egyptian regime resorted to launching propaganda campaigns in order to mobilize opposition forces in other Arab states to revolt against the established regimes (Iraq and Lebanon in 1958).

Lebanon's constraints outnumbered its capabilities during the period under study. First, Lebanon was a fringe state in both the Arab and the Middle East systems (which included Israel, Turkey and Iran). This limited its policy choices in time of conflict. Secondly, Lebanon was dependent on Syria as the gateway (by land) for its commercial activity with the Arab hinterland. This factor acted as a major constraint since it was impossible to establish links with Lebanon's second neighbour, Israel, in view of the complexities of the Arab–Israeli conflict. Thirdly, Lebanon's military capability was inferior to that of Israel and Syria. This fact created uncertainty and forced Lebanon to resist interference from either of these two neighbouring states, as it was certain to invite a reaction from the other side. Fourthly, the Lebanese political system was fragile and was threatened paradoxically by both Arab unity projects and inter-Arab conflict. This fragility was intensified by the fact that the Lebanese regime did not adopt a clear ideology, save a token consensus on national unity between Muslim and Christian communities. Therefore it was easy for any external power to appeal and support one or more of the various communities, in order to apply pressure on the Lebanese government.

The Lebanese laissez-faire economic system allowed Lebanon to make up for the deficit in its balance of trade. This was achieved through the invisible income resulting from banking services and tourism. However, the positive element here was conditional on the maintenance of internal stability and favourable regional circumstances (e.g. the flow of Arab petro-dollars).

The relationship between Egypt and Lebanon passed through different phases of co-operation and conflict. Chapter 1 deals with the impact of the regional defence pacts on the relationship between a core state (i.e. Egypt) and a fringe state (i.e. Lebanon). Chapter 2 deals with the impact of the Suez War and President Sham'un's acceptance of the Eisenhower Doctrine. Chapter 3 analyses the effects of the union between Syria and Egypt (the UAR) and the subsequent dispute between the Egyptian and Lebanese governments in its regional and international aspects. Chapter 4 focuses on the normalization of UAR–Lebanese relations and accounts for this era of co-existence. Chapter 5 accounts for relations following the break up of the UAR, and analyses the side effects of the Arab Cold War. Chapter 6 explores Lebanese–Egyptian relations after the June War of 1967, and pays special attention to Egypt's new role as a mediator between the Lebanese government and Palestinian guerrillas. Chapter 7 accounts for Egypt's withdrawal from Lebanese affairs due to Sadat's peace strategy with Israel and its legacy. Since 1990, efforts to revive mutual ties have focused on economic agenda under political guise. It is clear that the first six chapters covers in detail a period of two decades, while the last one deals with a period of near three decades. The reason lies in the fact that the Lebanese–Egyptian relationship during President Nasser's tenure (1952–70) was the subject of my Ph.D. thesis. This era was extremely important because Egypt was trying to undermine Western interests and the status quo in the region – with complex ramifications for Lebanon.

CHAPTER 1

The Battle over Regional Defence Pacts

Western response to Soviet challenges

In the early 1950s, the pre-occupation of the West was to counter the threat to its global interests from the Soviet Union, which used communist ideology as its spearhead. In the Middle East, it was thought that the long-term Soviet objective was to expand towards Asia Minor and the Persian Gulf. To this end, the Soviet Union adopted the short-term objective of denying the Western powers vital economic resources and strategic positions in the region.[1]

The Soviet Union employed two equally important tactics. First, while not attempting to promote communism as such, propaganda was used in an attempt to destabilize the Middle East and thereby disrupt oil supplies to the West. Two themes were popular at the time: the exposure of the destructive nature of the Western colonial legacy and its support for Israel; the other was to uncover the ways by which Western governments or their private companies exploited Arab oil.[2]

The second tactic the Soviet Union exercised sought to foster bilateral relations and co-operation with nascent nationalist movements in the region, whose aims were to achieve full independence. This elicited a mixed reaction from Western powers. While Britain, and the USA to some extent, held their suspicions about nationalism as a potential vehicle for communism, they tried to 'train it and divert it into the right channels'. However, France ruled out any dealings.[3]

The West's position came under heavy pressure when Great Britain clashed with the new nationalist regimes in Egypt and Iran, and came into controversy with Saudi Arabia over the Buraimy Oasis; France, too, faced immense difficulty with North African

1

nationalist movements. The USA, for its part, played a leading role in warding off the Soviet penetration through working at times with Great Britain, in particular, to conclude security pacts with the 'Northern tier' states, and sometimes substituting British influence as in the case of Iran.[4]

The British withdrawal from Suez in 1955 provided the Soviet bloc with opportunities to court the Egyptian regime and encourage it to adopt a neutral position between East and West. The West perceived this as inimical to its interests, at a time when it was busy rallying support for the Baghdad Pact to keep the Soviet Union at bay. Soviet diplomatic expansion in the Middle East reached Lebanon, Syria, Libya and North Yemen, thereby intensifying and enlarging the scope of Cold War conflict.[5]

What is Arab security?

The first Western proposal to establish a regional security organization was made public in October 1951, when the USA, Great Britain, France and Turkey invited Egypt to join the Middle East Defence Organization (MEDO) as a founding member. In November 1951, the four sponsoring powers informed Lebanon, Syria, Jordan, Iraq, Saudi Arabia, North Yemen and Israel about the principles of this organization. But after the Wafd government of Egypt rejected the proposal, branding it as 'an attempt to continue foreign occupation of Egyptian territory under a new guise', no Arab leader had the political strength to run counter to the Egyptian position and join the organization.[6]

The new regime in Egypt, which overthrew the monarchy on 23 July 1952, sought to achieve British withdrawal from the Suez Canal as a priority. To this end, it concluded an agreement with Great Britain under which Egypt dropped its claim over the Sudan in February 1953 and agreed to Sudanese self-determination. Concerning the membership of regional security pacts, Egypt continued to refuse to join and made it clear to other Arab states that their participation in any such arrangement would be better delayed until the Suez problem had been resolved.[7]

Iraq was the chief Arab state to challenge the Egyptian line by advocating an alliance with the West in order to defend the region against Soviet penetration. Moreover, the Iraqi government of Fadhil al-Jamali was seeking to achieve its own version of Arab unity by pursuing the scheme of 'Greater Syria' or even a more modest one such as establishing an 'Arab Union' of Iraq and Jordan. But the Iraqi scheme encountered immense opposition not only from the Egyptian government, which was fearful of being isolated, but also from Israel, France, and even Great Britain, Iraq's patron, in private – in spite of the popular belief to the contrary. As a result, the Arab League became an arena of conflict since various Arab governments competed to pursue 'Arab security'.[8]

Furthermore, a new Saudi–Egyptian front sought to oppose any Arab country wanting to join the Turco-Pakistani Pact which was established on 19 February 1954, and to ward off attempts to buy arms from the West (notably by Iraq and Lebanon) as this would lead eventually to alignment with the Pact. Egyptian and Saudi objections sprang from different motives. While Egypt thought any deal between an Arab state and the West would harm its bargaining power regarding the Suez Canal issue, the Saudis were concerned only with their rivalry with the Hashemite dynasty of Iraq.[9]

Eventually the Iraqi government joined Turkey, Great Britain, Iran and later Pakistan, in setting up the Baghdad Pact, which was signed on 24 February 1955. The Baghdad Pact represented, according to Adeed Dawisha, the single most important variable in regional power politics, which served to change the entire configuration of forces in the region, giving rise to new power alignments and constellations. To counter the influence of the Baghdad Pact, Egypt entered fully into regional Arab politics. To this end, Egypt formed an alliance in March 1956 with Syria, Saudi Arabia and later North Yemen in order to exhibit 'the free will of independent Arab states'. Lebanon and Jordan did not join either the Egyptian alliance or the Baghdad Pact despite the pressure brought to bear on them.[10]

Thereafter, President Nasser launched his bid to become a world statesman by jointly founding the Non-Aligned Movement in Bandung in April 1955. Moreover, he concluded the Czech arms deal in September 1955, which broke the West's monopoly of arms sales to the Arab states. As a result, Nasser's popularity and prestige soared in the Arab world, as he was perceived as spearheading the 'renaissance tide' and moving toward an independent 'Arab order'.[11]

Change in Beirut, too

The political crisis which engulfed Lebanon in the late summer of 1952, coupled with international and regional pressures, led to the downfall of the regime of Bishara al-Khuri on 18 September 1952. Internally, the regime was rife with corruption and nepotism, and lacked the will to tackle social problems such as poverty and unemployment. President al-Khuri tried unsuccessfully to appoint a prime minister with whom he could reach agreement on the make-up of a prospective government. As political and popular opposition mounted, al-Khuri was forced to call upon General Shihab to employ the national army to restore law and order and protect the regime. Shihab, however, refused and as a consequence President Bishara al-Khuri was forced to resign from office.

Regionally, the al-Khuri regime had been unable to resolve the tension with Syria resulting from the implementation of the Customs and Excise Co-operation Agreement signed between the two states on 14 March 1950.[12] Moreover, al-Khuri lost US support for his policies. Conflict arose between President al-Khuri's administration and America regarding conditional terms associated with US aid to Lebanon. Al-Khuri had prevaricated over the Point-Four Programme for economic and technical assistance, which his administration signed with the US government in May 1951. The al-Khuri regime blocked the implementation of the programme in June 1952, arguing that economic development should be nation-wide and not restricted to southern Lebanon (the Litani river area) as the USA had later revealed. This antagonized the USA which therefore decided to stand 'neutral' in the political crisis which culminated in al-Khuri's fall from office.[13]

Camille Sham'un was elected to the Lebanese presidency on 23 September 1952 and sought from the outset to reverse his predecessor's policies. First, the new government of Khalid Shihab issued laws to liberalize the Lebanese economy, and to reform the administration. Secondly, the new regime made warm and friendly gestures to neighbouring states of the region, with the exception of Syria with which Lebanon had poor relations over economic issues.[14] Thirdly, the Lebanese government concluded new projects with the USA under the Point-Four Programme on 15 January 1953 despite the opposition of the foreign minister, Mussa Mubarak, who was thought to be backed by France.[15]

Lastly, President Sham'un adopted a pro-Western line in his foreign policy in general, involving a special relationship with Great Britain in particular.[16]

By the summer of 1954, it seemed that the internal reform programme was superficial: it had failed to achieve concrete results in meeting the needs resulting from social mobilization and development. As a result, social cleavages surfaced in the form of sectarian tension in which some sections of the Lebanese Muslim community pressed to acquire more power. This elicited a reaction from the Christian community. The British ambassador described the situation as follows:

> The Moslims [sic] are undoubtedly increasing in numbers and are pressing for a census which they hope might lead to a revision of the unwritten 'Pacte Nationale' ... and both the president of the Republic and the papal nuncio have since spoken to me in serious terms of their apprehensions for the future of this country and of Christianity in the Arab world if the Moslims [sic] here ever succeed in getting the upper hand.[17]

President Sham'un sought to ease his regime's internal insecurity by joining the anti-communist crusade, with a view to enabling him to win more Western aid. The Lebanese ambassador to Washington, Charles Malik, lobbied the US government hard, trying to extract military aid by playing up the threat posed by communism and Muslim states to the Christians.[18] Simultaneously, Sham'un pursued a similar objective with Britain, whose assistance was offered to suppress communist activities inside Lebanon.[19] Furthermore, Lebanon co-ordinated its efforts with the Baghdad Pact members in the field of mutual security, although Lebanon did not join the pact formally. A report from Mr Bowker at the British Embassy in Ankara, on 9 January 1956, detailed a planned security meeting in Ankara for Baghdad Pact members in which Lebanon was represented for the first time despite being a non-member.[20] In other words, the Lebanese regime slid steadily towards the Western camp in order to preserve the internal political status quo from perceived internal as well as external threats. But it refrained from joining any pact or alliance openly, due to the regional political implications this would have.

Government contacts: who gets foreign aid first?

In early 1952, the Lebanese government was inclined towards joining an Arab security pact and postponing any decision concerning the Middle East Defence Organization (MEDO) until Egypt had reached a satisfactory treaty with the British government over the Canal Zone. But the British government viewed unfavourably an exclusive Arab pact propagated by Egypt since this carried the potential of being hostile towards Israel and the West's interests.[21] The new Egyptian regime was eager to maintain Lebanese support for the Egyptian position as part of its regional strategy to keep up pressure on the West. The new Egyptian leader, General Nagib, thanked the Lebanese for their support to his movement and requested the elevation of the Egyptian legation in Beirut to embassy status. The ancien regime had, in fact, demanded this just a few days before its downfall. However, the al-Khuri regime hesitated in granting its consent since it was unwilling to develop diplomatic ties with Cairo further. The status of the Egyptian legation remained unchanged until the new Sham'un regime took the decision to establish full diplomatic relations with Cairo. The first Egyptian ambassador to Beirut, Wagih Rustum, took up his post on 24 November 1952. Thus, Egypt became the first Arab country to have an embassy in Beirut, and in this joined the USA, Great Britain and France which already enjoyed full diplomatic representation.[22]

The first test of relations between the new Lebanese administration of President Sham'un and the Egyptian government came when the Lebanese delegation to the Arab League's political committee meeting suggested, on 24 September 1952, the establishment of an economic union between Lebanon, Syria, Iraq and Jordan. When the Syrian government suggested incorporating Egypt in this project, the Lebanese delegation showed little enthusiasm, citing 'political and geographical problems'. Eventually, the project was dropped after it became clear that Iraq was backing it in order to pursue its project of 'Greater Syria', thus eliciting Egyptian, Saudi and Syrian objections.[23]

The Egyptian government felt anxious about the Iraqi government's courting of Sham'un which would, if successful, strengthen the Iraqi argument that defence pacts with the West 'need not wait on a solution of the Palestine problem'. In a counter lobby, the Egyptian government invited Sham'un to visit Egypt in late March 1953, while he was in Iraq concluding an economic agreement at the invitation of the Iraqi government. The Egyptian government wanted to distract President Sham'un, in order to prevent him from joining a bloc with Iraq with Great Britain's encouragement. Iraq's prime concern was to prevent the development of Egyptian political hegemony over other Arab states.[24]

Sham'un, anxious to appear as a mediator between the Arabs and the West, accepted the Egyptian invitation and visited Cairo on 21 April 1953 for six days. The outcome was favourable to Egypt as Sham'un expressed publicly his support for the Egyptian position regarding the Suez Canal issue, and stressed that defence of the region was the responsibility of the Arabs. The Lebanese president declared that:

> The Lebanon will not hesitate to support Egypt in achieving the evacuation of British troops from the Canal Zone. The Arab countries are responsible for peace and security in their territories. Should anyone wish to co-operate with the Arabs to uphold the cause of righteousness and the protection of peace in this part [of the world] let him offer what he can. It will be possible then to weigh such help carefully so long as the independence and dignity of Arab countries is not affected.[25]

This Lebanese position was expressed privately, too, to the US Secretary of State, John Foster Dulles, who visited Beirut on 16 May 1953. President Sham'un expressed his concern about the hardening of Great Britain's position towards Egypt. A US memorandum summed up Sham'un's views as follows:

> The only answer in Egypt ... is complete evacuation of the British. The United States ... should find a solution and impose it on both sides. To make this palatable to the Egyptians, the United States should give military and economic aid to Egypt. ... [Sham'un] expressed himself as entirely in accord with the idea of a defence pact. The first step, however, is to find a solution for the Suez problem which would make it possible to set up such a pact and escape from the present vicious circle.[26]

Although Sham'un had the idea of acquiring economic and military aid from the USA, he was keen not to run counter to the pro-Egyptian tide at a time when even the US government was losing enthusiasm for the Middle East Defence Organization. Moreover, the Lebanese government persisted in supporting the Egyptian position in connection with the Suez Zone issue until the conclusion of the evacuation treaty with Great Britain in October 1954. Thus, Lebanese officials felt relieved at the removal of the obstacles between the West and the Arab countries.[27]

Nasser's regional agenda

The dispute between President Nagib and his prime minister, Nasser, which led to the resignation of the former in February 1954, was not a matter of concern for the Lebanese government, since Nasser was perceived as a 'known quantity'.[28] However, the granting of asylum by Lebanon to a prominent political opponent of Nasser, Mahmud Abu al-Fatih (the publisher of *al-Misri* newspaper) created a state of tension between the Lebanese and Egyptian governments by mid-May 1954, since Abu al-Fatih was thought to be instigating anti-Nasser press campaigns. The Egyptian government pursued two means to achieve Abu al-Fatih's expulsion from Lebanon. First, it applied economic pressure on Lebanon by hinting that Egyptian tourists would not be allowed to visit Lebanon. In fact, Lebanon had enjoyed a monopoly as the only tourist destination available to Egyptians due to regulations which the Egyptian government had introduced so as to save foreign currency. Secondly, Egypt exerted diplomatic pressure on Lebanon by dispatching a military officer to press Lebanon to apply fully its political asylum laws and silence or expel Abu al-Fatih.[29] This issue gained more importance, too, because it coincided with the boiling tension between the Egypt–Saudi camp and the governments of Syria, Iraq and to some extent Lebanon. A PRO report states that the Egypt–Saudi camp were plotting to change the regime in Damascus and bring back ousted President Adib al-Shishakli, and notes that 'the Lebanese can be counted upon to do everything possible to prevent such a development'.[30] Nasser commented on this situation by stating on 29 May 1954, that:

> I summoned the publishers and editors-in-chief of all Egyptian newspapers some days ago, and appealed to them not to reply to Syrian and Lebanese press campaigns, because I know they only wish to sow the seeds of discord between Arab countries, as they did by launching an unusual press campaign in Lebanon and Syria aiming at harming the reputation of the leaders of the revolution [in Egypt]. ...[speaking about the harm which Abu al-Fatih caused to the Lebanon by breaking the rules of hospitality], I wish to say that I do not

like to blame or moan at anybody, but after receiving assurances [from Lebanese officials] I consider this problem as over.[31]

In fact, it was the Lebanese prime minister, 'Abdallah al-Yafi, who moved to repair relations with the Egyptian government by ending the Abu al-Fatih affair and inviting a member of the Revolutionary Council, Major Salah Salim, to visit Lebanon. This was significant since Nasser had entrusted Salim with consolidating support for the Egyptian regime on the pan-Arab level. The end result was that Salim succeeded on 2 July 1954 in frightening the Lebanese government away from joining the Iraqi–Syrian efforts to 'isolate Egypt'. A face-saving formula was employed by which the Lebanese government undertook to mediate between Egypt and Iraq, thus confining Lebanon to its 'traditional role' of staying neutral in inter-Arab rivalries. Moreover, al-Yafi sought, according to Haikal, to 'co-ordinate its [Lebanese] policy with that of Egypt due to the existence of historical links between the two countries and that Egypt does not have any claims over Lebanon nor groups working on its behalf as is the case with Lebanon's neighbours'.[32]

By the end of 1954, Nasser appeared to have developed a new agenda in regional politics after achieving the evacuation treaty with Great Britain and consolidating his authority after Nagib's removal. This was clear in the regime's inclination to appear more nationalist and Islamic in its ideology, as was noted by the Lebanese ambassador to Washington, Charles Malik. The latter was reported to have told US officials that:

He [Malik] stressed as he had in previous conversations … that he himself was profoundly worried over the situation in Egypt because Nasir [sic] and the people about him were leading Egypt and the Arab world in an anti-Western direction in the cultural or 'spiritual' sense. He stressed that the present regime in Egypt tends to look to Mecca as its cultural centre, to lean to a revival of, or constant stress on Islam as opposed to Western values ….[33]

In short, Egyptian policy throughout 1954 emphasized that Lebanon should not join any regional defence pacts until after the settlement of the Suez Canal issue. This may be attributed to Nasser's new tactics, which posed a problem for the Western-oriented Lebanese regime. The latter, however, continued to work as the co-ordinator of Arab League meetings and maintain, in effect, a neutral position vis-à-vis quarrels between the Egyptian and Iraqi regimes.[34]

Baghdad Pact: a taboo?

Lebanon was the first country to be invited to join the nascent Baghdad Pact just after the Turco-Iraqi declaration of mutual defence in Baghdad on 13 January 1955. When this offer was presented by the Turkish prime minister, Adnan Menderes, in Beirut on 15 January 1955, Lebanon's prime minister, Sami al-Sulh, replied that 'the Lebanon would consult the Arab states before adopting any decisive attitude towards this pact'.[35] The Egyptian government was the first to voice its opposition to the pact, on the grounds that it challenged the spirit of the Arab collective security pact, and it moved to mobilize the Arab League in order to isolate Iraq and prevent more defections. As a result, the Lebanese government decided to accept Premier Nasser's invitation to debate the situation, hoping to mute Egyptian objections and perhaps find an acceptable compromise.

Lebanon's prime minister, Sami al-Sulh, headed an Arab League delegation which was dispatched by the Arab Premiers' Conference, held in Cairo on 30 January 1955, in order to convince the Iraqi government not to proceed with the pact with Turkey – for the sake of 'Arab unity'. When the Iraqi position remained unchanged, President Sham'un tried to step in personally to mediate by asking his prime minister to seek the Iraqi premier's consent to meet Nasser in Beirut. However, Nasser rejected the Lebanese proposal outright because it ignored, in effect, the Arab League and reduced the matter to a mere Iraqi–Egyptian dispute. In a speech given on 3 February 1955, he stated that:

> no new talks could have any effect on the present situation. The question at issue, that of joining alliances outside the Arab League, was a matter for all the Arab states, and not just for Egypt or Nuri al-Sa'id. Thus, any new talks on the basis of the [Lebanese] suggestion would be a waste of time.[36]

Premier Nasser appears to have been suspicious of the Lebanese role in mediation, and tried to cut a wedge between the Lebanese prime minister, Sami al-Sulh, and his foreign minister during the Arab Premiers' Conference in Cairo which was suspended on 3 February 1955. In addition, Nasser ignored Sham'un's request to

halt the anti-Iraqi propaganda campaign which, in effect, undermined and insulted the Lebanese president. The displeasure of the
Lebanese government at this was expressed on 8 February 1955 in
an official statement which stated that 'it would be difficult for the
Lebanon to go on trying to settle the Iraqi–Egyptian dispute if
Egyptian newspapers continued to attack the Iraqi authorities and
certain Arab politicians'.[37]

Nonetheless, Nasser could not have afforded to estrange the
Lebanese president completely, for two reasons. First, Lebanon
represented the second Arab candidate to join the proposed pact;
thus it was unwise to leave it prey to Iraqi, Turkish and even
Pakistani influence.[38] Secondly, as long as the Lebanese government remained in the self-made role of mediator, the government
in Cairo was able to manoeuvre politically and preserve open
channels with Iraq. This was especially important during the
sensitive period before the official signing of the Baghdad Pact on
24 February 1955. On 20 February 1955, the Egyptian minister of
national guidance, Major Salah Salim, was dispatched to Beirut to
appease Sham'un and canvass political support for Egypt at the
same time. It seems that President Sham'un favoured Salah
Salim's notion for Sham'un to be the 'spokesman of all the Arab
states' in discussing the issue of Middle East defence with the
West. But, when Malik invited the US Secretary of State, John
Foster Dulles, to visit Beirut to debate the situation with Sham'un,
Dulles turned it down. It is clear that Salim succeeded in fuelling
Sham'un's disappointment towards the USA for 'its frigidity and
immovability' regarding Lebanon's needs. Malik, in fact, empha-
sizes the point that by giving aid, Washington helped to lead the
Arab states 'to co-operate positively with the US' at this stage.
Malik is reported to have said that the refusal of the Arab states to
co-operate 'may cause their permanent withdrawal from the
support of the US'.[39] When Salah Salim requested that the
Lebanese government join the new Egyptian–Saudi–Syrian
agreement to counter the Turco-Iraqi Pact, this proposal was
turned down on the grounds that Lebanon's interests lay in
'preserving the Arab League'.[40]

Sham'un used the occasion of a visit to Turkey in early April
1955 to propagate a scheme for political and economic co-
operation between Lebanon and Turkey as a step toward a
rapprochement between the latter and the Arab world. The

Egyptian government interpreted this as a dangerous move by Lebanon toward Iraq and the West. As a result the Egyptian government threatened to sever economic and diplomatic relations with Lebanon. Also, Egypt directed attacks via the state media against Lebanese statesmen, which resulted in the withdrawing of the *al-Akhbar* newspaper from distribution inside Lebanon for a limited period. This Egyptian campaign succeeded in increasing the pressure on Lebanon, especially after Saudi Arabia and Syria, Egypt's allies, threatened the imposition of economic sanctions against Lebanon if it joined the Turco-Iraqi Pact. As a result, the Lebanese government faced staunch opposition in parliament, forcing it to change its mind and resort to its traditional policy of mediating between Arab states, i.e. being 'on the fence'.[41]

Thereafter, the Lebanese government moved closer to the Egyptian camp by signing an agreement on 1 September 1955, which stated that the two countries should consult together and exchange information on matters related to foreign policy, defence, trade and public security. Although this agreement, which was signed by Lebanese foreign minister, Hamid Franjieh, did not amount to a fully fledged alliance, it did signal Lebanese willingness, at this stage, to follow the Egyptian line concerning the Arab League and regional defence pacts. In other words, it represented a commitment by Lebanon not to join the Turco-Iraqi Pact, which became known as the Baghdad Pact.[42] This was very useful for both sides, though for different reasons. It was useful for the Egyptian regime in enabling it to gain support from the Lebanese government for its bold decision to buy arms from communist Czechoslovakia in late September 1955. The Lebanese foreign minister, Salim Lahud, gave this support by declaring in Cairo on 9 October 1955 that Lebanon had received no offer of Russian arms but would accept such an offer if, as with Egypt, there were 'no strings attached'.[43] President Sham'un found it useful as a means of frightening a reluctant West: unless given sufficient economic and military aid, he would be forced to follow Egyptian footsteps.[44]

Since the West was not as forthcoming as Sham'un had hoped, he continued to follow the Egyptian line, with caution, setting the agenda in conjunction with Egypt on regional issues in Arab League meetings until July 1956.[45] Furthermore, the completion of the evacuation of British troops from the Suez Canal and Nasser's election as president of Egypt earned the latter more pan-Arab credentials – and this coloured the Lebanese government's response. The prime minister, 'Abdallah al-Yafi, visited Egypt for three days in early July 1956, as a guest of the Egyptian government. Al-Yafi gave Nasser the highest Lebanese official decoration (al-Istihqaq al-Lubnani al-Mumtaz) and invited Nasser to visit Lebanon. Al-Yafi also paid tribute to Nasser by stating on 2 July 1956 that:

> We came here to congratulate Egypt for achieving the evacuation [of the British], and to congratulate President Nasser on his election as President of the Egyptian Republic. The evacuation from Egypt does not represent a liberation of Egypt only, but the liberation of the Arabs as a whole. Lebanon congratulates the President, as the man who achieved glory for the Arab people.[46]

In sum, the Egyptian government succeeded in its policy of preventing the Lebanese government from joining the rival Turco-Iraqi camp through applying political, economic and diplomatic pressure. Although it could not compel Sham'un to join the Egyptian camp, the Egyptian government was nonetheless able to influence deeply Lebanese foreign policy from September 1955 until July 1956.

Early contacts with potential Lebanese allies

The Egyptian regime's efforts to establish ties with political groups and personalities in Lebanon started in late 1954, more than two years after the overthrow of the ancien regime in Egypt. Initial moves began following the signing of the evacuation treaty by the Egyptian government with Great Britain in October 1954, freeing its hand to involve itself more in other foreign policy issues.[47] Following the political rise of Nasser to the forefront of the regime in Cairo (after Nagib's fall), the preaching of Arab nationalist ideology became a priority in order to attract Arab popular support beyond Egypt's borders. Egyptian intelligence officers were dispatched to establish contacts with political parties in the Arab East in general and Lebanon in particular. Ahmad Hamrush, a member of the ruling Free Officers Movement, states that Nasser was forced to rely on intelligence officers to canvass support secretly, because he did not have a well-trained political organization to establish open contacts with popular organizations. He mentions the names of the intelligence officers involved, such as Kamal Rif'at, Ahmad Lutfi Wakid, Izzat Sulayman, Fathi al-Deeb, and the military attaché's assistant in Beirut, Hassan Khalil.[48]

The first concerted campaign to win political support inside Lebanon by the Egyptian government was for the latter's anti-pacts policy. This was intended to pre-empt any defection by the Lebanese government to the Turco-Iraqi Pact, as Lebanon was considered a potential candidate. Thus, Major Salah Salim, Egyptian minister of national guidance, was dispatched from Cairo to Beirut on 20 February 1955. His aim was to lobby the Lebanese government not to look favourably toward the Turco-Iraqi Pact and to court the allegiance of political groups and leading personalities. Salah Salim met former premiers Sa'eb Salam, 'Abdallah al-Yafi and Husain al-'Uwayni, and former ministers Habib Abu-Shahla, Hamid Franjieh, Alfred Naccache, Rashid Karami and Charles Hilu. The ex-premiers, all Sunni Muslims, were clearly supporting Salim's opposition to the new pact.[49] The first outspoken supporters of Egyptian views were the political opponents of President Sham'un. Kamal Jumblatt, for instance, asked the Lebanese government to support the Egyptian position because:

> It includes the unification of the leadership of Arab armies, and the unification of foreign and economic policies of the Arab states. … This would benefit Lebanon immensely for it brings many opportunities, while our siding with the Turco–Iraqi Pact would subject the Lebanese economy to severe repercussions, especially if Egypt refuses to import our agrarian produce in general and apples in particular.[50]

Salim spent a week in Beirut, lobbying every significant political force whether left, right or centre, and also educational institutions, in order to win the support of the 'Arab masses'. The object was to isolate Iraq after it went ahead and signed the pact with Turkey on 24 February 1955. In a speech on 25 February 1955, at the Maqasid Muslim College, Beirut, Salim said:

> Egypt is ready to equip any Arab country with arms and ammunition. Egypt would work to … establish a unified Arab army on the basis of an Arab military pact to which the leadership is accorded to any country save Egypt. Egypt would also transfer its army and equipment to be under this unified Arab command, and it would encourage mutual Arab economic co-operation.[51]

A tendency developed whereby Egyptian official views were propagated by groups dissatisfied with President Sham'un's foreign policy. When it seemed that the Lebanese government was moving close to the Turco-Iraqi Pact in early April 1955, for example, pan-Arab and leftist groups voiced their opposition, calling instead for alignment with Egypt. A telegram was sent to the Arab League Council on 1 April 1955 by some Lebanese dignitaries stating that:

> The assembled [a collection of opposition parties and individuals] in the Najjadah Party House [the HQ of a Muslim and Arab Nationalist political party based largely in Beirut], today, oppose the Turco-Iraqi Pact and call for joining the Egyptian–Saudi–Syrian pact to establish the unified Arab army through the mobilization of Arab resources. [This is intended] to enable it [the Arab army] to defeat and uproot zionism. In addition, to strengthen the Arab nation [against] foreign conspiracies and colonial schemes.[52]

Egypt's decision to conclude the Czech arms deal in late September 1955 boosted its prestige on the popular as well as the political level in Lebanon. Lebanese political leaders praised the Egyptian initiative and perceived it as a warning to the West to respond to the Arabs' need for arms more positively. Consequently, the attitude towards Egypt was placed at the centre of Lebanese politics whereby President Sham'un was blamed by the opposition for his unwillingness to meet Egyptian demands. For instance, Hamid Franjieh expressed his dissent from the policies of the Lebanese government in terms of its lack of commitment to promoting relations with Egypt. Franjieh claimed that he had to resign as foreign minister mainly because he could not implement a bilateral co-operation agreement he had signed with Egypt on 2 September 1955. On 4 October 1955, Franjieh stated to the Lebanese parliament his reasons for departing from government as follows:

> I went to Egypt to discuss Lebanese–Egyptian relations at first, and after settling this matter I would then move to discuss wider Arab issues [i.e. pacts]. I did not encounter there a mere negotiator, but faced an Arab side which represented 22 million people saying to us that it does not wish to impose any conditions save to co-operate, consult each other, and stand as one bloc in order to prevent [outsiders] to divide and rule. I offered to be truthful to them, but after my

return, I found that the Lebanese government does not regard truth as an asset. This forced me to tender my resignation.[53]

The Egyptian ambassador, General Ghalib, tried to further the Egyptian aim of keeping Lebanon outside the Baghdad Pact by nurturing contacts with opposition figures and groups, thus keeping Sham'un under scrutiny. In fact, the fragile sectarian structure of Lebanon could easily be manipulated by any outside power to serve its own interests. Sham'un is reported to have complained to visiting Egyptian Minister of State, Anwar Sadat, about the Egyptian ambassador's close association with Lebanese opposition elements. A PRO document stated that 'the president asked him [Sadat] what the Egyptian government would think of a Lebanese ambassador in Cairo who cultivated the Moslem Brotherhood and other dissident elements in Egypt: he would not have been allowed to remain twenty-four hours in the country'.[54] It was clear that Muslim political figures, and the Sunnis in particular, were starting to compete among themselves to win Egyptian blessing in order to boost their Arab nationalist credentials. Those seeking political office, especially the office of prime minister, considered this useful. For instance, 'Abdallah al-Yafi visited Egypt and spoke publicly blessing a proposed union between Egypt and Syria, and implied that Lebanon might join. This was anathema to Lebanese nationalists especially since he was speaking in an official capacity. It was clear that al-Yafi intended to appear as Egypt's best ally when Nasser's prestige was soaring, which he [al-Yafi] hoped would increase his own popularity over his local rivals in Beirut.[55]

In short, Egyptian contacts with Lebanese groups developed from early 1955, when the Egyptian regime started its ideological, political and diplomatic offensive to pursue its quest for regional dominance. Some Lebanese groups found it useful to follow Egyptian leadership in political battles with Arab and foreign powers, hoping that this might reflect positively on their own interests vis-à-vis other groups and the Lebanese government.

The Egyptian foothold in Lebanese media

The role of the Egyptian media increased from late 1954, accompanying the widening influence of the Egyptian regime in Lebanon. The role of the Cairo-based radio station, the 'Voice of the Arabs' (Sawt al-'Arab), for instance, grew steadily from its inception in October 1953. It was aimed at propagating an Arab nationalist ideology and at feeding anti-imperialist feelings across the Arab world. The fact that it was controlled by Egyptian intelligence meant that it was prone to attack any country whose policy did not coincide with Egypt's.[56]

The Egyptian government used the radio and the press to attack perceived political shifts by the Lebanese government during the Baghdad Pact battle. This elicited official protestation from President Sham'un to visiting Sadat in early December 1955, as he deemed it harmful to his prestige.[57] Furthermore, the official Lebanese policy of neutrality in inter-Arab conflicts was attacked constantly and depicted as weak, ineffective and detrimental to Arab interests. The attacks did not go so far as to equate Lebanon with Iraq, but rather kept up the pressure on the Lebanese government and put it frequently on the defensive in the public eye.[58]

Until late 1954, official Egyptian influence on the Lebanese media was of negligible significance; rival Arab governments and other interested parties had a stronger presence. The role of the partisan media outlets was to boost the prestige of their paymasters, both at the level of Lebanese public opinion and more importantly Arab public opinion at large.

There were four media currents antagonistic to Egyptian policy. First, the Iraqi government, Egypt's regional rival, had maintained a strong presence since the early 1950s, advocating Iraqi views on different foreign policy issues such as Arab unity and the defence of the region. The Arabic daily, al-Hayat, and its sister publication in English, The Daily Star, supported Iraqi and, at times, British views which, in effect, ran against Egypt's.[59] Secondly, some internal opponents of the Egyptian regime conducted anti-military press campaigns from Beirut in mid-1954, at a time when Nasser was attempting to unseat President Nagib.[60] Thirdly, the Lebanese Christian right-wing press pursued an anti-Egyptian policy, concerned at what it perceived as Egyptian hegemony over the Arab League which reflected negatively on Lebanon in particular. These are the names of some anti-Egyptian newspapers: al-Ahrar, al-Zaman, al-'Amal, al-Nuhar, L'orient (French) and Le Jour (French).[61] Lastly, left-wing newspapers, such as al-Hadaf and al-Telegraph, criticized the undemocratic nature of the military regime in Egypt until mid-1954 when Egypt's open objection to imposed military pacts with the West was applauded.

The battle over the Baghdad Pact in early 1955 signalled the concentration of Egyptian efforts to cultivate supporters among the Lebanese media. This was deemed crucial since Egyptian strategy focused on the effective use of Arab nationalist propaganda. Three tactics were employed to win supporters among Lebanese journalists and writers generally. First, press delegations were invited to Egypt in order to establish contacts with officials of the regime and especially with Nasser directly. This was aimed at promoting his prestige as a true Arab leader. Nasser addressed one such Lebanese press delegation on 2 February 1955 in the following terms:

> We realize our own strength, and we work to develop it to the utmost; but in doing so we shall not ask any foreigner to give us support, since this would tie us. We must maintain the freedom for which our fathers and forefathers fought. Our strength is in our national cause and in our own resources, which we shall develop in the interests of the Arabs and of Arabism. This is the policy of Egypt, which we declare to all frankly and unambiguously. We shall go forward with you and for you until our strength is fully developed.[62]

Secondly, the Egyptian government tried to establish ties with some newspapers, which were openly hostile to the military regime in Cairo, but were not die-hard ideological foes. A case in point was the *al-Sharq* daily, which was sued by the Lebanese government on behalf of the Egyptian government in July 1953, following a complaint by the Egyptian ambassador in Beirut, but later turned to support Egyptian policy.[63] Thirdly, the Egyptian government also targeted journalists who had a pan-Arab tendency. This group was granted exclusive interviews with Egyptian officials and given access to the Egyptian media to comment on Arab affairs.[64]

Egypt's efforts to establish a sympathetic bloc with the Lebanese media did not produce a clear-cut and distinct pro-Egyptian current during this period, especially when the result is compared to that of other states such as Iraq and Saudi Arabia. This was perhaps related to the fact that Saudi Arabia, Egypt's ally in opposing the Baghdad Pact, provided direct financial backing to those publications most disposed towards the Egyptian line.[65]

Economic relations: a tilt in Cairo's favour

During the 1950s the Egyptian market represented the fifth most important market for Lebanese products after those of Syria, Saudi Arabia, Jordan and Iraq. Egyptian imports from Lebanon accounted for approximately 13 per cent of total Egyptian imports from the Arab states. Of the total Lebanese exports to Egypt, 80 per cent consisted of vegetables and fruit. The most important Lebanese export product was apples, which was granted preferential treatment by Egypt.[66] In fact, the Egyptian market was crucial for Lebanese apples in particular, as it was difficult for Lebanese apple exporters to penetrate other markets. In 1953 apple farmers exerted immense pressure on the Lebanese government to lobby the Egyptian government to exempt this particular product from imposed tariffs equalling about 100 per cent of its value.[67]

The Lebanese market accounted for 30 per cent of total Egyptian exports to the Arab states in the 1950s, making it second only to that of Saudi Arabia. Egyptian–Lebanese trade showed a substantial increase between 1954 and 1957. This was due to the granting of a tariff preference by Lebanon to Egyptian exports of vegetable products, and to a lesser extent textiles.[68]

In 1951, the trade balance between the two countries tilted in Lebanon's favour. Lebanese exports to Egypt totalled over L£9 million, while Lebanese imports from Egypt totalled L£4.6 million. This trend was maintained until 1954, though with varying degrees (see Tables 1a and 1b). In 1955, there appeared to be a slight change in Egypt's favour when its exports to Lebanon (L£7.33) exceeded, for the first time, Egyptian imports (L£6.83 million) from Lebanon (see Tables 1a and 1b).

Conclusion

The Egyptian regime's regional policy of exercising its hegemony over the Arab states gained momentum after Egypt had achieved its evacuation treaty with Great Britain. This shift restricted the Lebanese government's foreign policy options, and represented a strong factor in preventing it from joining the Baghdad Pact in 1955–56. Moreover, the Egyptian government endeavoured to gain political support with Lebanese groups and personalities as well as with sections of the Lebanese media. This strategy was employed not only to keep a check on Sham'un, but also to boost Egypt's prestige regionally.

CHAPTER 2

Lebanon Fails the Test at Suez

The Suez intervention

Nasser's decision to nationalize the Suez Canal Company on 26 July 1956 represented a significant juncture in world politics, which led to a new phase of conflict between regional and international powers in the Middle East. Great Britain intended from the outset to confront Nasser – not only so as to regain control of the Canal but also so as to prevent Arab nationalism sweeping across the Middle East and threatening British interests in the Gulf. France, too, hoped to solve its problems in North Africa by removing Nasser, while Israel found it useful to join both powers in order to open the Straits of Tiran to Israeli shipping.

The Israeli invasion of Sinai on 29 October 1956 and the subsequent British and French military intervention, succeeded in defeating the Egyptian army. However, Soviet threats and US economic pressure, applied on Great Britain in particular, halted the war on 7 November. This, in effect, deprived the attacking countries from exacting a political victory. Thereafter, the USA acted swiftly to substitute crumbling French and British influence in the Middle East by creating its own agenda of political action, necessarily rejecting British requests to join the Baghdad Pact.[1]

President Eisenhower promulgated his 'doctrine' on 5 January 1957 which stated his administration's readiness to fill the 'vacuum' in the Middle East and prevent the Soviet Union from gaining new ground. This presented Great Britain with no choice but to co-operate with America to stop the Soviet Union gaining more political influence in Egypt and Syria in particular. The USA sought to assume British and French influence in the Middle East after the Suez debacle, but at the same time working with them to prevent the Soviet Union from destabilizing their oil interests.[2]

21

The USA fills the vacuum

The US administration's public announcement on 18 July 1956, withdrawing its offer to assist Egypt through the financing of the Aswan Dam, and President Nasser's reaction in nationalizing the Suez Canal Company on 26 July 1956, set the stage for a major confrontation in the Middle East. President Nasser, on the one hand, tried to rally Arab public opinion to his side which forced Arab governments to support him at least publicly. France and Great Britain, on the other hand, led the Western effort to check Nasser's influence and force him to backtrack on his decision.

Although Nasser was defeated militarily by Israel, France and Great Britain in early November 1956, he was able to manipulate the political battle and emerge as a victor in Egyptian and Arab eyes. Moreover, he maintained the Suez Canal under his control, and succeeded in forcing the pro-Western regimes in the Middle East, notably those of Iraq and Jordan, on to the defensive. This was the beginning of Nasser's high tide in the Arab world, in which he enjoyed popular support and made his brand of Arab nationalism a political force to be reckoned with.[3]

The Eisenhower Doctrine was perceived by Nasser as a US manoeuvre to isolate Egypt and prevent it from leading an Arab bloc capable of extracting favourable terms for economic and technical assistance. It was clear that the USA was suspicious of Nasser's tactics of playing East against West which might eventually result in the Soviet Union establishing a formidable base in the Middle East. This triggered a new regional conflict through which Nasser tried to stop Arab states adhering to the prevailing US doctrine, while America encouraged them to do so.[4]

The Lebanese government was the first to accept the US offer. This acceptance was made public in mid-January 1957, at a time when Nasser's position towards the Eisenhower Doctrine was ambivalent as he was pre-occupied with securing an Israeli withdrawal from Sinai. The Jordanian domestic political crisis of April 1957 eroded Egyptian influence, as King Hussein dismissed the pro-Egyptian government of Sulaiman Nabulsi and asked for the protection of Saudi and Iraqi troops against his internal foes. This represented a Saudi departure from the Syrian–Egyptian camp, which was helped by effective Western pressure on Israel not to intervene militarily in Jordan.[5] The USA reacted to Syria's closer ties with the Soviet Union by orchestrating a diplomatic campaign in order to 'save it from communism'. Therefore the

Turkish government threatened to intervene militarily, while the Egyptian government led a political and diplomatic campaign in support of Syria. As a result, the Syrian regime moved towards a close relationship with Egypt in order to cover its internal rifts and ease the external pressures.[6]

Sham'un goes west

The Lebanese regime was exposed to the forces of political polarization between Egypt and the Western powers. Sham'un ignored a British request in early September 1956 to replace the al-Yafi government. According to the British ambassador to Beirut, George Middleton, Sham'un said that in the last resort all authority lay with him under the constitution and 'he would ensure that Lebanese policy remained friendly to the West'.[7] However, al-Yafi tendered his resignation on 16 November 1956 as a result of President Sham'un's obstruction of al-Yafi's attempt to steer Lebanese foreign policy on a pro-Egyptian course. This ignited an internal crisis, which expressed itself in sporadic sectarian clashes. Despite these incidents Sham'un's choice of Sami al-Sulh as prime minister signalled a definite shift towards a more pro-Western stance in Lebanese foreign policy.[8]

Subsequently, the Lebanese government's acceptance of the Eisenhower Doctrine escalated the rift between government and opposition. While the opposition argued that Sham'un had violated the spirit of the National Pact of 1943, which stipulated Lebanon's neutrality, the government charged the opposition with collaboration with communism to undermine internal stability. Sham'un employed heavy handed methods to ensure the election of a loyal parliament in June 1957, in order to pave the way for the renewal of his second term of office.[9] The government and opposition differed on every aspect of foreign policy, which was translated into divisions over internal affairs.

Rhetorical support for Egypt

Nasser's nationalization of the Suez Canal Company earned him considerable praise from the Lebanese government in spite of President Sham'un's guarded caution. This seemed to confirm the West's pre-crisis suspicion that 'Prime Minister Yafi's willingness to follow a neutralist and even anti-Western line and his propensity for "playing to the street" will further Lebanon's drift into the Egyptian camp'.[10] Al-Yafi expressed total support for Nasser's decision to nationalize the Suez Canal, announcing on 27 July 1956, that:

> The Lebanese government gives unqualified support for the Egyptian decision to nationalize the Suez Canal. It is time that the world recognizes that Arab states have acquired conscience and might, to the extent that no party will be allowed to impose hegemony and squander their resources. ... I declare that we are to be counted on Egypt's side whether through our intentions or our actions.[11]

Nonetheless, Sham'un was fearful of the repercussions of an Arab–Western military conflict which would threaten the entity of Lebanon. Therefore Sham'un sought to 'look realistically' at the crisis and offered to mediate on 5 August 1956, on the basis of the following points:

1. That the decision to nationalize the Suez Canal Company constituted a natural right under Egyptian sovereignty; thus it was indisputable legally since the Egyptian government offered to pay compensation to shareholders.

2. That the recognition of Western concerns that the freedom of navigation in the Suez Canal should be maintained.

3. That both sides should refrain from issuing threats and instead commit themselves to solving the crisis through negotiation.

4. That the West should refrain from embarking on a military attack on Egypt. According to Sham'un, this could result 'in losing now, in the future and perhaps forever, all trust for the West in this region [the Middle East] and write off any hope for co-operation even with friendly states regardless of pacts and treaties'.[12]

Consequently, the Lebanese government moved on the diplomatic front employing a two-pronged plan. First, it contacted Iran, Iraq and Turkey, and requested them to support Egypt's position diplomatically. To this end, it was clear that President Sham'un was keen to gain the Egyptian Embassy's consent in order to avoid misunderstandings since all three states were members of the Baghdad Pact. For instance, Sham'un dispatched the Mayor of Beirut, 'Adil al-Sulh, to Turkey on 14 August 1956 under the pretence of 'winning over the Turks to support the Arabs in the

Suez Canal issue, and to inaugurate a new era based on under-standing'.[13] Secondly, while keeping close contacts with the Egyptian government and granting it support at Arab League meetings, the Lebanese government acted as a channel of com-munications between Egypt and other states, notably Great Britain.[14]

President Nasser was satisfied at this juncture with Sham'un's position – especially because of his awareness of British pressure on the Lebanese government to adopt a neutral stance in the crisis. Nasser said on 21 August 1956, that:

> Some Western politicians might have had dreams to see the neutrality of Lebanon and its president fulfilled, but President Sham'un's speech [on 5 August 1956] dispelled their dreams and undermined their plans. ... Moreover, President Sham'un worked with great ef-fort to back Egypt's position, and this is still giving us benefits due to noble Lebanese diplomacy. Thus, the West's representatives in Beirut understood that aggression on Egypt would be seen as an aggression on Lebanon as well.[15]

Sham'un sensed Great Britain's readiness to send naval units to Lebanese waters 'to discourage any Syrian attempt to intervene in Lebanese affairs' in the event of hostilities with Egypt.[16] This showed, in fact, that Sham'un was not prepared to go all the way with Egyptian policies to confront the West, notwithstanding his government's denunciations of the French and British massing of troops in Cyprus. In the meantime, the Lebanese government continued to support every Egyptian initiative aimed at solving the crisis peacefully.[17]

The start of the rift

The Lebanese government condemned the tripartite attack on Egypt, declared a state of emergency, and called for a meeting of Arab heads of state in Beirut to 'co-ordinate their efforts'. Moreo-ver, it adopted the symbolic measure of not allowing British and French ships to transport oil from Lebanese ports. President Sham'un was reluctant to follow Egypt and Syria by cutting diplomatic relations with Britain or France despite strong pressure from his prime minister, 'Abdallah al-Yafi, and minister of state, Sa'ib Salam.[18]

Sham'un, in fact, followed a controversial course of action during the Arab heads of state meeting in Beirut on 13–14 November 1956, which was perceived as inimical to Egyptian interests. First, Sham'un not only refused to support Egypt and its Syrian ally in their moves towards severing diplomatic relations with Great Britain and France, but sought to stress the role of the United Nations in solving the crisis. This undermined Sham'un's Arab nationalist credentials since he failed to orchestrate an 'Arab reaction' to the attack on Egypt as he had promised, but endeared himself to the USA, in particular, for his 'moderation'. A State Department document stated on 23 November 1956, that:

> Inform Chamoun [sic] USG [US Government] deeply appreciative his consistent efforts exercise moderating influence, especially in connection with current NE [Near East] crisis, and hopes Lebanon will continue to support UN actions to restore and preserve peace in NE. Steps which it has taken in Egypt indicate manner in which UN can be effective. UN thus provides [a] measure of protection to Lebanon as regards its own security.[19]

Secondly, President Sham'un dropped his prime minister, 'Abdallah al-Yafi, and his government – replacing al-Yafi with the pro-Western Sami al-Sulh. This was because al-Yafi wanted to sever relations with Britain and France as a measure of sympathy with Egypt during the Arab leaders meeting in Beirut. It is noted that details of that meeting were not revealed at the time due to Lebanese censorship. Later, Emile Bustani MP defended President Sham'un's position against Lebanese opposition and Egyptian claims, saying that Sham'un had agreed with the opinion of the majority of Arab leaders, while al-Yafi and Sa'ib Salam 'had promised' the Syrian government to sever relations at least with France. But they had to resign after falling prey to Syrian pressures which ran contrary to Sham'un's wishes.[20] This signalled a change in the direction of Sham'un's foreign policy. He feared the threat to his regime emanating from Egyptian and Syrian regional influence, coupled with the increased Soviet involvement in Middle East affairs.[21]

Furthermore, when the Lebanese authorities uncovered agents working with the Egyptian military attaché in carrying explosives and conducting bomb attacks on British institutions in Beirut, Sham'un sought to embarrass the Egyptian government by exposing its involvement. This was achieved with the collaboration of the British, since Lebanese censorship permitted no direct reference to Egypt's role. The British ambassador to Beirut, George Middleton, reported on 21 November 1956 that:

> The President of the Lebanon ... has asked that this news [the culpability of the Egyptian Embassy] should be publicized in the above terms by all possible means. He insists on adding the following comment: We understand that the Lebanese government, despite this subversive activity, intends to remain loyal to resolutions passed at recent meeting of heads of Arab states. Nevertheless, the uncovering of these subversive activities by Egypt in a sister Arab country has created a very violent popular reaction in Lebanon.[22]

The Egyptian government retaliated by banning Lebanese civilian aeroplanes from flying to Cairo on the grounds that the French and British national airlines both owned shares in Lebanese airline companies. Thus, the Egyptian ban on French and British planes extended to Lebanese ones also. Although this issue was resolved by mid-December 1956, it was clear that relations between the Egyptian and Lebanese governments were on a collision course following the Suez War.[23]

The battle over the Eisenhower Doctrine

The Lebanese government's open declaration that it intended to co-operate with the Eisenhower Doctrine made it the first Arab country to do so, which put it at odds with the 'non-aligned' Arab camp, namely Egypt and Syria.[24] This signalled the beginning of a new chapter of political and ideological rifts with the Egyptian regime.

Lebanese foreign minister, Charles Malik, tried from the outset to conclude a trade-off with President Nasser. The Lebanese government would support Egypt in its request for the withdrawal of Israeli forces from all Egyptian territory, and would try to mediate with the British and French governments to settle the after-effects of the Suez crisis. In return, it was expected that the Egyptian government would understand Lebanon's need to secure foreign aid, especially since Egypt was not capable of providing it, while Lebanon's Arab commitments would not be violated (i.e. towards the Arab League and the Palestine question).[25]

However, Nasser turned down Malik's offer for two apparent reasons. First, he aimed to deny Malik gaining a diplomatic coup by performing as 'the spokesman of the Arabs' in Western capitals and in the UN. An official Egyptian statement denied that Charles Malik was entrusted with any mission on Egypt's behalf. Despite this, Malik continued to announce his readiness to 'help according to Lebanon's capability with dignity and wisdom'.[26] Secondly, Nasser did not intend to estrange Syria, whose government stood firmly with him on the Suez crisis, by allowing Lebanon to be a special case in adhering to the Eisenhower Doctrine. This would have boosted the Lebanese government's position in its open political, economic and ideological rift with Syria.[27]

Therefore Malik impressed on the Western powers the necessity of co-ordinating actions to achieve Nasser's downfall as well as that of his ally, the Syrian regime, in order to achieve stability in the Middle East. He told British officials on 14 January 1957, that:

> Syria was the most urgent and important problem in the Middle East. The second was the problem of Egypt and the third Israel. If we could do something in Syria, we should open the way to useful action in Egypt and later to a settlement of the Israel dispute.[28]

Malik spoke on the same lines to US officials, but devoted more attention to finding substitutes to Nasser, as the USA was, in effect, the protector of Western interests. According to a US memo, Malik told John Foster Dulles on 5 February 1957, that:

> He [Charles Malik] wished to speak on the subject of Egypt. On his way to the United States recently he had talked with Nasser for four hours and had given more than a hundred hours of thought to the situation of Nasser and his activities. ...[Malik] believed it necessary to search for an effective alternative to the type of nationalism which Nasser represented. ... He considered this type of nationalism as a virulent and morbid type which was constantly fanned and agitated by the communists. ...We [the USA] were mistaken if the Middle Eastern situation could be improved by assisting Saudi Arabia. Only a political change in Syria and Egypt would achieve the desired result.[29]

The Lebanese government's formal adherence to the Eisenhower Doctrine came in mid-March 1957, thus making Lebanon the first country to do so. While this act was rewarded with much needed economic and military grants from the USA, it created an open rift with the Egyptian government. Lebanon could no longer be considered neutral, but was in fact aligned to America in particular. President Eisenhower's special envoy, James Richards, concluded a programme of economic and military assistance with

Lebanon, which included grants totalling $12 million. The following are some of the factors influencing his decision:

1. Lebanon prior to my visit endorsed president's proposals and has strongly reaffirmed this stand in public statements since my arrival. These acts required considerable political courage which we should recognize.

2. Public impact achieved in Lebanon as first country visited by mission important to success of mission's trip as a whole.

3. Real fear evident among Lebanese officials (confirmed by Embassy) over growing subversive activities in country by communists supported by Syria and Egypt.[30]

Subsequently, the Egyptian government launched a political crusade against the Sham'un regime by supporting Lebanese opposition groups. The Egyptian ambassador to Beirut, General Abdul-Hamid Ghalib, worked to co-ordinate the opposition's efforts to win the general elections of June 1957.[31] Furthermore, the Egyptian media conducted a concerted campaign to undermine the legitimacy of the regime of President Sham'un due to his 'passive attitude' towards Egypt during the Suez crisis and his later alliance with the West, thus trying to swing public opinion to the opposition's side. A commentary on the 'Voice of the Arabs' radio delivered by an Egyptian popular propagandist, Ahmad Sa'id, on 5 April 1957 stated that:

> The Lebanese Government has accepted the Eisenhower doctrine for the Middle East, while the Opposition, like the ever-vigilant Arab people has decided to oppose and not to accept any aid which might restrict the freedom of the Lebanon in her foreign policy. ... This is the battle which is being waged today in the Lebanon. ... It is the Lebanese people who will gather the fruits of this battle. They are the people who may enjoy peace or suffer from war, who may be enriched by the American alliances mentioned in Eisenhower's doctrine, who may be colonized and be destroyed as a result of the very same American aid.[32]

The Lebanese government was thus publicly thrown on the defensive by the intensity of Egyptian political attacks. It was also aware that it lacked the means to retaliate similarly by supporting Egyptian opposition groups since they were more or less defunct. Therefore it resorted to the use of counter-propaganda measures and diplomatic protests in an attempt to neutralize official Egyptian pressure. First, Charles Malik attacked communism by linking it to zionism, thus depicting the close relationship between Egypt and the Soviet Union as fruitless and inimical to Arab interests, and contrary to the US role. He also denied the popular view held in the Arab street that the Soviet Union was the real saviour of Egypt by suggesting that President Eisenhower had, in fact, stopped the war. Malik said that 'if a single Soviet aircraft were to carry out a raid, Moscow itself would be demolished'.[33]

Secondly, by mid-April 1957, the Lebanese government had resorted to the use of selective censorship against Egyptian publications distributed in Lebanon which attacked Sham'un and other Lebanese officials. When these attacks increased in the build-up towards the Lebanese general elections in June 1957, the Lebanese authorities banned all Egyptian newspapers for two months between early May and 12 July 1957.[34] Thirdly, the Lebanese government expelled Egyptian journalists for violating the Lebanese legal code pertaining to attacking heads of state.[35] Lastly, the Lebanese government used diplomatic channels to protest against the inaction of the Egyptian government to prevent Egyptian newspaper campaigns against Charles Malik for his alleged contacts with the Israeli ambassador to Washington, Abba Eban. The Lebanese memorandum was delivered on 22 June 1957, and listed the following points in complaint:

> (i) the unanimity of the Egyptian newspapers in publishing the al-leged documents in the form in which they were published on 15.6.57; (ii) the unanimous or almost unanimous failure of these papers to publish the statement of denial issued on 13th June; (iii) also their failure to publish the statement of the Lebanese chargé d'affaires at his press conference on 19th June or even refer to it ... [therefore] and in view of what it knows of the close relationship between the official authorities and the press in Egypt, the Lebanese Government strongly protests against what was published and what has not been published on the subject.[36]

The two countries now maintained completely opposing posi-tions: the Egyptian government committed itself to 'neutrality', while the Lebanese government persisted in its commitment to the Eisenhower Doctrine and its attached political agenda. However, Sham'un did seek to mend fences with Nasser in mid-July 1957. He had two objectives. First, he and his government were seeking political backing for the candidature of Charles Malik for the post of president of the United Nations General Assembly, as elections were due in late September 1957. Secondly, he was trying to prepare the ground for economic co-operation with Cairo, especially as regards the export of Lebanese apples to Egypt.[37]

President Nasser, aware of Sham'un's manoeuvres to by-pass the pro-Egyptian Lebanese opposition, decided to 'defer the re-negotiation of the relationship between the two countries to the newly elected Egyptian parliament'.[38] Moreover, Nasser pre-empted pressure to support Charles Malik by attacking, in a speech in Alexandria on 26 July 1957 'the betrayal of certain Arab countries which committed themselves to the Eisenhower Doctrine'. Despite efforts in the Lebanese cabinet to play down Nasser's outbursts, it was clear that Egypt and its allies, Syria and the Yemen, were firmly against Malik.[39]

Furthermore, the Egyptian government decided to escalate the crisis in relations between the two countries by boycotting the second Arab sport tournament held in Beirut on 12 October 1957. Egyptian tourists were instructed to avoid visiting Lebanon while on their way to Damascus, on the grounds that 'this measure has been prompted by the Lebanese government's action in helping some tourists to travel to other foreign countries by giving them special permits separate from their Egyptian passports'.[40]

Although the dispatch of Egyptian troops to Syria in early October 1957 was meant to help assist in repelling any Turkish threats, the Lebanese government was shaken. While Prime Minister Sami al-Sulh paid lip service to this development, saying that it was 'done in accordance with the military accord which had already been concluded between Syria and Egypt', the fact remained that the growing Egyptian influence in Syria was inevitably bound to affect Lebanon.[41]

The Lebanese government was thrown further on to the defensive in mid-December 1957 when it was accused by the Egyptian–Syrian axis of permitting hostile activities to be organized on Lebanese territory. Nasser complained publicly of a 'conspiracy' being hatched in Beirut against the Egyptian government by Egyptian political refugees in Lebanon. Despite the Lebanese government's declaration of innocence and its sending a diplomatic note 'requesting the necessity to arrange a meeting of Lebanese and Egyptian officials to resolve the disputed issues', it was clear that the rift between the two countries had reached a new dimension.[42]

Nasser: a hero of Lebanese opposition

The impact in Lebanon of Nasser's nationalization of the Suez Canal Company varied widely among sectarian communities and political groupings. This single act was met with immediate support and jubilation from both Muslim political leaders and popular bodies. Muslim leaders, whether inside or outside government, competed with each other in sending telegrams of support to President Nasser full of grandiose Arab nationalist and anti-imperialist rhetoric. The pro-Egyptian deputies within the Lebanese parliament ensured the adoption of a resolution on 30 July 1956 which expressed appreciation of 'the vast effort which the sister-country, Egypt, is taking to strengthen its political and economic independence, ... [the parliament] fully supports President Nasser in his action and wishes Egypt complete success'.[43]

Popular demonstrations were organized in major Muslim cities such as Beirut, Sidon and Tripoli, with Sunni organizations in the forefront. In Beirut, for instance, the Najjadah Party held processions in support of Egypt, and then visited the Egyptian Embassy to 'congratulate' the ambassador, General Ghalib, for his country's stance. The leader of the Najjadah party, 'Adnan al-Hakim, went to Cairo in mid-August 1956 to 'represent Lebanon' in the Conference of the Struggling Society for the Liberation of Arab and Muslim Peoples, which comprised personalities from the Muslim world and was used by Nasser as a vehicle for propaganda. As a result, al-Hakim offered Nasser the political allegiance of the Najjadah party, which continued until well after Nasser's death.[44]

The occasion of 'Egypt Day', which was organized in protest against the London Conference debate on the Canal issue on 16 August 1956, provided an opportunity for Muslim political parties, Arab nationalist groups and leftist organizations to force a general strike in Lebanon in support of Egypt. Moreover, various rallies were staged, carrying Nasser's portraits and chanting pan-Arab and anti-imperialist slogans. This forced government officials to ride the wave of popular support for Nasser and join in with the rhetoric.[45] The British ambassador to Beirut, George Middleton, summed up the situation by saying:

> There is no doubt in my mind about the tremendous impetus which the Nasser bandwagon has now gained. All the latent anti-Western resentments, Arab xenophobia and 'anti-imperialist' hysteria is being given free rein. ... Pro-Nasser sentiments are the order of the day and undoubtedly popular. Portraits of the Egyptian dictator are beginning to appear in all the shops and I should think that nearly half the taxis in Beirut also have his portrait displayed on the rear window.[46]

The tripartite attack on Egypt on 30 October 1956 unleashed emotional feelings among pro-Egyptian Lebanese, and boosted their affiliation and sympathy with Nasser as a pan-Arab hero. The pro-Egyptian camp rushed to 'help' what it perceived as the Arabs' legitimate cause on three fronts. First, it mobilized supporters, especially students, to stage demonstrations in support of Egypt and submit petitions to the Lebanese government to implement certain policies in aid of Egypt. These included the imposition of military training on the Lebanese populace, a total boycott of France and Britain, and the sequestration of French and British institutions on Lebanese soil.[47]

Secondly, Muslim and left-wing political parties demanded that the Lebanese government vigorously denounce the attack on Egypt and depart from its cautious 'wait and see' position. President Sham'un and the right-wing Christian leaders, countered this by paying lip-service expressions of sympathy to Egypt, while leaving major decisions to be determined at the Arab Heads of State Summit in Beirut in mid-November 1956.[48] When Sham'un failed to satisfy the pro-Egyptian camp by severing diplomatic relations with Britain and France, the Sunni prime minister, 'Abdallah al-Yafi, and his minister of state, Sa'ib Salam, resigned abruptly. It was argued that even Iraq cut off diplomatic ties with France despite being a member of the Baghdad Pact, while Lebanon stood idle. This signalled the will of some Muslim politicians to follow the guidelines of Egyptian foreign policy regardless, while Christian parties feared the tide of Arab nationalism. Therefore Muslim–Christian communal tension intensified despite its negative repercussions on the coherence of the Lebanese regime.[49]

Thirdly, pro-Egyptian groups expressed solidarity with the Egyptian people in material and humanitarian fields as a sign of political support for Nasser's government by setting up 'the Popular Committee to Help Egypt' on 21 November 1956, designed to deal with the aftermath of the Suez War. This committee was headed by Haj Hussein 'Uwayni, a Sunni leader, and Sheikh Butrus al-Khuri, a Maronite industrialist, and adopted the slogan 'take revenge on colonialism by helping Egypt'.[50] Leaders of parties, groups and popular organizations succeeded in drawing the commercial elite in their communities to respond positively. In Tripoli, for instance, the local leader, Rashid Karami, led a committee in person and conducted door-to-door collections in the commercial areas 'to help our brothers in Egypt'.[51] In Beirut, too, similar exercises were applied, with the Society of al-Maqasid Islamic Schools making the largest donation of L£25,000. In the final count, there were 26 lists of donations which made a total of L£500,000 donated to the battered city of Port Sa'id.[52]

Fanning opposition to Sham'un

In early 1957, the Egyptian government moved quickly to contain President Sham'un's foreign policy shift by consolidating its contacts with its newly acquired supporters in Lebanon. First, it invited to Cairo ministers from the previous government of al-Yafi, which was sacked by Sham'un during the Arab Summit in Beirut in mid-November 1956. This was intended to expose Sham'un's deviation from the Arab consensus. Ex-Minister of State, Sa'ib Salam, visited Egypt in mid-January 1957 'to congratulate dear Egypt in the person of Nasser', and to call for Arab co-ordination before rushing to decisions regarding the Eisenhower Doctrine.[53]

Secondly, the Egyptian government encouraged Lebanese Muslim politicians – who had long held the view that Lebanon was an Arab country but had compromised over the identity of the new state after independence in 1943 – to air their views as a counter-balance to Sham'un and right-wing Christians. The Egyptian media were placed at the service of these Muslim politicians to counter official Lebanese censorship. Ex-premier Rashid Karami, for example, was quoted by the 'Voice of the Arabs' as saying on 24 February 1957 that:

The Lebanon entered the realm of Arab circles ever since the Arab wave extended to the country of Al-Shaam [Syria]. No country in the Arab east could claim to be more Arab than the Lebanon. ... It is regrettable to find that those who are deceived by colonialism still adhere to the saying that the Lebanon has a Phoenician origin; that the Lebanon has an Arab face but its blood, heart and soul are matter for debate. ... At the present time, neutrality is represented by a large bloc, consisting of 27 Afro-Asian countries ... which have decided to open 'a third avenue' between the East and West. Why should we leave the 'avenue' of this large international bloc ... and join the West in order to protect ourselves from an alleged danger, and protect Israel, which usurped the land of our dear Palestine?[54]

Thirdly, Nasser personally preached, on occasion, Arab nationalist rhetoric to the rank and file of his camp in Lebanon. His charisma facilitated the spread of his ideological doctrine as well as developing the image of Egypt as the leader of other Arab states. On 24 April 1957, Nasser told a delegation of some 300 Lebanese students visiting Cairo at the expense of its government that:

I welcome you in your country Egypt. The duty shouldered by the Lebanon, the Arab State, is great; and the duties which are yours at this early stage of the Arab Revolution are enormous and are fundamentally based on brotherhood and whole-hearted collaboration with other Arab youth in the Lebanon, Syria, Jordan, Egypt and in other Arab countries.[55]

Furthermore, Nasser canvassed for good relations with anti-Sham'un Christian religious and political leaders. This was aimed at widening Egypt's political base in Lebanon and pre-empting any charge of sectarianism. In other words, Nasser was keen not to appear in the eyes of Lebanese Christians as conspiring to change the Lebanese regime in favour of the Muslim population. In fact, Dr Boutros-Ghali, who was a political observer during this period, ruled out any possibility that the nature of the Egyptian government's co-operation with Lebanese groups was based on religious grounds, but stressed that it was on ideological principles – i.e. Arab nationalism and not Islam.[56] The Maronite Patriarch, Bulus Ma'ushi, was bestowed with the title 'the Patriarch of the Arabs' in the Egyptian media, which focused on his statements calling on Sham'un to 'nurture good relations with Arab sister states, work for their welfare and adopt a united stance with them'.[57] Hamid Franjieh, a political rival of Sham'un, blamed the Lebanese government alone for Lebanon's deteriorating relations with Egypt and its loyal ally Syria. Franjieh said that this deterioration was caused by the tilt of Lebanese foreign policy towards the West. He said in an open letter to Pierre Jumayyil, the leader of the Phalange Party who was pro-Sham'un, on 14 February 1957, that:

> The Lebanon did not agree with Egypt that the Canal question was the foremost problem of the Arabs. When the aggression against Egypt occurred, many in France and Britain denounced it. Please tell me at what time you or anybody else has seen a British prime minister resign while controlling a majority in parliament. ... Is it in our interest and the interest of all in this part of the world to reopen the door for [Western] intervention?[58]

Hence, while the Lebanese government was attempting to seek US assistance in confronting 'Egyptian, Syrian and communist conspiracies' to topple the Lebanese regime, the newly formed Lebanese opposition bloc relied on Syrian–Egyptian support, especially after the Lebanese government ratified the Eisenhower Doctrine in mid-March 1957.[59] However, it seemed that Syria's material support for the Lebanese opposition was greater than that which Egypt could provide, perhaps due to the fact that Syria was engaged in a prolonged dispute with the Lebanese government which motivated it more than Egypt. In addition, Syrian support was more feasible given its geographical proximity to Lebanon.[60]

The Lebanese opposition continued to support the co-ordination of foreign policy with Egypt and Syria, despite its failure to achieve much success in the Lebanese elections held in June 1957. The leader of the Socialist Progressive Party, Kamal Jumblatt, accused the Lebanese government on 23 July 1957 of exaggerating the alleged threat of the Egyptian and Syrian regimes to the Christians of Lebanon in order to reap material and military benefits from the USA. Jumblatt denied that communism was on the brink of seizing power in these two countries and was ready to jump on Lebanon. He stated:

> The Eisenhower Doctrine and the visits of the US Sixth Fleet to Beirut were employed by the Head of State [Sham'un] before the Lebanese elections in order to deceive the people, to score a victory and prepare the ground for his re-election for a new term. ... Nobody can claim that Egypt has become a communist country. President Nasser's wise decision to restore diplomatic relations with France and Britain has, in fact, proved his real desire to bring balance

to this area. However, this was not done on the basis of serving colonialism as we are witnessing now in Lebanon.[61]

President Nasser perceived the Lebanese opposition as the real
representative of the Lebanese people, especially after it became
clear that the Lebanese government's tilt towards the West was
irreversible.[62] Relations between the regimes of Egypt and Syria
headed towards closer political and military co-operation, especially after the dispatch of Egyptian troops to Syria in October
1957. Consequently, Lebanese opposition delegations embarked
on visiting Damascus to voice their support for Syrian and
Egyptian policies as well as Nasser's leadership of Arab nationalism.

Nasser's media strategy

President Nasser used his propaganda machine to its fullest extent
from July 1956 in order to mobilize the 'Arab masses' in Egypt
and other Arab countries against the West. This was thought to
offer him considerable leverage with which to transfer the battle
outside Egypt's borders and put pressure also on pro-Western
regimes in the Middle East. Regarding Lebanon, the full thrust of
Egyptian media attacks on the Lebanese regime escalated after the
acceptance of the Eisenhower Doctrine in early January 1957. The
Egyptian commentators and journalists who concentrated on
Lebanese affairs included Ahmed Sa'id on the 'Voice of the Arabs'
radio programme, Anwar al-Sadat in *al-Jumhuria*, and Muhammad
al-Tabi'i in *al-Akhbar*.

Nasser was eager to establish links with the Lebanese media
and journalists in order to widen his appeal. It was recognized that
Beirut hosted many publications and news agencies which were
hostile to his regime. That meant fighting media wars with Egypt's
enemies and rivals in the Beirut arena.[63] Thus, the reaction of
Lebanese newspapers to Nasser's decision to nationalize the Suez
Canal Company was expressed in editorials of unanimous approval and praise for Egypt in general and Nasser in particular.[64]
But this supportive trend started to shift in mid-August 1956 with
the right-wing Christian newspapers criticizing the way in which
the pro-Nasser camp inside Lebanon was disrupting public life
through popular demonstrations. However, direct criticisms of
Nasser's leadership were not aired at this stage.[65]

The political crisis which erupted between Sham'un and his prime minister, 'Abdallah al-Yafi, over Lebanese foreign policy led right-wing Christian newspapers to start criticizing Egyptian arson activities against Western targets on Lebanese soil as well as other 'unwise' actions in Egypt itself.[66] This criticism developed into two main trends in Lebanese newspapers following the acceptance by the Lebanese government of the Eisenhower Doctrine. The newspapers of the Christian Maronites, the Syrian Socialist Nationalist Party and pro-Iraqi factions welcomed co-operation with the West. The Arab nationalist newspapers and those of the political left wing supported the Egyptian policy of positive neutrality. Each trend thus propagated completely different political opinions regarding Egyptian policies and President Nasser.[67]

Furthermore, particular publications were encouraged by the Egyptian government and given unlimited support. For instance, *al-Hawadiss* was launched in Beirut on 19 October 1956 by a Lebanese Egyptophile, Salim al-Lawzi, who defined its mission as 'to serve the Arab revolution at a time when it was embarking on confronting its enemies'.[68] The *al-Ahad* magazine, a pan-Arab publication edited by Riad Taha and opposed to the Baghdad Pact, also joined Nasser's camp, which enabled it to enjoy special favours.[69] Sai'd Frayha, publisher of *Dar al-Sayyad*, also enjoyed a special relationship with Cairo since he was opposed vehemently to Sham'un.[70]

The trade balance shifts in Egypt's favour

The Lebanese and Egyptian governments signed a new trade agreement on 27 June 1956 to replace an earlier one that had been in force since 2 September 1951. The new agreement was aimed at organizing trade relations, currency exchange and payments between the two countries. It also called for the free exchange of mutual trade. To this end, certain products were exempted from customs duties in order to encourage local industry in both countries, while duties of 50, 25 and 20 per cent were imposed on other products. Moreover, the Lebanese government committed itself to giving preferential treatment to Egyptian tourists by paying them an exchange rate of no less than L£8.5 for every Egyptian pound. This accord was adapted and renewed every year, and served as the basis for trade relations between the two countries until 1992.[71] However, there was a dispute on the application of this accord in two fields. The first concerned Egyptian requests to alter the terms of the tourism section in the new agreement in the summer of 1957. This was related to the Egyptian authorities' insistence that the exchange rate for an Egyptian pound should stay at L£8.5, in spite of the Lebanese government's view that the real exchange rate was L£5.75 (due to economic difficulties resulting from the Suez War). As a result, the Lebanese government offered a favourable 25 per cent increase to the rate of exchange, which made every Egyptian pound equivalent to L£7. But the Lebanese government refused to accept the view that every Egyptian visitor to Lebanon should be classified as a tourist with a right to reap prescribed benefits. However, this compromise was rejected by Egypt who therefore kept its tourists away from Lebanon.[72]

The second point concerned Egyptian government moves to restrict the import of Lebanese apples to the vital Egyptian market in July 1956.[73] This factor contributed to the ensuing 'apple crisis' in Lebanon which prompted the apple lobby to exert pressure on the Lebanese government to convince the Egyptian authorities to comply with the free trade rules, and also to balance the trade between the two countries.[74] Furthermore, the political crisis over the Suez Canal and Egyptian fears over being subjected to a Western economic blockade deferred the issue.[75] The licences to import Lebanese apples were eventually granted after the Suez War for a limited period, allowing for the export only of a third of the usual imported quantities. It is estimated that apple exports to Egypt for the 1956–57 season were 250,000 boxes, while the quantity was 600,000 boxes prior to that.[76] The Lebanese government's identification with the Eisenhower Doctrine and its tilt towards the West played a great part in forcing Lebanon to look for new markets in the West, especially after Egypt's refusal to import Lebanese apples in the late summer of 1957. In fact, the Lebanese minister of national economy, Kazim al-Khalil, claimed that Iraq, Britain, France, West Germany and the US Sixth Fleet had agreed to import Lebanese apples. It was clear that al-Khalil, who was also a close political ally of Sham'un, was saying that the loss of the Egyptian market was not harmful, since Lebanon's 'friends' would help in this respect.[77]

The two mentioned issues were part of a general austerity policy in Egypt, which led to encouraging exports and restricting imports. Quantitative restrictions were imposed which, in effect, negated tariff preferences accorded to some Lebanese products. As a result, Egyptian exports to Lebanon were boosted, reaching a record level of over L£10 million in 1956, and L£13 million in 1957 (see Table 2) of which 82 per cent consisted of vegetable, cotton and paper products.[78] By contrast, Lebanese exports to Egypt shrank to L£6 million in 1956, and L£5 million in 1957 (see Table 2). This shift in the trade balance signalled a reversal of the trend prior to 1955, when Lebanese exports to Egypt amounted to twice those of Lebanese imports from Egypt (see Chapter 1).

Conclusion

The confrontation between Egypt and the West over Suez caused a deep dilemma for the Lebanese government. After sitting on the fence from July until the Suez War, Sham'un opted not to be carried away by Egyptian and Syrian hostile tendencies towards the West. To this end, Sham'un's decision to ally Lebanon with the Eisenhower Doctrine signalled the beginning of a process of strained relations between the Lebanese and Egyptian governments. This process continued throughout 1957 and took on new aspects with the increase of Egyptian influence in Syria – Lebanon's only Arab neighbour. To counter this trend, the Egyptian government strengthened its contacts with Lebanese groups and media which opposed Sham'un's foreign policy drive. Despite the political discord, bilateral trade grew and worked in Egypt's favour, while the latter prevented its tourists from visiting Lebanon.

CHAPTER 3

The Lebanese–UAR Dispute of 1958

The West on the defensive

The Lebanese political crisis, which exploded on 8 May 1958, evoked considerable international interest. The Soviet Union accused the West, particularly the USA, of using the crisis as a pretext to interfere militarily in the affairs of Lebanon and as a means of applying pressure on the Arab states of the Near East.[1] America, for its part, observed the situation with concern but refrained from implementing the relevant section of the Eisenhower Doctrine which called for military intervention. Moreover, the USA entrusted the UN to determine whether there was evidence of communist interference in what was seen as a civil disturbance.[2]

The West was disturbed by the Iraqi coup d'état of 14 July 1958, which threatened not only to sweep away the pro-Western regimes in the Middle East but also to directly threaten Western economic interests. Great Britain and the USA reacted swiftly by sending troops to Jordan and Lebanon to contain the advance of Arab nationalist and communist forces. The US Secretary of State, John Foster Dulles, had suggested in May two possibilities to contain Nasser in the Middle East. The first was to prevent the Egyptian president from blackmailing Europe over oil, including plans for the holding of vital oil facilities and for transport round the Cape. The second was to put pressure on Nasser through the Nile waters in conjunction with the Sudan.[3] President Eisenhower told the US Congress on 15 July 1958 that:

> On July 14, 1958, I received an urgent request from the President of the Republic of Lebanon that some United States forces be stationed in Lebanon. ... I have replied that we would do this and a contingent of United States Marines has now arrived in Lebanon. ... We share

with the Government of Lebanon the view that these events in Iraq demonstrate a ruthlessness of aggressive purpose, which tiny Lebanon cannot combat without further evidence of support from other friendly nations.[4]

The Soviet reaction to Western military intervention in the Middle East was purely symbolic and restricted to diplomatic and political spheres. This was related, perhaps, to a Soviet desire to avoid a nuclear confrontation with the West at a time when the West's oil lifeline was at risk. Instead, the Soviet government moved to consolidate its position in the area by demanding the immediate withdrawal of Western troops on the grounds that they violated the UN Charter. In addition, the new Iraqi regime was recognized outright in order to show the Soviet commitment to help 'liberation movements' in the Third World.[5]

On 5 August 1958 the two superpowers agreed to debate the problems of the Middle East before the UN General Assembly. As a result, the Assembly adopted Resolution 1237 on 21 August 1958, which requested the Secretary General to make practical arrangements with various countries to 'facilitate the early withdrawal of the foreign troops' from Lebanon and Jordan. Consequently, the USA completed the withdrawal of its troops from Lebanon on 25 October 1958. The US government perceived their mission and that of British troops in Jordan as successful in stabilizing the Middle East area without invoking a confrontation with regional powers or the Soviet Union. Although the West lost the friendly regime in Iraq, a pivot of the Baghdad Pact, it was able to preserve other pro-Western regimes and guard Western interests in the Middle East.[6]

Nasser spreads north

The fusion of Egypt and Syria into the United Arab Republic (UAR) which was declared on 1 February 1958 represented a major regional development affecting the political map of the Middle East. The Egyptian government saw three benefits of such a union. First, it would act as a balance to the non-Arab states in the region which pursued active pro-Western policies, namely Israel and Turkey. Secondly, it ensured that Syria would be kept outside the communist dominion and maintain its internal stability. Thirdly, this new entity would enjoy a better bargaining position with the West, in order to meet its political and economic needs due to the fact that the UAR controlled 90 per cent of oil lines either through the Suez Canal or the Syrian pipelines.[7]

Professor P. G. Vatikiotis argues that Arabism was not essential for authorizing the political power of the military in Egypt proper. But the union with Syria catapulted Arabism into an efficacious formula by which Egyptian rulers could transfer their leadership into a Syrian national context and secure a measure of popular allegiance. The army officers ruling Egypt recognized that Arab nationalism was a source of strength, while the people in Syria appeared to hail it as the essential requirement for change.[8]

As soon as Nasser established his base in Syria, a rival Arab federation, the Arab Union (AU), was formed in mid-February 1958 between Iraq and Jordan in order to counter Egyptian influence. King Faisal of Iraq became head of state, and his prime minister, Nuri al-Sa'id, presided over the Federal Cabinet, which meant that Jordan joined the Baghdad Pact in all but name. Thus, a new battle commenced between the UAR and the Arab Union, with both aiming to gain influence over undecided Arab states. Saudi Arabia decided to withdraw a £5 million subsidy to Jordan as a sign of disenchantment with unity projects, while Lebanon was to become the first ground of conflict.[9] The Iraqi government lobbied the US and British governments in mid-April 1958 to facilitate Lebanon's joining the Arab Union.[10] But the Western powers opposed such an idea even after the eruption of the Lebanese civil war in May 1958. In fact, the West was reluctant to challenge Nasser and the Lebanese opposition in this respect because it would make reaching a solution more difficult.[11]

On the morning of 14 July 1958, Brigadier Abdul Karim Qassim led a successful coup attempt in Baghdad and proclaimed Iraq a republic. The US president reported that the head of the CIA, Allen Dulles, briefed him about the nightmare scenario in the region as follows. First, Dulles doubted the future of Jordan as Israel might be tempted to seize the West Bank. Secondly, Kuwait could also be in the balance. Thirdly, the Lebanese government had officially requested the West's intervention. Lastly, King Sa'ud of Saudi Arabia secretly demanded that the Baghdad Pact powers intervene in Iraq. Therefore the US and British military intervention in Jordan and Lebanon was defensive in nature since it sought to protect the shaky pro-Western regimes in the Middle East and not to restore the Iraqi regime.[12] This signalled the end

of pro-Western security systems such as the Baghdad Pact and the Arab Union. Turkey, for instance, refrained from intervening either in Syria or Iraq unless it obtained guarantees from the West against possible Soviet action on their common borders.[13]

The West's military intervention in Lebanon and Jordan to contain the perceived advance of Nasser's Arab nationalism seemed to succeed. According to Nasser's confidant, Muhammad H. Haikal, Nasser sent 'advice' to the new Iraqi rulers just hours after their coup. First, the new regime in Baghdad should promise to keep oil flowing to the Western markets uninterrupted. Secondly, the appearance of independence of the 'Iraqi revolution' should be maintained, even from the UAR. Lastly, there was no need to rush into unity with any Arab country in order not to antagonize the West against 'the revolution in its first vulnerable days'.[14] Nasser visited Moscow secretly in the wake of the US military intervention in Lebanon on 15 July 1958 in order to assess the position of the Soviet Union. Khrushchev cautioned Nasser against any escalation, in view of the possibility of nuclear war between the superpowers. He informed Nasser that any confrontation with the West should be restricted to the political, and not military, arena.[15]

Accordingly, the Egyptian government sought to achieve the withdrawal of Western troops from the Middle East through the Arab League framework. The conjunction of international and regional efforts was expressed at the UN General Assembly leading to an acceptance of the Arab states' pledge to respect the existing borders.

The roots of internal crisis

The Lebanese crisis which began in earnest with murder of Nasib al-Matni, an anti-Sham'un journalist, on 8 May 1958, was caused, according to Fahim Qubain, by a division in the soul of Lebanese society. This division involved the concept of national identity as well as relations with Arab Muslim neighbours and the Christian West.[16] In the event, the opposition held the government responsible for Matni's murder and called for a nation-wide strike. Soon after, hostilities flared up all over the country.

The main reason of the crisis lay in the Muslim and Arab nationalist opposition to President Sham'un's bid to stand for a second term despite a constitutional prohibition. This was seen as disrupting the sectarian balance since Sham'un tried to strengthen his own powers and reduce the power of the Sunni prime minister's office and the influence of non-Christians in general. As a result, the Christians rallied broadly behind the Maronite Christian president who followed a pro-Western policy, while the Muslims sought assistance from the UAR.[17]

Following US military intervention in Lebanon, Robert Murphy, Eisenhower's special representative, arrived in Beirut on 19 July 1958 in order to clarify the new US policy objectives. Murphy found that much of the conflict concerned personalities and rivalries of a domestic nature, with no relation to international issues. Therefore he sought to mediate between the Lebanese government and the opposition after making it clear that the US marines had not come to meddle in Lebanese politics. Moreover, Murphy facilitated the election of General Fu'ad Shihab, commander of the Lebanese army, as president on 31 July 1958.[18]

The formal hand-over of power to President Shihab on 23 September 1958 signalled the beginning of the process of defusing the internal crisis in Lebanon. Shihab nominated Rashid Karami, the leader of the opposition in Tripoli, as prime minister. Karami sought to build the new regime on the basis of the National Pact of 1943. A new 'balanced' government was formed and consisted of two Sunni Muslims, including Karami, and two Maronite Christians, and adopted the conciliatory slogan 'no victor, no vanquished.[19]

Prelude to conflict with the UAR

The relations between the Egyptian and Lebanese governments were so tense in early January 1958, that any action by one side was interpreted as hostile by the other side. This atmosphere of mistrust led to mutual attacks in the press and radio and the prohibition of distribution of each other's newspapers and magazines. The Lebanese government refused entry to Egyptian publications on two occasions in less than a month. The first was because Egyptian newspapers published news stories about the marriage of President Sham'un's son to an 'English dancer'.[20] The second related to a statement made by Egypt's foreign minister, Mahmud Fawzi, in the Egyptian parliament in which he accused Lebanon of being 'the centre of conspiracies directed at Egypt'.[21]

The real reason for Egyptian grievances was that the Lebanese government had turned a blind eye to the activities of the Free Egypt Committee, which opposed Nasser's regime, from Lebanese soil. Moreover, the Lebanese government turned down an Egyptian request to suppress this committee after it had sent a memorandum to the UN Secretary General criticizing the policies of Nasser's regime. The Lebanese government argued that the granting of refuge to 'some Egyptian personalities' was based on individual grounds – therefore it did not recognize that their activities had any political tinges.[22]

The Lebanese government tried to exploit this episode with its regional allies to its full advantage. First, Sham'un lobbied Great Britain to grant Lebanon more arms in order to match Soviet generosity to both Egypt and its Syrian ally. Sham'un's opinion was understood by the British ambassador in Beirut to be that 'it was impossible for him [Sham'un] to support the pro-Western policy of the Lebanon unless he received some practical support in return'.[23] Secondly, Lebanese foreign minister, Charles Malik, gave the British government the impression that it would be useful to diffuse Egyptian propaganda in the region – even if it meant embarking on some measure of reconciliation with Cairo in the short term. The British ambassador to Beirut, George Middleton, reported on 14 January 1958, that:

> Malik's intense dislike of Nasser and the present regime is of course undisguised. But he seems to have been influenced by his most recent talks with the Persians and now to incline to the view that sooner rather than later the Nasser regime will quietly disappear and that meanwhile we might as well try to get on terms with Egypt, if only thereby to silence the voice of their propaganda.[24]

The impact of UAR formation

The formation of the United Arab Republic (UAR) between Egypt and Syria on 1 February 1958 led to new pressures on the Lebanese government to join or at least affiliate with the new republic. This new factor threatened the internal stability of Lebanon especially since its Muslim element had wanted to back Nasser's anti-Western policies since 1956, while the Christian element sought the opposite.[25]

The Lebanese government was informed officially of the forming of the UAR on 4 February 1958, but it deferred the recognition of the new state until after the referendum to elect the head of the new state on 21 February 1958. The Egyptian authorities saw this position as a ploy to co-ordinate efforts with Egypt's Arab rivals (Jordan and Iraq) under the cloak of seeking Arab consensus on this issue. The reason for the Lebanese government's anxiety was perhaps related to two factors. First, the new entity was not only created outside the framework of the Arab League, but also UAR officials did not notify the League about the new development as was required. This was seen as a threat from the tide of Nasser's pan-Arabism to other Arab states' sovereignty, and Lebanon's in particular, which was enshrined in the League's constitution. Secondly, the Lebanese government complained that it was not consulted by the Syrian and Egyptian governments over this affair. Moreover, it was feared that Syria's traditional reluctance to recognize Lebanon's independence in clear terms might influence the view of the new state. Thus, it was not clear whether Lebanon had to re-negotiate mutual agreements with the new state, which controlled its access to the Arab hinterland, or not.[26]

Lebanese officials moved quickly to voice their suspicion and fears of the intentions of the UAR. President Sham'un asked the leaders of other Arab countries not to meddle in the internal affairs of Lebanon, while Charles Malik stressed the will to remain independent. In parliament on 11 February 1958, Malik said that:

> We pray to God that the unification declared between Egypt and Syria will bring about an increase in the living standard of the peoples of the two countries, and that it may augur well for the parties concerned ... whether these countries be called Syria, Egypt or the UAR, or called Iraq, Saudi Arabia. ... While the Lebanon – which continues to exist for ever as a nation – would keep a standard, a sovereignty, an independence, and a message, and will continue to play its international role.[27]

The Lebanese government maintained its aloofness from the new developments in the UAR by using two tactics. First, Beirut did not spare any effort to keep up the facade of unity within its ranks in the face of pressures to recognize the UAR. To this end, the Lebanese prime minister, Sami al-Sulh, denied categorically on 6 February 1958 that the resignation of the finance minister, Jamil al-Makkawi, was caused by the rejection of his proposal to recognize the UAR immediately.[28] Secondly, on 11 February 1958 the Lebanese government reiterated the view that it had not yet decided whether to send official emissaries either to Syria or Egypt to congratulate the new state. This was a clear attempt to quash the claims of the Lebanese opposition that it represented Lebanon in the many delegations it sent to congratulate President Nasser.[29]

The Lebanese government lived up to its promise and recognized the UAR officially on 27 February 1958. Nasser replied to the greetings of Lebanon's prime minister, Sami al-Sulh, by saying that:

> We hope for this new republic [the UAR] to be a strong fortress to defend Arabism and its peoples against conspiracies and bad intentions. We still remember Lebanon's [positive] attitudes towards Arabism. We also look forward to the moment when the Lebanese people join other Arab peoples and us in strengthening the bonds of co-operation and fraternity.[30]

Consequently, on 15 April 1958, the Egyptian ambassador to Beirut, General Abdul Hamid Ghalib, presented his credentials to the Lebanese government as the UAR ambassador.[31] But the Lebanese move to recognize the UAR was timed to come out simultaneously with the recognition of the rival Arab Union of Jordan and Iraq. This was aimed at depriving Nasser of the opportunity to present his UAR as taking precedence to other unity projects. Despite the political gloss that the Lebanese government maintained – it intended to stand at an equal distance from the rival unions – it was clear that it pursued policies aimed at counterbalancing the perceived threats posed by the UAR on Lebanon.[32]

The persistence of Sham'un's loyalists to press ahead with their intention to amend the Lebanese constitution in order to allow Sham'un to run for a second term as president inflamed the internal political crisis in Lebanon. This factor added to the already strained relations between the UAR and the Lebanese government, since the UAR had offered backing and inspiration to the Lebanese opposition against President Sham'un.[33] The Speaker of the Lebanese Parliament, 'Adil 'Ussayran, visited Cairo on 28 March 1958 to mediate between Nasser and Sham'un. 'Ussayran tried to win Nasser's support for Sham'un's desire to amend the constitution, since one word from Nasser could do much to quieten the Lebanese opposition. Furthermore, 'Ussayran sought to extract guarantees from Nasser regarding Lebanese independence and national unity. The Speaker said in a press conference on 28 March 1958 that:

> I found that this man [Nasser] is a wise leader who wishes every good for all Arab countries, ... does not in any way contemplate forcing any Arab country to unite with him, and does not wish his name to be thrust into the domestic affairs of any Arab country. President Nasser assured me that he was as anxious as the Lebanese themselves to preserve Lebanon's independence and its national unity.[34]

'Ussayran succeeded in extracting statements from Nasser to calm and reassure Lebanese Christians over their fear of a possible takeover of Lebanon by the UAR. Nasser was quoted as telling 'Ussayran that 'there is no truth to the talk that nationalist agents are plotting to make trouble to annex Lebanon to the UAR. We have great respect for Lebanese Christians ... it was they who brought Arabism to Egypt and it was they who preserved the language of the Koran'.[35] The fact that the Nasser–'Ussayran meeting lasted five hours shows that they dwelled on the internal and external implications of a dangerous state of affairs in Lebanon. But President Nasser seemed not interested in concluding a deal with Sham'un, fearing this would enable the Lebanese president to save his political future. More importantly, Nasser did not buy the idea that keeping Sham'un in office would represent a guarantee for Lebanese Christians and the independence of Lebanon. This was related to the fact that the dispute between the two presidents involved foreign policy orientation since the Suez War as well as differences in their personalities. Nasser gave the impression that Lebanese opposition groups had a cause of their own and thus he could not be held responsible for their actions. The UAR president explained this by saying 'I only listen to what they [the Lebanese opposition] say ... I do not have a school here to make good citizens out of them. Their visits here do not mean that I do what they say'.[36]

Subsequently, Lebanese–UAR relations started to deteriorate at the same time as the internal political crisis in Lebanon escalated between supporters and opponents of Sham'un. The Lebanese government resorted to banning Egyptian news publications in Lebanon on the grounds of their opposition bias. On 5 April 1958, all Egyptian publications were banned in Lebanon for describing some internal unrest in the south of the country as being 'the vanguard of sweeping popular revolution'. When the Lebanese prime minister, Sami al-Sulh, drew the attention of the Egyptian ambassador, General Ghalib, to this matter, the latter replied that the material published in Egyptian newspapers 'does not differ much from what is published in Lebanese newspapers'.[37] However, Egyptian publications continued to support the cause of Lebanese opposition with increasing fervour despite Lebanese bans. For instance, *al-Ahram* criticized Sham'un and his government's policies on 14 April 1958 in the following terms:

> Is it possible that the present battle in the Lebanon will precipitate a civil war? ... Is President Sham'un pleased to see such things [internal clashes] happening in the Lebanon's streets ... while he sits in his palace brooding over plans for suppressing a free people and silencing its citizens? It is time the Lebanon turned toward Arabism and stood in the new Arab ranks in order to assume a notable position in the Arab nation. ... The Lebanese Government is banning Egyptian papers from the Lebanon but it will never be able to ban our prayers that the Lebanon and its people may be preserved.[38]

The Speaker of the Lebanese Parliament, 'Adil 'Ussayran, tried again to mediate between Nasser and Sham'un. He visited Cairo on 19 April 1958, and stayed there for a week trying to strike a deal with Nasser. But 'Ussayran's mission failed to produce concrete results and he found himself embroiled in an Egyptian exercise to drive a wedge between him and Sham'un. On 22 April 1958, the UAR official news agency (MENA) attributed comments to 'Ussayran in which he called on Lebanon to join the UAR and denounced reported moves by the US Sixth Fleet to protect the status quo in Lebanon.[39]

UAR intervention in the revolt

The UAR government and media encouraged the Lebanese opposition in its revolt against President Sham'un following the murder of Nasib al-Matni, an anti-Sham'un journalist, on 8 May 1958. Sham'un dispatched 'Adil 'Ussayran on the same day to Damascus in order to mediate with UAR officials in the northern region (Syria) and the visiting Secretary of the National Union in Egypt, Anwar Sadat. This proved a futile exercise as every side refused to compromise.[40]

On 13 May 1958, Charles Malik held a press conference in Beirut in which he accused the UAR, for the first time, of intervening directly in the internal affairs of Lebanon. Malik enumerated many examples of UAR actions and held it responsible for Lebanese internal disturbances. The most controversial event was the arrest of the Belgian Consul General in Damascus, Louis De San, on the Lebanese border with Syria, while trying to smuggle arms and instructions to the Lebanese opposition. However, Malik blamed the UAR, not Belgium, for this incident and for the following attack by 500 men, mostly Syrian, on the border post of al-Massna' in an attempt to press the release of the Belgian official. Malik also stated that the Lebanese authorities had arrested scores of armed Syrians in Beirut, together with two boats carrying Palestinian gunmen and weapons from the Gaza Strip, then under Egyptian control. Moreover, he noted that Lebanese police had confiscated about 100 rifles with Egyptian army markings which had been sent to mutineers in Tripoli, North Lebanon.[41]

Subsequently, the Lebanese and UAR governments were engaged in a diplomatic confrontation, protesting at each other's actions and refusing to receive diplomatic notes. On 14 May 1958, the UAR government refused to receive a Lebanese memorandum protesting at UAR interference in Lebanese affairs on the grounds that it was baseless. At the same time, the UAR ambassador to Beirut, General Ghalib, protested to the Lebanese authorities at the forcing down of two Egyptian civilian planes in Lebanese airspace and the mistreatment of their passengers.[42]

On 15 May, the UAR government protested to the Lebanese government at the mistreatment of Egyptian diplomats and the arrest of many UAR citizens. The Lebanese government rejected, in turn, the Egyptian accounts of these events and instructed its chargé d'affaires in Cairo to return Egyptian memoranda to the UAR Foreign Ministry.[43] Meanwhile, the Lebanese government protested at the apparent inaction of Egyptian authorities over the occupation of the Lebanese Embassy in Cairo by anti-Sham'un Lebanese students. This issue was aggravated by the burning of Sham'un's posters along with the Lebanese flag, and the erection of a new plaque on the Embassy entrance bearing the name of 'the United Arab Republic – the Lebanese Region'.[44]

The Lebanese government raised the stakes and issued a statement on 16 May 1958 which accused Egypt and Syria of plotting against Beirut by using Lebanese opposition groups ever since the Suez war of 1956. The aim of these acts, it was alleged, was to cause riots and disturbances inside Lebanon because of Lebanese government opposition to breaking off diplomatic relations with Britain and France (see Chapter 2). The statement ended by saying that:

> All these actions [examples of UAR interference in Lebanon] clearly indicate that official and unofficial quarters in Syria and Egypt aimed at spreading terror and fear in the Lebanon and carrying out sabotage with a view to undermining the Lebanon. These actions, however, are not the only evidence of ill intentions by United Arab Republic quarters. Official broadcasts and press campaigns against the regime in the Lebanon have lately aimed at sowing sedition and have called upon the Lebanese people to oppose the present regime and revolt against the government.[45]

Nasser commented publicly on the Lebanese–UAR dispute for the first time on 16 May 1958, upon his return from an official visit to the Soviet Union. First, Nasser accused the Lebanese government and its ally, the Syrian Socialist Nationalist Party (SSNP), of killing Nasib al-Matni, thus instigating the civil war. Secondly, Nasser denied that the UAR government had interfered in the internal affairs of Lebanon. Thirdly, he restated his respect for Lebanese independence and the absence of a plan to annex it to the UAR. He said:

> In the name of the people of the United Arab Republic I repeat what I have said before. We uphold and respect the independence of the Lebanon; that we will not allow interference in its internal affairs; and that the things said by those people [the Lebanese government] are nothing but fabrications. They constitute, however, a clever move to transform the internal strife into an external one between the Lebanon and the UAR. It is a skilful move to deceive the big powers and induce them to intervene.[46]

Consequently, the war of words escalated between Lebanese and UAR officials with each side laying responsibility at the door of the other. A case in point was that of Akram al-Hurani, UAR vice-president, who said on 21 May 1958 that the Lebanese rulers made Lebanon 'an imperialist base in the last few years to spread poisonous propaganda against the Arab cause, as well as to threaten the independence of the UAR'. Al-Hurani accused Charles Malik personally of conspiring with imperialism and the Syrian nationalists who killed Colonel 'Adnan al-Maliki in Syria in

1955. The implication was that Lebanese governments had conspired against Syria and Arab nationalists well before 1956.[47]

The dispute before the Arab League

On 21 May 1958, the Lebanese government requested an urgent meeting of the Arab League Council in either Libya or the Sudan, to discuss its complaint of interference by the UAR in the internal affairs of Lebanon. A day later, the Lebanese government lodged a similar complaint against the UAR in the UN Security Council. But the Lebanese government proceeded with its complaint at the Arab League level after the Egyptian government accepted in principle on 24 May 1958 that it would attend.[48] This paved the way for the Arab League Secretary General, 'Abdel Khaliq Hassuna, to request that the UN Security Council postpone its discussion of the Lebanese question, in accordance with Article 52 of the UN Charter, which stipulates settling disputes by regional organizations (i.e. the Arab League). The Iraqi foreign minister, Fadhil al-Jamali, also asked the Council on 27 May 1958 to defer the discussion of the Lebanese complaint until the League had had chance to debate it.[49]

The UAR government persuaded the Arab League Council to meet in Benghazi, Libya, on 31 May 1958. The UAR's aim was to deny the Lebanese government exacting possible gains on two counts. First, the UAR played down the importance of the meeting and thus was represented by the assistant under-secretary of its Foreign Ministry, Sayyid Fahmi. Lebanon was represented by Minister Bashir al-A'war, while Iraq was represented by its ambassador to Cairo, Ibrahim al-Khudayri.[50] Secondly, the UAR government persuaded the Arab League's Secretariat to change the venue of the meeting from Tripoli to Benghazi. The reported aim was to deny the Lebanese side a propaganda coup due to the lack of facilities for direct reporting from Benghazi.[51]

The League Council met for six closed sessions in Benghazi from 31 May until 6 June 1958. The UAR and Lebanese delegates traded charges and counter-charges of interference in each other's affairs. The Lebanese chief delegate, Bashir al-A'war, asked the League to take effective measures to stop UAR propaganda and to prevent arms and terrorists from infiltrating Lebanon. The UAR chief delegate, Sayyid Fahmi, concentrated on describing the

Lebanese crisis as a mere internal affair. Moreover, Fahmi accused the Lebanese government of undermining the Arab League by resorting to the UN Security Council to resolve a problem between two Arab states.[52] Eventually, the League Council adopted a Libyan draft resolution on 4 June which stated that:

First: All [activities] likely to disturb, in any way, the cordial atmosphere among the member states [of the League] should cease;

Second: The government of the Republic of Lebanon should withdraw its complaint from the UN Security Council;

Third: An appeal should be addressed to the various Lebanese factions to halt the disturbances and disorders and to work towards the settlement of [their] internal conflicts by constitutional peaceful means;

Fourth: The dispatch of a commission to be appointed by the Council of the League of Arab States, from amongst its own members, in order to appease sentiments and to implement the resolution of the Council.[53]

The Lebanese government rejected this draft resolution outright and instructed its delegation to withdraw from the meeting if Lebanese grievances were not addressed. The Lebanese government stated that the draft resolution was very broad and did not address the substance of the crisis – UAR interference in Lebanese affairs. Moreover, the scope of the proposed commission was, in the Lebanese government's view, devoid of any binding recommendations, thus making its mission useless. As a result, the Lebanese delegation argued on 6 June 1958 that the draft resolution requested Lebanon to withdraw its complaint from the Security Council while asking the UAR to do nothing. This led to the collapse of the meeting as the Jordanian and Iraqi delegations withdrew their support for the proposed resolution.[54]

The UAR government was content with the Lebanon's failure to win an outright condemnation of suspected UAR interference in Lebanese affairs. However, some UAR officials criticized the League Council for committing a 'legal blunder', namely ending the session without issuing the draft resolution formally, due to the Lebanese rejection.[55]

The dispute before the UN Security Council

As early as 14 May 1958, the Lebanese government decided to present to the UN Security Council a complaint against UAR interference in the internal affairs of Lebanon. But the official request to the UN was not made until 22 May 1958 when the Lebanese government was able to overcome some opposition in parliament.[56] The representative of Lebanon at the UN, Karim 'Azqul, stated in his letter to the President of the Security Council on 22 May 1958 that:

> The said intervention consists *inter alia* of the following acts: the infiltration of armed bands from Syria into Lebanon, the destruction of Lebanese life and property by such bands, the participation of the United Arab Republic in acts of terrorism and rebellion against the established authorities in Lebanon, the supply of arms from Syria to individuals and bands in Lebanon rebelling against the established authorities, and the waging of a violent radio and press campaign in the United Arab Republic calling for strikes, demonstrations and the overthrow of the established authorities in Lebanon, and through other provocative acts.[57]

The Security Council deferred the debate on this issue three times (27 May, 2 and 5 June 1958) at the request of the Lebanese government and the Arab League. This was intended to allow the Arab League Council time to reach a solution. But just after the reported failure of the League, the UN Security Council began its session on 6 June 1958 (the same day the Arab League's Council meeting ended). The chief of the UAR delegation to the Arab League's meeting, Sayyid Fahmi, joined the UAR delegation in New York, while the Lebanese delegation was instructed to send the proceedings of the Arab League Council meeting to New York.[58]

During the UN Security Council meeting, Charles Malik, and the UAR representative at the UN, 'Umar Lutfi, were engaged in lengthy arguments. The Lebanese foreign minister reiterated his government's charges against the UAR and enumerated many examples of UAR intervention. Malik said that this took the form of waging propaganda campaigns and providing arms and guidance to the Lebanese opposition. Malik ended his speech by appealing for UN protection:

Of all countries in the Middle East, then, Lebanon primarily depends upon the United Nations for its safety. The [UN] Charter is our primary protection. We cannot protect ourselves alone: we are much too small and fragile for that. We resorted to the League of Arab States and we gave it all opportunity to act, but no decision was taken, and the intervention, far from abating, has actually increased in intensity in the last day or two. The [Security] Council is our last recourse.[59]

The UAR representative rejected Malik's accusations and charged the Lebanese government with playing the Arab League against the Security Council in order to extract a favourable resolution from the League. Lutfi argued that the Lebanese government, in rejecting the League's resolution, had violated Arab consensus:

> The present government of Lebanon has striven to give an international aspect to what is a purely domestic problem and to divert the attention of its own public opinion and that of the world from the situation now prevailing in Lebanon. It appears that the Lebanese Government was not very serious in submitting the complaint to the Arab League and that this was merely a device to show that, before coming to the Council, it had exhausted local remedies. ... According to information I received today, six states of the Arab League ... submitted a resolution, which was unfortunately not accepted by the Lebanese Government.[60]

Lutfi produced extracts of statements by numerous Lebanese statesmen, former officials and Muslim and Christian clergymen to prove that the conflict was internal. Secondly, he charged the Lebanese government of mistreating UAR diplomats and expelling thousands of its citizens. Finally, he accused Lebanon of hosting anti-UAR groups, especially the Free Egypt Committee, and allowing hostile press campaigns to be staged by certain publications and clandestine broadcasting stations.[61] On 10 June 1958, Malik and Lutfi elaborated on their cases and entered into polemics concerning the proceedings of the Arab League meeting at Benghazi. The Security Council meeting turned into a stage for Cold War politics as the USA supported the case of the Lebanese government, while the Soviet Union supported the case of the UAR.[62] The Iraqi foreign minister, Fadhil al-Jamali, joined in the fray by vehemently attacking Nasserism and communism and charged both ideologies with wreaking havoc not only in Lebanon but also in Iraq and Jordan:

We believe that the problem which Lebanon has raised in this Council does not affect Lebanon alone. It is the design of President Nasser to dominate the Arab world, or at least to turn the Arab states into satellites of Egypt by fomenting revolutions. President Nasser applies practically the same communist method of subversion from within as that used in Eastern Europe, Korea and Vietnam.[63]

On 11 June, the Security Council adopted a Swedish draft resolution, with the abstention of the Soviet Union, which called for the dispatch of a UN observation group to Lebanon in order to investigate the Lebanese claim. The Lebanese government had, in fact, initially rejected the Swedish draft on 10 June 1958, for two reasons. First, the resolution failed to condemn the UAR in clear terms, which meant that the draft was similar to that of the Arab League's. Secondly, the draft suggested the dispatch of a mere observation group and not an international police force as the Lebanese government had hoped. But Lebanon found it ultimately impossible to oppose the draft, especially after it became clear that it had already won the approval of the UN Security Council. Thus, the Lebanese government approved the draft on the grounds that 'it included all Lebanese concerns implicitly'.[64]

The Lebanese government felt disenchanted by the mission undertaken by the UN Secretary General, Hammarskjold, during his visit to the Middle East lasting from 19 to 25 June 1958. Hammarskjold tried to mediate between Nasser and Sham'un under the guise of stopping the press and radio campaigns between the UAR and Lebanon – a first step to clearing the atmosphere between the two countries. But on 25 June 1958, Sham'un expressed his opposition to these efforts, which included a request to withdraw or freeze at least the Lebanese complaint at the Security Council. Moreover, Sham'un hinted that he might ask for military intervention under the provisions of Article 51 of the UN Charter. This proved that he was impatient with the mediation efforts of the UN and wanted speedy results.[65]

Sham'un suspected that the UN Secretary General had reached an understanding with Nasser to freeze the Lebanese issue until after the Lebanese presidential elections, scheduled for 24 July 1958. This became apparent when the Lebanese delegation to the UN failed, on 28 and 29 June, to win the approval of the Secretary General for recalling the Security Council.[66] Meanwhile, it seemed that President Nasser was not unhappy with the work of the UN observation group. On 29 June 1958 he said:

> The United Arab Republic did not object to the resolution taken by the Security Council to send UN observers to Lebanon because this will show the truth which Lebanon's rulers are trying to hide. ... As to Egyptians, there is no Egyptian community in Lebanon for Lebanon's rulers to level fabricated accusations at. As to Syrians, 70,000 of them live in Lebanon and are working in various fields. Lebanon's rulers expelled 25,000 of them in order create an appropriate atmosphere for their accusations.[67]

The first report of the UN observation group in Lebanon, published on 1 July 1958, failed to blame the UAR outright for providing any significant support for Lebanese opposition groups. This provided a diplomatic victory for the UAR government which stressed on 3 July 1958 that the UN report denied Lebanese government claims and proved the non-intervention of the UAR in the internal affairs of Lebanon.[68] President Sham'un criticized the UN and charged it with helping Nasser establish control over the whole Middle East. On 6 July 1958, Sham'un said:

> Mr Hammarskjold's statement and the observers' report give carte blanche to Col Nasser to step up infiltration into Lebanon. I am deeply disappointed both in the Secretary General and the observer group here [in Lebanon]. They have given the 'go ahead' signal to the United Arab Republic to take over the Middle East without fear of any objection by the UN.[69]

However, Sham'un refrained from requesting the departure of the UN observation group. Instead, on 4 July 1958, the Lebanese government expelled seven members of the UAR Embassy staff in Beirut for 'activities not in accordance with their duties, and in particular contacts with certain groups which they have provided with information, arms and money'.[70] The Egyptian ambassador to Beirut, General Ghalib, denied the charges and questioned the wisdom of this decision at a time when 'the UN report discharged the UAR from allegations of interference in the internal affairs of Lebanon'.[71] This was the first time the Lebanese government had expelled UAR diplomats since the beginning of the dispute. The UAR Embassy staff in Beirut was now reduced to four diplomats.

Furthermore, on 8 July 1958, the British government instructed its ambassador to Beirut to suggest to the Lebanese government that they take tougher measures against the UAR

Embassy in Beirut. The stated aim was that the Lebanese case against the UAR would carry more conviction in the UN. These measures included the breaking-off of diplomatic relations with the UAR or at least expelling its military attaché and restricting the cipher facilities in its Embassy.[72] When the British ambassador put this suggestion to Victor Khuri, director of the Lebanese Foreign Ministry, Khuri replied that 'the Lebanese government had already discussed the desirability of declaring the UAR ambassador persona non grata, and it will be done soon'.[73] In fact, the Lebanese government expelled the UAR ambassador, General Ghalib, on 24 July 1958. Ghalib protested that the Lebanese officials did not explain to him the reasons for his expulsion. The Lebanese authorities stressed, however, that his expulsion did not signify the rupture of diplomatic relations between Lebanon and the UAR. Nevertheless, the UAR government did not retaliate in kind.[74]

Solution in the UN General Assembly

President Sham'un's swift decision to invite the US military intervention of 15 July 1958 was intended to save his regime from collapsing under pressure from pro-UAR opposition groups. In fact, the fall of the Iraqi regime on 14 July 1958 had deprived Sham'un of a significant regional ally to check Nasser's policies. Therefore Sham'un sought the protection of a superpower (the USA) under the rules of Article 51 of the UN Charter.

Lebanese prime minister, Sami al-Sulh, perceived the US intervention as a correction of an earlier mistake by the UN observation group when it absolved the UAR on 1 July 1958 from the charge of interfering in the internal affairs of Lebanon. In fact, Western capitals had previously lacked enthusiasm even for sending an international police force to Lebanon for a limited period.[75]

Nasser was aware that the Lebanese–UAR dispute had been transferred from a mere regional conflict to an international issue involving both superpowers and their respective allies. This factor imposed restrictions on Nasser's room to manoeuvre, as the UAR itself was unable to substantiate previous vows to intervene in Lebanon in the event of Western intervention.[76] On 16 July, Nasser criticized the US intervention by saying that:

The American forces' occupation of the Lebanon constitutes a threat to peace in the Middle East, a serious aggression against the UN Charter and a flagrant threat to the Arab states which have refused to succumb to imperialism and are determined to pursue an independent policy. It is evident that the US Government has used the internal revolution in Lebanon ... as a pretext for realizing its objective, which is to occupy Lebanon and to threaten the independent states of the Middle East.[77]

The US warning to the UAR on 18 July 1958 that it would bear the consequences of any attacks on US forces stationed in Lebanon gave President Nasser a clear message that the USA was the prime authority in Lebanon. The Egyptian ambassador to the UN, 'Umar Lutfi, stated on 18 July 1958 that the US ambassador in Cairo delivered a *note verbale* to the Egyptian government which asserted that:

> The [US] troops have no hostile intentions. It was necessary to come to the assistance of Lebanon because of the change of government in Iraq. The United Arab Republic should realize that if the United States forces are attacked by military units of the United Arab Republic or by elements which the United States knows to be under control of the United Arab Republic or ready to carry out its instructions, there will be a danger that the problem may be enlarged and assume major proportions.[78]

The US threat meant that violence was no longer a viable option for President Nasser to force political changes in Lebanon. Moreover, his efforts to change the status quo in the Middle East were checked further as the security of the regimes in Lebanon and Jordan had become a Western domain. This led Nasser to look for prospects of co-operation with the new regime in Baghdad rather than risk a confrontation with the West over Lebanon. He declared that any attack on the new regime in Baghdad would be regarded as 'aggression against the UAR' in accordance with the Arab Collective Security Pact.[79] As a result, Nasser pursued the diplomatic option over Lebanon by two means. First, the UAR president co-ordinated his efforts with the US government in masterminding the election of General Fu'ad Shihab, the commander of the Lebanese army, as a new president for Lebanon on 31 July 1958. Mahmud Riad, Nasser's adviser and later his foreign minister, said that Nasser accepted the suggestion of Raymond Hare, the US ambassador to Cairo, that General Shihab was the best choice to succeed President Sham'un.

Shihab's strong point was, according to Riad, his 'wise decision' not to use the Lebanese army against the opposition in Lebanon.[80] Secondly, the UAR government showed readiness to offer guarantees respecting Lebanon's independence during the special session of the UN General Assembly debate on the Middle East crisis, 8–21 August 1958. Sham'un recognized this and vowed not to stand in the way of any proposed formula, whether in the Security Council, as he would have favoured, or the General Assembly.[81] The UAR government endorsed a face-saving formula presented by the Arab League to the UN General Assembly session by which all Arab states pledged to respect their existing frontiers. Although the draft did not specify the UAR by name, it implicitly carried a UAR undertaking not to interfere in Lebanese and Jordanian internal affairs after the withdrawal of Western forces.[82] Likewise, the draft called for the UN Secretary General to contact the different parties to facilitate the withdrawal of foreign troops from Lebanon and Jordan – a UAR request. Thus, the UN General Assembly adopted the Arab League draft unanimously on 21 August 1958.[83]

Consequently, the UN Secretary General met Nasser on 4 September 1958, and asked him to scale down his propaganda war against the Lebanese and Jordanian governments. But Muhammad H. Haikal, Nasser's confidant and informal spokesman, recounted that the president protested at this specific request by telling the UN Secretary General that:

> If you deprive me of my radio, then I am left defenceless. … The only way to reach my source of strength, the Arab masses, is through the airing of my principles and opinions. The Egyptian newspapers are prevented from entering Lebanon and Jordan, and my Embassies there are under siege. Therefore the radio is the only medium available for me to communicate with the people.[84]

However, the UN Secretary General succeeded in negotiating a compromise between the Lebanese and UAR governments. On 5 September 1958, the day after the UN official met Nasser, the Lebanese government reversed its decision to prohibit the distribution of Egyptian newspapers in the country.[85] Nonetheless, the process of restoring normal relations between the UAR and Lebanon had to await Sham'un's departure from the presidential office. In fact, the UAR opposed the candidature of Charles Malik for the post of president of the UN General Assembly in favour of the Sudanese foreign minister, Muhammad Mahjub. This position was maintained throughout even after the election of Malik for the UN post on 17 September 1958.[86]

Normalization of relations

President Shihab started the process of normalizing relations with the UAR government just after he succeeded Sham'un on 23 September 1958. To this end, Shihab's new administration reversed virtually every measure taken by his predecessor against the UAR. On 5 October 1958, Philip Takla, Lebanon's new foreign minister, met the UAR chargé d'affaires in Beirut to express 'the necessity to restore the traditional and cordial relations between the two countries'.[87] Later, the Lebanese foreign minister instructed Lebanese diplomatic missions, particularly in South America, to call off the campaign against the 'activities of UAR missions in these countries'.[88]

Furthermore, the Lebanese government took the initiative on 31 October 1958 to 'revive' the diplomatic relations with the UAR on two levels. First, the Lebanese government suggested Joseph Abu-Khatir as new Lebanese ambassador to Cairo. Secondly, it requested the return of former UAR ambassador General Ghalib to Beirut.[89] This gesture was intended to preserve his dignity and that of his country by wiping out the effects of declaring him persona non grata by the previous government. In fact, the Lebanese government had overcome an objection to Ghalib's return, which was tabled by Pierre Jumayyil, Minister of Agriculture and leader of the right-wing Phalange Party. The latter explained that some Lebanese perceived Ghalib as one of those responsible for the civil war in Lebanon.[90]

The UAR government accepted these gestures and dispatched its ambassador to Beirut on 9 November 1958. The new Lebanese ambassador to Cairo, Joseph Abu-Khatir, took up his post on 12 November 1958. He made clear that the new Lebanese government was ready to start a new era of relations with the UAR government. First of all, it recognized that the UAR held the leading role in Arab affairs 'under the wise leadership of the great man [Nasser] who is pursuing the Arabs' dignity and rights'. Secondly, the Lebanese government would respect and abide by collective Arab decisions regarding Israel.[91] In short, the Lebanese government undertook to co-ordinate its foreign policy in conjunction with the UAR.

The withdrawal of US troops from Lebanon on 25 October 1958 ushered in the beginning of the process of winding down the international dimension of the UAR–Lebanese dispute. The Lebanese foreign minister, Hussein 'Uwayni, sent a letter on 16 November 1958 to the President of the Security Council demanding the deletion of the complaint against the UAR.[92] Consequently, the UN Secretary General gave his instructions on 17 November 1958 to the President of the Security Council to liquidate the operation of the observation group in Lebanon.[93] This paved the way for the restoration of normal political contacts between the two governments.

The last step which the Lebanese government adopted in order to clear relations with the UAR, was the abandonment of its commitment to the Eisenhower Doctrine on 10 December 1958. This declaration was conveyed to William Rountree, the US under-Secretary of State, during his visit to Beirut. Rountree replied that the Eisenhower Doctrine was a 'unilateral declaration' and thus no government should feel bound by it. Therefore the Lebanese government mirrored the UAR position on aid by stating that it would only accept forms of aid which were unconditional. As a result, Lebanese prime minister, Rashid Karami, was promised a $10 million grant from the USA without incurring any protest from President Nasser.[94]

The impact of the UAR on Lebanese communities

The declaration of the creation of the United Arab Republic on 1 February 1958 sent different messages to the Muslim and Christian communities of Lebanon. For Muslims, the appeal of Arab unity became stronger when the Egyptian regime suddenly was invited to unite with Lebanon's neighbour, Syria. For Christians, this development re-awakened the old fears of being engulfed by a Muslim empire, which inevitably would reflect negatively on their political and social position. Desmond Stewart, a British observer who lived in Beirut at the time, depicted accurately the popular mood of both communities:

> To the Arab nationalists [inside Lebanon] the achieved goal [of unity] was two hours away by taxi; to the 'Libanists' [i.e. the majority of

Christians] the menace was at the door: not a seedy republic ... but one wing of a great pan-Arab state presided over by the most effective Arab personality to have appeared for centuries [i.e. Nasser]. The appeal of this state was visible and audible in many quarters of Beirut, Tripoli and Sidon. The walls of cafes and private houses were decorated with portraits of Nasser, while radios blared the stirring Egyptian anthem 'Allahu Akbar!'. The threat of this state revived in the 'Libanists' a traditional tendency to look to the West for support.[95]

Consequently, Lebanese society was split on religious lines to a great extent, which fuelled the civil war. While the Christians, by and large, rallied behind Sham'un to oppose Nasser's threat, the Muslims revolted against Sham'un with the encouragement of the United Arab Republic. Muslim political leaders celebrated the UAR creation by sending cables of congratulations to President Nasser. Moreover, a strike was organized on 5 February 1958 in Muslim cities and towns whereby popular demonstrations called for Arab unity under Nasser's leadership.[96]

When Nasser visited Damascus in late February 1958, political leaders (Arabic *za'im*, pl. *zu'ama*), mainly Muslim, flocked to greet him along with tens of thousands of their followers. Rashid Karami, Tripoli's Muslim leader, offered his loyalty to Nasser on 27 February 1958:

> We in the Lebanon believe that the Lebanon is of the Arabs and for the Arabs. The Lebanese people, O President, believe in your principles and mission, and are following your footsteps and example. ... You can rest assured, O President, that when the hour strikes we will all leap up as one man to hoist the banner to which all the Arabs will rally.[97]

Although Nasser replied in kind and avoided calling Lebanon to join the UAR outright, it was clear that he was drumming up Arab nationalist fervour in Lebanon. He told a Lebanese delegation that:

> Arab unity is now an actual fact – it is a unity of hearts and sentiments – a unity of souls. Events have united the Arab peoples ... their struggle for the suppression of pacts, for the consolidation of the foundations of freedom and equality, this true and deeply rooted unity. Dear Lebanon is now a neighbour, adjoining the shores of the UAR. ... The UAR will ever be a strong support and aid to the people of Lebanon against Israeli menace. ... It will also stand by

Lebanon against imperialistic danger, as well as against attempts at sowing the seeds of discord or hatred.[98]

Meanwhile, the twin issues of Muslim loyalty to Nasser and opposition to any constitutional changes which would enable President Sham'un's re-election became entangled. On 24 February 1958, at a rally of the Najjadah Party in Beirut, various political leaders congratulated Nasser on his election to the presidency of the UAR, while at the same time attacking Sham'un bitterly. Most subsequent political rallies and demonstrations organized by the opposition to Sham'un followed this position with increasing participation from Muslim religious leaders.[99]

Sham'un and the majority of his Christian Maronite supporters regarded Muslim loyalty to Nasser, rather than to Sham'un, as a clear indication of their repudiation of the National Pact of 1943. Moreover, this conveyed the impression that Lebanese Muslims were not interested in preserving Lebanon's independence any longer, and perhaps aimed at joining the UAR. Michael Johnson attributed this phenomenon to the disappointment felt by the Muslim community towards the socio-economic regime, which took over from the French in 1943. By 1958, the grievances of the Sunni *menu* people played a great part in re-activating dormant sectarianism. According to Johnson, when President Sham'un's regime failed to appease the Sunni Muslim petty bourgeoisie, it joined the sub-proletariat of the Sunni community in turning to Nasser. This forced the Sunni traditional leaders (*zu'ama*) to join the lower echelons of the community in requesting fairer distribution of opportunities in the Lebanese state. But since the answers to these demands were slow to materialize, the Sunni community turned to popular Nasserism en masse.[100]

Therefore when the Sham'un regime could not respond to the mobilization of the Sunni community, it resorted to blocking UAR attempts to build a power base in Lebanon. On 6 February 1958, Sham'un announced the setting up of a new law school in the Lebanese National University. The object of this was to give the Lebanese government grounds for refusing a request from the UAR to establish a law school of its own in Beirut.[101]

Backing the Lebanese opposition

The civil war which erupted in Lebanon on 8 May 1958 cut through religious lines. While the majority of Christians supported President Sham'un, the majority of Muslims, particularly the Sunni sub-proletariat, opposed him. However, the Lebanese opposition included some Christians opposed to Sham'un for personal or 'exceptional' reasons, according to Michael Johnson. For instance, Sulaiman Franjieh was the most important political leader to carry his followers with him to fight Sham'un, though for internal reasons preceding the civil war. Other Christian leaders opposed Sham'un politically, but not militarily, such as the Maronite Patriarch Ma'ushi, former President Bishara al-Khuri and Nasim Majdalani.[102]

The UAR government supported all opposition parties and political leaders whose aims were identical to its own. While the UAR wanted a change in Sham'un's foreign policy, the Lebanese opposition struggled to prevent Sham'un from being elected for a second term. According to Amin Huwaidi, ex-head of Egyptian Intelligence, UAR officials accommodated every opponent of Sham'un in order to serve the interests of the UAR in Lebanon. Moreover, the concept of unity between Lebanon and the UAR was never put forward, in order to keep the coherence of Lebanese opposition.[103]

The Lebanese opposition contested Lebanese government accounts of UAR interference in the internal affairs of Lebanon. This enabled UAR officials to quote from opposition statements when the UAR–Lebanon dispute was internationalized. Here is an extract from an opposition statement made on 17 May 1958:

> Neither the United Arab Republic nor the Palestinian refugees have any connection with the internal dispute in the Lebanon today. From the Lebanon and the Land of the Lebanon intrigues and plots were directed against the United Arab Republic. The dispute in the Lebanon is an internal matter which concerns the Lebanon, and in which the Government stands alone on one side and the people on the other. Infringements upon the constitution, the sanctity of law, public freedoms, and the innocent souls of the citizens – because of the [government] policy of alignment [with the West] and the plans for intrigue, assassination, and terrorism pursued by officials in authority – all these matters combined are the true cause for the overwhelming wrath of the people; and this the Government statement ignored.[104]

The Egyptian government, in turn, provided the Lebanese opposition with material and military assistance in order to balance what the pro-Sham'un parties received from Western sources. For instance, the British ambassador to Beirut commented on the Turkish supply of arms by saying:

> I hear from my Turkish colleague that the Turks are sending in 1800 rifles and 200 sub-machine guns, with ammunition. These are being delivered, (as have been other consignments from other countries), to the gendarmerie, who, in turn, hand them over to the President's entourage.[105]

Salah Nasr, ex-head of Egyptian Intelligence, wrote later with regret that millions of Egyptian pounds were wasted on arms and propaganda given to the Lebanese opposition. While Nasr did not specify the relevant sums, he stated that Rashid Karami and Sa'ib Salam received financial help through Syrian Intelligence (Deuxieme Bureau). Moreover, the UAR ambassador to Beirut, General Ghalib, distributed funds to other figures in the Lebanese opposition.[106]

Lebanese opposition figures were, however, more open about giving details of received UAR funds. Sa'ib Salam, for instance, stated later that he received L.£1.3 million from General Ghalib, only to be spent on 120 men sent from Syria to help Salam's forces in Beirut. However, Salam denied receiving any other funds or any of the 14,000 rifles claimed to have been sent by Syrian Intelligence. Salam said these may have been sent by Colonel Sarraj, head of Syrian Intelligence in the UAR, either to the Karamis and the Franjiehs in North Lebanon, or to Kamal Jumblatt in Mount Lebanon.[107]

Most opposition leaders voiced support for the selection of General Shihab to succeed Sham'un, as recommended by President Nasser. In fact, it was Kamal Jumblatt who called on some of his radical colleagues in the opposition to drop the issue of amending the constitution until after the election of a new president. Jumblatt feared that his colleagues, particularly the Sunni Muslims, would arouse Christian fears by seeking to abrogate sectarian quotas in the state. Moreover, in an effort to maintain opposition unity he stated that 'even Egypt itself does not want us to "pour more oil on fire" and thus increase the complexity of the Lebanese crisis'.[108]

Nasser: a power broker

President Shihab's nomination of Rashid Karami, the opposition's candidate and favourite of Nasser, to serve as prime minister signalled a symbolic victory over the ancien regime. President Sham'un retired to a remote village on Mount Lebanon, his prime minister, Sami al-Sulh, departed for Turkey, and Charles Malik remained in New York where he presided over the UN General Assembly.[109]

Karami moved quickly to declare on 25 September 1958 his intention for a better application of the National Pact of 1943, thus dispelling any tendency towards joining the UAR. By the end of 1958, Karami was able to carry out the promises of the opposition, which were in a sense identical with the declared goals of the UAR government concerning Lebanon. First, the opposition succeeded in preventing Sham'un from amending the Lebanese constitution in order to get re-elected. This was achieved in spite of the fact that Sham'un had enjoyed the support of a majority in the Lebanese parliament. Secondly, the election of President Shihab, a relatively neutral figure, prevented Sham'un from choosing one of his loyalists. Thirdly, the Karami government achieved a speedy evacuation of US troops and UN observers from Lebanon. Fourthly, the opposition insisted and succeeded in securing the return of General Ghalib as UAR ambassador to Beirut. Lastly, Karami declared on 10 December 1958 the adoption of the doctrine of 'peaceful neutrality' in foreign policy, while at the same time abrogating Lebanese commitment to the Eisenhower Doctrine. Although Karami was at pains to explain the difference between his 'peaceful neutrality' and 'positive neutrality', which was adopted by the UAR, it was clear that he set out to steer Lebanese foreign policy in a direction more congenial to the UAR.[110]

Nasser became a powerful power-broker in Lebanese politics through his hold over the Muslim community, and the Sunnis in particular. Political leaders of the community (*zu'ama*) understood this factor and, therefore competed among themselves to win Nasser's favour which could ensure for them political office in Lebanon. By this, Nasser, as a political patron, was able not only to exercise influence on the Muslim community but also to keep the Lebanese government in check. A good example of this appeared during December 1958, when there was a deadlock in UAR–Lebanese economic talks. Kamal Jumblatt, a Druze; 'Ali

Bazzi, a Shi'a; Sa'ib Salam and 'Abdallah al-Yafi, Sunni Muslims, all visited Cairo at the same time, in order to 'help solve the economic issues between the UAR and Lebanon'.[111] It is significant to note that none of these figures held any post in the Lebanese government at the time.

The UAR stake in media and education

After the formation of the UAR, the Egyptian media was keen to reflect the popular support enjoyed by President Nasser in Lebanon. Although there was abundant reporting of rallies and speeches of Muslim leaders supporting the new state, there was also a keen desire to show Lebanese Christian support. The intention behind this action was, arguably, to dispel any accusation that Nasser fostered 'Muslim unity'.[112]

The UAR–Lebanese dispute involved the employment of aggressive propaganda tactics against Lebanese officials and pro-Sham'un parties.[113] This campaign reached its peak just after the latter's invitation to US troops on 15 July 1958. Ahmad Sa'id, the most notorious Egyptian propagandist, commented on this in the 'Voice of the Arabs' by saying that America had intervened to 'save Sham'un from the fate which overtook Faisal, 'Abd al-Ilah and Nuri as-Sa'id'.[114]

By contrast, Shihab was portrayed as being endowed with all the good qualities, just after his election as president on 31 July 1958. For instance, al-Mussawar magazine emphasized the fact that Shihab 'is a prince whose family relates to the Prophet's tribe of Quraysh'. Moreover, Shihab's grandfather lost his Emirate when he collaborated with Egypt (a reference to Emir Bashir Shihab who ruled Mount Lebanon in the early nineteenth century).[115]

The UAR support for the Lebanese opposition made the task of creating a pro-UAR section in the Lebanese media much easier. Opposition leaders ensured that pro-UAR policies were reported in their particular publications. Moreover, they collaborated with the Egyptian media in making adulatory statements about Nasser while cursing his Arab rivals. For instance, Sa'ib Salam said in a statement of 10 March 1958 to the UAR official news service, Middle East News Agency (MENA), that:

> The era of kings and dictatorial regimes is gone forever as a result of the modern Arab renaissance. ... The recent plot [supposedly by

King Sa'ud] was not so much directed against President Abd an-Nasir [sic] as against the Arab nation. ... I expect that certain people in Saudi Arabia will move to put an end to King Sa'ud and his actions, and then fully co-operate with the United liberated Arab states.[116]

There were three important pro-UAR publications which expressed, in one way or another, the will of the Sunni Muslim community in Beirut. The al-Siyassa newspaper was owned and edited by 'Abdallah al-Yafi, a za'im and former prime minister. Sawt al-'Uruba was owned and edited by 'Adnan al-Hakim, leader of the populist Najjadah Party. Beirut al-Massa was owned and edited by 'Abdallah al-Mashnuq, a protégé of Sa'ib Salam.[117]

Moreover, President Nasser won the unquestioned support of three Lebanese journalists whom he rewarded in different ways. Riad Taha was the only Lebanese journalist chosen by Nasser to attend the ceremony of signing the UAR documents in Cairo. Salim al-Lawzi, owner and editor of al-Hawadiss magazine, was given special mention, during the UAR inaugural celebrations, for the loss of his son in an accident in Damascus. Sa'id Frayha, owner of Dar al-Sayyad, which published al-Anwar daily, was favoured for his persecution at the hands of Sham'un, which led him to take refuge in Cairo during the Lebanese civil war. Moreover, these journalists were given the opportunity to write in Egyptian publications on issues relating to political events in Lebanon.[118] No doubt the UAR government offered these journalists material and moral support during 1958. Anwar al-Jamal, UAR press attaché in Beirut from 1957 to 1978, acknowledged this but declined to give specific figures.[119]

In short, the UAR's influence in Lebanon was at the end of 1958 in the ascendant. This was not restricted to the political and press fields, but spread also to other areas such as education. A report from the British High Commissioner to Bahrain on 7 September 1958 deals with the subject of loaning Egyptian teachers to Arab and Muslim countries during the school year 1958–59. It concluded that 'it is significant that Lebanon got 90 teachers, while the Syrian region of the UAR got only 105. This is far more important than North Yemen 3 and Jordan 48.'[120] It is important to note that Egyptian teachers were assigned to Sunni Muslim institutions in Lebanon, while Egyptian teachers in other countries were assigned to government institutions.

Economic gains for the UAR

The Lebanese economy recovered quickly after the five months of internal crisis which paralysed commercial activity in particular. Some of the 'invisible' exports on which Lebanon was dependent to bridge her trade gap (L£474 million in 1957) were hit hard. These exports consisted of the transit and entrepôt trades and tourism, all of which were hampered by Syria's restrictions on transit and uncertainty in Iraq and Jordan. Beirut port statistics for 1958 showed a movement of 1.4 million tons compared with 2 million tons in 1957.[121] Also, Lebanese total imports shrank to L£518.34 million (L£629.99 in 1957), and Lebanese exports were reduced to L£110.5 million (L£152.18 million in 1957). As a result the Lebanese trade gap in 1958 stood at L£407.84 (see Table 3).

The union between Syria and Egypt did not alter, at first, the nature of Lebanese economic relations with the new state. In fact, the UAR government informed the Lebanese government that it needed a period of three months at least to sort out Syria's previous economic agreements with its neighbours. The Lebanese government's concern stemmed partly from Syria's position as a trading partner (14.6 per cent imports and 12 per cent exports in 1957), but more importantly from its control of Lebanese trade routes and petrol pipelines with the countries of the Arab East.[122]

The Lebanese–UAR dispute affected economic relations between the two countries in two ways. First, the UAR government did not endorse a trade agreement between Lebanon and Egypt prior to the latter's union with Syria. Secondly, UAR officials imposed a halt on transit trade via Syria.[123] After the departure of President Sham'un, the Karami government tried to solve economic problems with both regions of the UAR. This was done through the good offices of two pro-UAR members of the cabinet – Rashid Karami and Hussein 'Uwayni. However, no concrete results were achieved by the end of the year, in particular no new agreements with the Syrian region of the UAR.[124]

The Lebanese government succeeded in late October 1958 in convincing UAR officials to let the Egyptian region lift the ban on the import of Lebanese apples and subscribe to a quota worth E£200,000. This issue was very important to Lebanon, especially after Great Britain and France had cancelled their quotas of this produce. London justified its decision to cancel a quota worth £100,000 on the grounds of the abundance of British produce in

the 1958–59 season. However, there were some hints that it was
also motivated by political considerations due to the change of
regime in Beirut.[125] Despite many requests by Lebanese officials
and opposition figures, it seemed that the UAR was reluctant to
import any substantial quantities. In fact, Cairo imposed higher
taxes on imported Lebanese apples, which made them impossible
to market.[126] This policy was applied in general to Lebanon, thus
increasing Egyptian exports to Lebanon while keeping imports
from the latter to a minimum. Therefore in spite of the dispute
between the two countries, Lebanon imported goods from Egypt
worth L£8.71 million in 1958, while Lebanese exports to Egypt
were restricted to L£1.89 million (see Table 3).

Conclusion

The Egyptian union with Syria on 1 February 1958 accentuated
the existing differences in foreign policy between these two
countries and Lebanon. Moreover, the Lebanese regime feared the
ramifications of Lebanon being swallowed into an Arab and
Muslim super state. The UAR government backed implicitly the
internal revolt which erupted on 8 May 1958 under the banner of
preventing Sham'un from being elected for a second term as
president. The Lebanese government complained to the Arab
League and then the Security Council against UAR interference in
Lebanese affairs. However, the Lebanese government failed to
produce a situation through which UN or Western troops would
interfere to close Lebanon's border with the UAR.

The US intervention in Lebanon on 15 July 1958 was intended
to stabilize the Sham'un regime and prevent a takeover by the
UAR or the pro-UAR opposition. This situation transferred the
UAR–Lebanese dispute from a mere bilateral one into a regional
crisis involving the superpowers. The expressed concerns for
regional stability led to the conclusion of a solution reached at the
UN General Assembly in conjunction with the Arab League. As a
result, the UAR undertook, implicitly, to respect the status quo in
the region and Lebanese independence in particular. Later, the
Shihab regime included the pro-UAR opposition in its government, which oversaw the normalization of Lebanese relations with
the UAR.

CHAPTER 4
The Era of Co-existence

The West and regional stability

The US and British intervention in Lebanon and Jordan in July 1958 succeeded in preventing these two countries from falling into Nasser's sphere of influence, and thereby pre-empted any potential gains by the Soviet Union in the region. However, during 1959 relations between the governments of the Soviet Union and Iraq improved. NATO perceived the Soviet strategy to accrue allies in the Middle East as consisting of the following elements: first, to fan anti-Western and anti-Israeli sentiment by propaganda and diplomacy calculated to make the Soviet government appear as the champion of the Arabs against the Israelis, the Turks, the Western imperialists and the oil companies; secondly, to exploit the hatreds thus encouraged by supplying arms, training facilities and advisers; thirdly, to build up pro-Soviet sentiment in the Arab countries by economic help 'without strings'; fourthly, to build up communist cadres (by scholarships in the Soviet Union etc.) for use at a later date; fifthly, to weaken the Central Treaty Organization (CENTO) internally; lastly, to consolidate their gains in Iraq and to exploit them as bases for further advances, while remaining in the background as far as possible.[1]

Although the members of the Western alliance were united in a common aim to confront the Soviet Union and the communist ideology, the alliance was divided on how best to achieve it. The most important difference lay between the USA and Great Britain. In early 1959, for instance, America was pursuing a policy of pragmatism regarding Egypt. The then US Secretary of State, John Foster Dulles, informed his British counterpart, Selwyn Lloyd, that in the Middle East 'Nasser was a lesser evil than communism'.[2] Despite the US emphasis suggested in Dulles's remarks, Britain opted to aid Iraq's Qassim by passing on information pertaining to a 'possible coup'. In fact, Selwyn Lloyd encouraged

Qassim discreetly to 'resist pro-Nasser and pro-communist forces equally'. Lloyd justified Britain's assistance as 'not been taken from any wish to enter into inter-Arab quarrels', but to protect the lives of British citizens in Iraq, given the probability of civil war erupting there.[3]

This difference in approach between Britain and the USA became more evident in late April 1959. The British were displeased that America regarded Nasser as the champion of anti-communism in the Middle East. For the British, Nasser was more anti-Qassim than anti-communist, especially in the light of arms shipments from the Soviet Union to Egypt. In essence, Britain was concerned to support its anti-communist Arab allies and protect its oil interests, thus refusing to regard Nasser as a reliable bulwark against the influence of communism in the region.[4]

The Soviets, unlike the British, supported Qassim overtly, as they perceived Iraq to be a possible communist foothold in the Middle East. However, they were keen to keep their distance from the competition between Baghdad and Cairo for leadership of the Arab world. The British explanation for this was that Nasser was still the only possible rallying point for the Arab world and to break with him completely would 'jeopardize the Soviet Union's profitable role as "friend of the Arabs"'.[5] Although the Soviets could have pressurized Nasser into submission, they were reluctant to do so because both sides had an interest in undermining Western influence in the Middle East.

The USA, for its part, was keen to co-operate with President Nasser from a distance in order to keep communist influence out of the Middle East. This US priority to 'stabilize' the region was expressed candidly by President Eisenhower in his memoirs:

> During 1959 the attitude of President Nasser seemed to become progressively less aggressive. From October 1959 to the end of 1963, stability in the Middle East and northern Africa improved remarkably. Although two governments were overthrown by coup d'états, the Menderes regime in Turkey in 1960 and the Kassim [sic] regime in 1963, such leaders as King Hussein, President Nasser, General Shihab, the Shah of Iran, President Habib Bourguiba of Tunisia, and the ruling house of Morocco have retained their positions and influence. ... The peoples of the Middle East, inscrutable as always to the West, have remained outside the communist orbit.[6]

Nasser's supremacy

Nasser was able not only to survive but also to manipulate the international situation to his advantage, thus making Egypt a prominent regional power in the Middle East. The interaction of three factors worked in his favour. First, the US government was content for him to be the champion of Arab nationalism and the enemy of communism. Secondly, the Soviets were satisfied with Nasser working as a tool to attack Western imperialism in the region. Thirdly, as the British influence continued to wane and US influence grew, the British animosity to Nasser was held in check by the new international political structure. Malcolm Kerr described this period in Arab politics, with the exception of two peripheral instances, as a period in which the crucial decisions governing Arab affairs lay in Arab hands.[7]

Turkey who was a major player in Middle East affairs during the 1950s, as a member of NATO as well as a signatory to the Baghdad Pact, was forced to leave the scene of inter-Arab politics. The Turks were antagonized by the Italian offer of economic assistance to Nasser in early 1959, which included selling 50 per cent of their Egyptian phosphate shares. The Turkish government perceived this action as a possible shift in Western policy, which would bolster Egypt as a regional power at the expense of Turkey. The Turkish delegate to NATO warned his fellow representatives on 21 January 1959 that:

> We should remember that it was Nasser who introduced Moscow [into] the Middle East. His [Nasser's] attempts to get rid of local communists did not mean a change of policy. He saw the Iraq communists, for instance, as an obstacle to [the] reduction of Iraq to the status of a satellite of Egypt ... in fact the Turkish Government had evidence that many of the so-called communists whom Nasser had arrested were conservatives who opposed union with Iraq.[8]

Nevertheless, the USA felt that Nasser's stand on communism was a priceless advantage to the West since he had saved Syria from communism by forming the UAR in February 1958, and moreover, had led the crusade against Qassim in Iraq. This contest between the two leaders started to appear publicly in early 1959, and continued to explode in varying degrees until Qassim's fall on 9 February 1963.[9] As a result, King Hussein of Jordan was placed in a precarious position. On the one hand, Nasser's brand of Arab nationalism challenged the legitimacy of Hashemite rule in Jordan. Moreover, the kingdom's close ties with Britain placed the Hashemites in a potentially vulnerable position in an anti-imperialist atmosphere. On the other hand, it was impossible for King Hussein to ally himself with Qassim's government in Iraq, given the murder of his Hashemite cousins by Qassim's forces during the coup d'état of 14 July 1958. In an attempt to strengthen the monarchy's position, diplomatic moves were made by Amman to encourage the Lebanese government into an informal alliance to withstand Nasser's political influence in the region. Lebanon, however, preferred to remain on the sidelines of Arab politics, unwilling to jeopardize its new relationship with the UAR.[10]

Shihab in control

In fact, President Shihab resorted to a traditional policy of neutrality concerning inter-Arab affairs, and moved to rebuild the country after the civil war of 1958. However, Shihab's policy of reconstruction, which subsequently became known as 'Shihabism' or al-Nahj (the Path), failed to take into account Lebanon's mosaic of sectarian and political cleavages. Shihabism had four major elements:

— The affirmation of Lebanon, as a whole, as an Arab country which belonged to the Arab world.

— The encouragement of secularism as the first step towards achieving national unity.

— Discouraging political extremism, notably in the Arab nationalist and right-wing Christian camps.

— The employment of the Lebanese army to underpin the overall strategy.

Shihab, also, attempted to address the issue of identity in Lebanese society. Walid Faris asserts that Shihab acted in the light of the National Pact of 1943, working to 'Lebanonize' the Lebanese Muslims and 'Arabize' the Lebanese Christians.[11] Munah al-Sulh confirmed this view and went further by calling this policy 'the new isolationism'. Al-Sulh added that to win the support of the Lebanese Muslims, the Shihab administration resorted to developing the infrastructure of the Muslim areas.[12]

In June 1960, new elections took place under the neutral prime minister, Ahmad Da'uq. He introduced a new law increasing the number of deputies from 66 to 99, which brought a new openness to the political system. It seems that the USA requested its Western allies not to intervene in the elections by aiding their respective allies financially. This policy aimed to discourage Egyptian intervention, and thereby stabilize the Lebanese regime. This caused deep concern among the pro-Western Christian elements, which were surprised not only by the negative response of the USA and Britain, but also the hesitancy of France and the Vatican.[13] As a consequence Shihab reduced the power of hard-line Maronite leaders like Camille Sham'un and Raymond Eddy. These two leaders retained their seats in parliament but many of their supporters did not. The results were favourable to 'populist' leaders such as Pierre Jumayyil for the Christian camp, and Salam and Karami for the Muslims.[14]

The Nasser–Shihab summit

On 26 March 1959, Shihab and Nasser held a summit in a specially erected marquee on the frontier between Lebanon and Syria. Lebanon's minister for the interior, Raymond Eddy, suggested this arrangement in order not to 'annoy anybody' and to 'respect the dignity of Lebanon'.[15] Thus, the location of the summit was a deliberate compromise between the two leaders. It avoided, on the one hand, antagonizing Lebanese Christian opinion by Shihab's not visiting Damascus, and, on the other, avoided giving a boost to Lebanese Muslim opinion should Nasser be received in Beirut. It also prevented the stirring up of the historical Christian fear of Lebanon joining a pan-Arab union.

The resultant joint communiqué was interpreted as being a victory for Shihab, for he gained a promise from Nasser to respect Lebanon's independence and not to interfere in its internal affairs. Also, the Lebanese president won a promise to help solve outstanding economic problems between the two countries. Shihab offered, in return, a broad reaffirmation of solidarity with the Arab cause, without having to support Nasser in his dispute with Qassim or Moscow. This signalled Lebanon's acknowledgement of Nasser's leading role in the Arab world. It put an end to the dispute of 1958 and marked a return by Lebanon to the traditional policy of neutrality in inter-Arab affairs which had been violated by Sham'un. The Lebanese government wanted Nasser to help lift the trade, travel and transit restrictions imposed on Lebanon by Syria, particularly since early 1958.[16]

Furthermore, this summit was seen as a trade-off between Shihab and Nasser. While Nasser endorsed Shihab in order that the latter would gain the support of Lebanese Muslims, Shihab undertook to develop Muslim areas economically. Nasser requested that Lebanon would undertake not to enter into any alliances with other regional actors. Furthermore, Lebanon would not get involved in political intrigue which might undermine the position of Syria within the UAR. Shihab had promised, through his control of Lebanese intelligence, to stop conspiracies against the UAR being launched from Lebanese territories. In return, Nasser would defend Lebanon against interference from Arab radicals in its internal affairs. This policy survived until the Cairo Accord of 1969, which Nasser sponsored between Palestinian guerillas and the Lebanese government.[17]

Mahmud Riad, who participated in the summit, praised Shihab for his sincerity in executing the accord 'one hundred per cent' and by doing this, he secured stability for Lebanon. Consequently, Lebanese foreign policy was co-ordinated so as not to conflict with UAR interests, specifically concerning inter-Arab disputes and general Arab issues.[18] In other words, a passive foreign policy ensured Lebanon did not challenge or clash with UAR pre-eminence in the Arab world.

Where to stand in the Iraq–UAR dispute?

Since the beginning of the Iraq–UAR dispute in late 1958, the Lebanese government had stayed away from any involvement in order not to jeopardize its trade links with the two countries or its role as a transit centre for the Arab East. The pro-Nasser prime minister, Rashid Karami, and the Phalange Party leader, Pierre Jumayyil (the latter had sympathy for neither Nasser nor Qassim), agreed on this neutral policy. According to Jumayyil, the Lebanese government's purpose was 'to create a spirit of conciliation between feuding parties in the explosive Arab world'.[19] In line with this policy, the Lebanese government prevented popular demonstrations by pro-UAR elements in protest against the death sentence pronounced upon Colonel 'Arif, Qassim's second in command, in an effort to avoid offending Qassim.[20]

The Lebanese government adopted the role of 'honest broker' at the Arab League meeting, convened to discuss the Iraq–UAR dispute, in Beirut on 2–7 April 1959. This role involved lobbying the League members to attend the meeting and working with Cairo and Baghdad separately to 'soften' their media war.[21] However, the British ambassador to Beirut, Moore Crosthwaite, said that Iraq, Libya, Jordan and Tunisia did not attend in order to avoid contributing to UAR propaganda attacks on Iraq and on the perceived communist menace. Lebanon joined the Sudan and Morocco in determining 'not to line up with the UAR in open condemnation of Iraq, while sheltering behind them was Saudi Arabia'.[22]

Nevertheless, none of these countries challenged the UAR openly, leaving it to dominate the scene and colour the communiqué. It called on all Arab states to follow a policy of non-alignment and non-dependence. It expressed the committee's wish for the reinforcement of the national ties uniting the Arabs and condemned all foreign influence from whatever source, which tended to prejudice Arab rights. It appealed to Iraq to conform to the decisions taken at the meeting, and concluded by setting up a sub-committee to study, in collaboration with the Arab League Secretariat, means of achieving the objectives expressed in the communiqué.[23]

The Lebanese government was accused that by accepting the communiqué, it had compromised its self-professed neutrality, just established by President Shihab at the summit with Nasser on 26 March 1959. But, Shihab was quoted as saying, in a British document, that in reality 'nobody had any illusions on the subject; nothing would happen, [and] he [Shihab] thought that 'Uwayni [Shihab's foreign minister] had been clever in accepting the chairmanship and that it had enabled him to abstain from taking sides'.[24]

The Jordan River row

This dispute was centred on the issue of diverting the River Jordan and then on how to resolve the Palestine problem. The UAR called for a meeting of the Arab League foreign ministers in

Cairo on 8 February 1960 to discuss Israel's project of diverting the waters of the Jordan, and to identify ways to pre-empt this by diverting the sources of the river. This project concerned the Syrian region of the UAR, Jordan and Lebanon as they bordered Israel and controlled most of the sources of the River Jordan. Although the three countries agreed on the need to prevent Israel's project being implemented and the need to divert the water, they differed markedly on the means of approach. The Lebanese government, for instance, paid lip service only to the Arab diversion project while trying to wriggle out of any collective stance. Indeed, the Lebanese government attempted to distance itself from the Arab project by suggesting an exclusively Lebanese plan to be financed and executed by the Lebanese army. This demonstrated Lebanon's reluctance to be involved in a conflict with Israel, especially since its foreign minister, Golda Mayer, criticized the pan-Arab project.[25]

The UAR government, for its part, was keen to hold the meeting in Cairo and used its hegemony over the Arab League to execute its political will. The justification for this decision was that Cairo was at 'the centre of the Arab world' and that the UAR foreign minister wanted to take part in the proceedings, but could not leave Cairo because of 'important political circumstances'.[26]

The meeting ended in failure since Jordan, who considered Palestine as its political domain, joined Iraq and Morocco in requesting the amendment of the Arab League Charter. The amendment was supposed to ensure that the League headquarters be moved from Cairo to other Arab capitals on a rotation basis, thus checking Egyptian hegemony over the League.[27] Lebanon stayed on the sidelines, despite the growing tension on the frontiers between the UAR and Israel. Moreover, the Lebanese government took no measures to implement its own project of diverting the Hasbani River (one of the headwaters of the River Jordan) into the Litani River – an exclusive Lebanese river.[28] Although nothing stood in the way of the Arab diversion plan, it was put on the shelf because of technical and political complexities. Arab opposition to the Israeli scheme was conveyed formally to the UN Secretary General, while trying to work out a military strategy to protect the diversion facilities. According to Arnon Medzini, if the Arab plan was implemented, it would have deprived the Sea of Galilee of 25 per cent of its water, and the salt content of the lake would have increased significantly.[29]

The Lebanese government was too busy attempting to improve its economic relations with the UAR and Iraq to deal with the dispute between Jordan and the UAR. This dispute was deferred to an Arab League meeting at the level of foreign ministers held in Lebanon on 23 August 1960.[30] Before the meeting took place, President Shihab mediated between Nasser and King Hussein, sending two letters to each of them requesting a cessation of their attacks on each other and ensure their countries' representation at the meeting.[31] Although the Arab League meeting reached a consensus concerning the Algerian war of liberation, it failed to do so regarding the issue of Palestine.[32] While the Lebanese government secured the participation of both parties to the dispute, it did not ensure that differences were buried and the conflict re-surfaced during the Arab League session.

The mutual animosity between the Jordanian and UAR leadership was deepened further as the dispute took on a violent character. The Jordanian prime minister, Haza' al-Majali, was killed when a bomb exploded in his office in Amman on 30 August 1960, prompting King Hussein to accuse the UAR of direct involvement. This heralded a reciprocal terror campaign, which escalated on Lebanese territory, during which the UAR Consulate in Beirut was bombed on 10 September 1960 (presumably by agents of Jordan).[33]

King Hussein brought the dispute to the United Nations General Assembly in early October 1960 in an attempt to embarrass Nasser. He informed the British prime minister that the Lebanese prime minister, Sa'ib Salam, while sympathetic, declined to support King Hussein publicly in order not to antagonize Nasser.[34] Salam, in order to distance his government from the Jordan–UAR dispute, denied his role as mediator between Nasser and King Hussein, stating that he only advised the Arab delegates not to carry their disputes to the UN.[35]

Despite its efforts to stay out of the Jordan–UAR dispute, the Lebanese government became entangled when a senior UAR officer, General Muhammad al-Jarrah, complained that Syrian exiles in Lebanon were plotting freely against Syria. He also accused Lebanese authorities of supplying the Syrian exiles as well as Jordanian plotters with Lebanese identity cards so that they could cross the Syrian border freely.[36] The Jordanian government was implicated directly when Jordan's military attaché in Beirut was accused, by the Lebanese authorities, of organizing terror acts against the UAR. Thus, Lebanon became increasingly caught up in hostilities and feared negative repercussions for Lebanese domestic politics and trade with both countries.[37]

The Lebanese government perceived the gravity of the situation to be such that it recalled its ambassadors from Amman and Cairo for consultations. Subsequently, Lebanon took steps which satisfied the UAR in particular. First, the Lebanese government tightened its controls over Syrian refugees residing in Lebanese territory, forcing them either to reside in the remote town of Jizzin, south Lebanon, or to leave the country. Secondly, Shihab asked the British Embassy in Beirut to bring pressure to bear on Jordan to cease committing acts of sabotage against the UAR on Lebanese territory. Shihab's anxieties over the matter were reported by the British ambassador to Beirut, Moore Crossthwaite, as follows:

> He [Shihab] did not criticize the Jordanians for trying in the face of provocation to organize anti-UAR activities. But they [the Jordanians] had a common frontier with Syria, and he strongly deplored their using Lebanese territory for that purpose. It was embarrassing and created difficulties for the Lebanon both internally and with the UAR.[38]

Thirdly, the Lebanese government conveyed to the Jordanian government a message stating that 'it would be wiser to withdraw the military attaché before he was declared persona non grata'. This was accepted and he was recalled directly by his government.[39] The final episode in this sequence of events came when Sa'ib Salam accused unspecified persons of plotting against the UAR and using Lebanon as a base. He then promised to counter such activities since 'every sincere Lebanese does not accept his country to be a plotting centre, and we recognize our role in this respect'.[40] In other words Lebanon, of necessity, appeased the UAR without necessarily damaging its relationship with Jordan.

Walking on a tightrope

The Lebanese government supported the UAR's foreign policy position on issues relating to Arab and Third World affairs such as the war of liberation in Algeria, the continuing stalemate in Palestine, and the crisis in the Belgian Congo. Beirut distanced itself from Lebanon's representative at the UN (and President of the UN General Assembly), Dr Charles Malik, for his visit to the Israeli section of a trade fair in New York in mid-May 1959. Prime minister Rashid Karami and foreign minister Hussein 'Uwayni deplored this behaviour but stopped short of expelling him from his post for fear of antagonizing the Christian ministers in the Lebanese government.[41]

When Karami visited the UN in September 1959, he met President Eisenhower and spoke in support of the 'Palestinian struggle' and the Algerian war of liberation from France. Moreover, Karami asked Eisenhower for the USA to supply Lebanon with 'unconditional economic aid'.[42] Eisenhower stated that Karami expressed views not unlike those of Nasser:

> Mr Karami, a confirmed Arab nationalist and admirer of Nasser had, in the terms of his office, developed a reputation for moderation. He was strictly an orthodox Arab, and was far from convinced, even at the time of his visit, that the communists constituted a worse threat to the Arabs than did Israel. He passionately supported the Algerians against the French. ... He claimed that President Nasser was now fighting the communists as hard as he had formerly fought the imperialists.[43]

Sa'ib Salam adopted the same line when he visited the UN in the autumn of 1960. He, too, saw no contradiction when requesting unconditional economic aid or agreeing with the USA on confronting 'the alien ideologies', namely communism, in line with Nasser's approach.[44] However, he distanced himself from Nasser's position on three issues. First, he abstained from voting on a UN proposal put forward by the non-aligned movement, calling for a summit between Eisenhower and Khrushchev. Despite being asked to vote positively by Nasser, Salam gave a somewhat feeble excuse that 'we [the Lebanese delegation] were invited for a dinner during the voting session'. Secondly, Salam did not support a proposal to accept Communist China into the UN, on the grounds that Lebanon had already recognized the National Chinese government. Thirdly, Salam supported the UN Secretary General Hammarskjold's position on the Congo issue, thereby contradicting the stance taken by the Arab and non-aligned countries.[45] This independent spirit of the Salam government was an attempt to demonstrate Lebanese neutrality in order to secure US economic assistance. Salam also tried to distance Lebanon from the UAR and the non-aligned camp generally in order to present Lebanon as a potential ally with which America could work. Lebanon's apparent support for the UAR in the UN involved rhetoric and political manoeuvring – it was never an obedient client.

The Lebanese government avoided a serious crisis with President Nasser when he attacked the Phalange Party and the Syrian nationalists, branding them 'imperialist agents' in a public speech in Damascus on 23 February 1960. According to the British ambassador to Beirut, Moore Crossthwaite, Nasser found it useful to divert Syria's attention from worsening economic conditions by focusing attention on Lebanon in order to impress opinion in Syria. Secondly, although Nasser's attack was instigated by the publication of a series of essays in the Phalange Party mouthpiece, al-'Amal, which criticized the economic policy in Syria, he hoped to get an embarrassed Lebanese government to impose restrictions on the Lebanese press in general. In fact, anti-UAR newspapers represented a source of irritation to Nasser for spreading reports about his problems controlling Syria. Nasser perceived this as part of a 'conspiracy' against the UAR itself. Thirdly, by applying political pressure on the Lebanese regime, Nasser hoped to get rid not only of the leader of the Phalange Party, Pierre Jumayyil, who was a minister, but to bring down Sa'ib Salam's government itself. This was related to Salam's reported failure to co-operate with the Egyptian ambassador to Beirut, General Ghalib, to increase Nasser's influence inside Lebanon.[46]

The situation escalated when Pierre Jumayyil, supported by other Christian parties, replied that Nasser wanted 'agents' not 'friends' in Lebanon. He also accused the UAR president of interfering in Lebanon's internal affairs. Nasser justified his attacks as being defensive when he said on 26 February 1961:

> I chose in the past not to retaliate [to anti-UAR press campaigns] in order to safeguard Lebanese national unity, but today I am speaking out [against hostile press campaigns] in order to safeguard national unity in the UAR. ... They [the anti-UAR press] say that our republic is suffering from hunger, ... and the Syrian people want to secede from the union and get rid of Nasser's rule. [They say also] the Syrian people resist Egyptian colonialism, and Nasser rules Syria [against its will].[47]

Neither Shihab nor the Lebanese government as a whole dared to react publicly to President Nasser. Instead, they opted for behind-the-scenes diplomacy to calm the situation. Haikal reported that Shihab handed over to General Ghalib a report detailing the activities of Belgian and other foreign intelligence agencies based in Beirut working against the UAR.[48] Moreover, the Speaker of the Lebanese Parliament, Sabri Hamadi, and Prime Minister Sa'ib Salam visited Damascus to 'congratulate' Nasser on the third anniversary of the UAR. Salam used his rhetoric to calm the political waters, saying that 'if we had ignored in the past what harm had befallen our brothers' unity ... it is then not in our interest to allow this to continue as from now'.[49] Furthermore, the Lebanese government restrained the press by applying penalties equally to pro- and anti-Nasser newspapers, thus averting the worst crisis between the two countries since 1958.[50]

The UAR reaches for all Lebanese groups

Nasser emerged as the undisputed popular Arab leader who commanded the support of Lebanese Muslims since he backed their revolt in 1958 against Sham'un. Nasser represented the external patron of Lebanese Muslims through whom they tried to enhance their own interests inside the Lebanese regime. Moreover, Qassim's challenge to Nasser's leadership of the Arab world had failed by early 1959, since most of the Muslims in Lebanon sided with Nasser.

Nasser's influence created three different categories among Lebanese political groups, according to Dr Hamdi al-Tahiri: first, the Arab nationalists, who expressed their support for the UAR president as the sole pan-Arab leader; secondly, Muslim traditional leaders, the *zu'ama*, who traded on Nasser's friendship as a means of acquiring political capital inside Lebanon; thirdly, the right-wing Christians who found it beneficial to have Nasser as an enemy in order to promote their political interests within their own communities.[51]

Arab nationalist groups

The Arab nationalists could not be described as a coherent party but, more accurately, as a mixture of intellectuals and Muslim sub-

proletariat leaders who were loyal to the tenets of Arab nationalism. After 1958, Nasser enjoyed an unquestioned hold over them
despite being least represented in parliament. Bassim al-Jisr, a pan-
Arab Lebanese intellectual, ascribed this to the fact that the UAR
government used this group directly, which worked to its disad-
vantage. He also said that it was good to meet Nasser personally
but when one ended up dealing with the military attaché in Beirut,
then 'one felt being treated like an agent, which was unpleasant'.[52]

The case of 'Adnan al-Hakim was, however, different in that
he succeeded in becoming a member of parliament on the Arab
nationalist ticket in July 1960, but failed to become a mainstream
force in Lebanese politics. Although al-Hakim was a leader of a
Lebanese party, *al-Najjadah*, since 1943, he adopted the Nasserist
line unquestioningly to further Muslims' political rights in Lebanon. An Egyptian diplomat described him as being 'the most
daring Muslim leader who attacked the Maronites in parliament
and raised his voice according to Cairo's instructions – but lacked
wisdom'.[53] Another diplomat went as far as saying that al-Hakim
'was treated as a lightweight because he did not represent real
popularity but merely exploited the Nasserist trend'.[54] Al-Hakim
himself stated that he met Nasser several times every year, and
that Nasser granted him special favours and executed all his
requests such as financial help to treat the sick.[55]

While the UAR was involved in a bloody campaign against
communism and Iraq, the Lebanese pan-Arabists were the ideal
ally in this battle. In early 1959, UAR agents were implicated in a
notorious incident involving the abduction and murder of a
Lebanese communist leader, Farjallah al-Hilu. Despite repeated
denials by UAR officials, it was thought that UAR Intelligence
executed him secretly.[56] This group undertook to propagate the
UAR's influence in Arab affairs by mobilizing students as well as
the deprived stratum of society in order to dominate 'the street'.
Their activities spread to other cities whose people harboured
pro-Nasser sympathies, namely Tripoli and Sidon.[57]

Traditional Muslim leaders

This group consisted of traditional Muslim leaders who were
members of parliament attempting to enhance their internal
influence by co-operating with the UAR after 1958. Sa'ib Salam,
for instance, returned to Beirut on 13 January 1959 after spending

five weeks in Cairo for 'deliberations' with UAR officials, to be received in Beirut as a victor and to have his portraits shown shaking hands with Nasser.[58] Another tactic adopted by this group was to repeat what President Nasser had said in his speeches.[59]

This traditional group joined other Arab nationalist delegations which visited Damascus every year in February to congratulate Nasser on the anniversary of the UAR. This enhanced Nasser's prestige as the leader of Arab nationalism and offered him a platform to express his 'feelings' towards Lebanon.[60] In turn, Muslim traditional leaders welcomed the assistance of the UAR in the establishment of the Arab University of Beirut, as part of a larger education package. In fact, the UAR backed the issue of establishing a Lebanese college to teach law in Arabic, while the Christian Maronites had sought, since 1958, to oppose it through legislation (see Chapter 3). After visiting Cairo, Prime Minister Karami, though sympathetic to the idea, took great care not to offend his Christian ministers.[61] A delegation representing the Society of al-Maqasid Islamic Schools visited Cairo in April to probe the issue. The UAR Minister of Education supported their efforts to establish a new university, and promised to send teachers and publications 'until the need for foreign schools disappears'.[62]

Lebanese Christian leaders

The majority of Christian leaders were determined to ignore UAR overtures of friendship, since their fears of Lebanon being engulfed in the 'Arab Sea' were confirmed by UAR support for the Muslim community during the 1958 revolt in Lebanon. This fear was widespread, in spite of assurances by the UAR's ambassador to Beirut, General Ghalib, that Lebanon's sovereignty was not in jeopardy. Symbolic of this unease was Raymond Eddy's reluctance to accept the *Republic* decoration from General Ghalib in gratitude for Eddy's protection of the Egyptian Embassy during his service as minister of the interior in 1958–59.[63] Likewise, the leader of the Phalange Party, Pierre Jumayyil, was granted the *Nile* decoration in February 1961. But Nasser attacked him a week later and branded his party 'imperialist agents' who owed their loyalty to France.[64]

The UAR maintained its hostility towards ex-President Sham'un and his 'henchmen'. Sham'un, in turn, grabbed any opportunity and attacked Nasser in mid-May 1959 for receiving in his office 'a notorious zionist', Dr Elmer Berger. This was a reaction to pro-UAR media attacks on Lebanon's representative at the UN, Charles Malik, for visiting the Israeli stand at the New York trade fair. General Ghalib accused Sham'un of 'wilful confusion' between the anti-zionist American Council of Judaism, to which Berger belonged, and the American Jewish Agency.[65]

Emile Bustani was the only Christian politician who continued to enjoy a strong relationship with Nasser. Although Bustani was a member of parliament, he relied more on his role as a regional businessman to mediate between Nasser and the British government. For Instance, Bustani conveyed to Foreign Office minister John Profumo, on 29 January 1959, that after holding long talks with Nasser, he concluded that Nasser was 'very anxious' to mend his fences with them.[66]

But the British felt unhappy when they suspected that Bustani conveyed to Nasser their true intentions. Thus, Bustani's request to meet the British prime minister, Harold Macmillan, in June 1959 was turned down for two reasons. First, it was thought that it was not desirable 'to allow him to go away with the impression that he bears a message from the P.M. to President Nasser, since we cannot rely on his presentation of such an interview'. Secondly, the British government did not want to allow Bustani to use such an interview to improve his prestige in internal Lebanese politics at the expense of other friends.[67] Instead, Bustani was granted an interview with Foreign Office minister, John Profumo, in which Bustani conveyed Nasser's views on communism, the Arab Development Fund (made of capital from 5 per cent of Arab oil sales) and improving relations with Great Britain.[68] In short, Bustani attempted to act as a mediator between Nasser and the British, using his professed pan-Arab sympathies as well as his Western leaning. For Nasser, the situation was satisfying in that someone who was not too closely associated with Cairo articulated his thoughts on certain difficult regional issues, such the Arab Development Fund. This enabled Nasser to test the regional waters and perhaps avoid any negative repercussions.[69]

Media battles in Beirut

Beirut continued to be used by competing governments as a central post of observation in the Arab East for information gathering, misinformation campaigns, espionage and propaganda. The British Embassy in Beirut, for instance, used Beirut as a post for gauging Arab public opinion on regional and international issues, since the Lebanese press represented different competing regional political currents.[70] Moreover, Beirut was useful in monitoring Syria's political and economic situation, since the UAR had shifted all diplomatic missions to Cairo.[71]

The UAR continued, during this period, to use Beirut in order to influence Lebanese and Arab public opinion. A British diplomat complained that Beirut had become 'a hot-house for rumours, many of them planted by Egyptian propagandists' which led foreign correspondents to send inaccurate stories to their editors in London.[72] Likewise, its rivals used this technique against the UAR. Nasser complained to Harold Macmillan on 28 September 1960 about the action of the BBC in taking up a hostile article about General 'Amer in an 'obscure Lebanese paper and publicizing it round the world'.[73] The UAR employed its own press as well as a sizeable section of the Lebanese press to propagate its policies.

The Egyptian press

The UAR press changed its strategy towards Lebanon during this period, reflecting the detente between Shihab and Nasser. This new strategy consisted of three elements: the positive coverage of relations between the two governments, the focusing on the 'popular' support the UAR enjoyed inside Lebanon, and a policy of non-intervention in Lebanese internal affairs.

The Egyptian press concentrated on the 'friendship' and 'good hospitality' of the Lebanese president and government. Moreover, disputes over policies were not aired but debated behind the scenes. During the summit held between presidents Shihab and Nasser on 26 March 1959, the former was praised and flattered in al-Ahram for his respect for Nasser's fasting, despite Shihab's normal habit of smoking a hundred cigarettes a day.[74] Also Shihab's qualities of statesmanship, sincerity and fairness were over-emphasized in an effort to express Egyptian pleasure with his leadership.[75] Nevertheless, lip-service statements, typical of pro-UAR politicians, caused a crisis on 5 August 1960, when the new prime minister of Lebanon, Sa'ib Salam, was reported in the Egyptian daily, *al-Jumhuria*, as saying:

> My cabinet is a natural extension of the [1958] revolution ... we wage all our battles in the name of Arab nationalism and on its behalf. ... Tell the UAR people that the Lebanese people support them heart and soul in all their battles. The strongest weapon the Arabs have is One Word, One Front.[76]

In protest at this statement, the Phalange Party threatened to withdraw from government. However, Salam's denial of the report's legitimacy was sufficient to appease the Phalange deputies in parliament.[77]

The second element of the Egyptian press strategy focused on the contribution of the pro-UAR element in Lebanon to Arab nationalism. Thus the freed Lebanese prisoners who had been involved in the 1958 civil war were hailed as noble 'Arab strugglers' who wanted to continue supporting Arab nationalism.[78] Moreover, every Lebanese politician and public figure of every hue was portrayed in a way which served the UAR role of 'taking care' of this Lebanese branch of the movement, in line with its role as the vanguard of Arab nationalism.[79] For instance, a great deal of elaborate coverage was given to the return to Lebanon, from Brazil, of the respected expatriate Lebanese poet, Rashid Salim al-Khuri, at the end of 1958 to witness the 'Arab awakening'. After writing some bitterly anti-British poetry, he received an invitation to visit Syria and stay there as long as he liked with a government grant of S£1,000.[80]

The third element of the UAR press strategy followed the line of non-intervention in Lebanese affairs, leaving it instead to Lebanese pro-UAR publications. Incidents of violence inside Lebanon were reported but not exaggerated, in keeping with the UAR's intention of not encouraging civil strife. In fact, attention was directed towards other issues such as the war of independence in Algeria, and the fight against communism in the region. One exception to this generally held rule occurred on 24 February 1961, when Nasser attacked bitterly 'the newspapers of imperialism in Lebanon edited by imperialist agents'. This was in reaction to reports in the right-wing section of the Lebanese press concerning the deterioration of Syria's economic position.[81] The ensuing press campaign went as far as saying that Beirut had succeeded Istanbul as the imperialist centre for espionage, whose sole aim was to attack Nasser and the UAR.[82]

The Egyptian media retaliated by seizing the opportunity offered by the campaign of the pro-UAR Minister of Education, Kamal Jumblatt, who called for the closure of the Middle East Centre For Arabic Studies (MECAS) in Shimlan, on the grounds that it was a British spying centre in Lebanon. This caused deep embarrassment for the Lebanese and British governments because the pro-UAR Lebanese and Egyptian media unearthed some loopholes in the charter and administration of MECAS as a basis to prove that it performed as a spy centre with the implicit knowledge of the Lebanese authorities.[83] Therefore Michael Adams, the Beirut correspondent of the *Guardian* and a teacher in MECAS, wrote an article on 23 March 1961 entitled 'wild imaginations by Cairo: British school for spies'. Adams replied to Egyptian propaganda in detail, and ended up saying that even if it were supposed that this institute is a spying school, then 'it has an enviable record in that throughout its 15 years of active useful life not one of its many graduates has ever been caught'.[84]

The pro-UAR press

The pro-UAR press consisted of two major factions, reflecting the political positions of their proprietors and/or editors. The traditional UAR allies included figures such as 'Abdallah al-Mashnuq, proprietor of *Beirut*; 'Abdallah al-Yafi, proprietor of *al-Syassa*; and 'Adnan al-Hakim, proprietor of *Sawt al-'Uruba*. Such figures used their respective publications to promote UAR policies. The second group consisted of proprietors and/or editors who found allegiance to the UAR advantageous at this point – for example Sa'id Frayha, publisher of *Dar al-Sayyad*. Both groups were used as a tool in the propaganda war to influence Arab public opinion generally and boost UAR prestige.[85] Moreover, pro-UAR quotes appearing in the Cairo press, taken from the 'free' Lebanese press, enhanced the credibility of the Cairo regime at home, despite the fact that some of these stories originally emanated from within UAR circles.[86]

The UAR's press attaché in Beirut, Anwar al-Jamal, played a central role during this period, building relationships with any journalist who was ready to co-operate. He acknowledged paying regular sums of money to many Lebanese journalists who were supporting the UAR political line.[87]

Relations such as those outlined above gave Cairo a lead in influencing the Lebanese press over its regional rivals. When Prime Minister Karami visited Cairo on 4 June 1959, four senior Lebanese journalists accompanied him. They were Salim al-Lawzi, Riad Taha, Wafiq al-Tibi and Farid Abu Shahla, all of whom were described by Karami as 'friendly' to the UAR.[88] However, when the Iraqi government invited the Lebanese press syndicate to Baghdad, to attend the celebrations surrounding the first anniversary of the Iraqi revolution, the offer was declined. Colonel Mahdawi, Iraq's chief propagandist, responded angrily and discredited Beirut newspapers, stating that they 'lived off subsidies from the Americans, the UAR and others'.[89]

The pro-UAR press in Lebanon followed faithfully President Nasser's battles against communism and Qassim and even the Egyptian government line on Lebanese internal affairs. When Nasser began his campaign against communism in his Port Sa'id speech on 23 December 1958, commentaries on his attack took 'pride of place' in the majority of Lebanese newspapers.[90] Also, the impact of Nasser's use of religion in propaganda was reflected in Beirut newspapers, as this commentary in *Beirut al-Massa* stated:

> Arabs from the Atlantic to the Arab Gulf must realize that communists in Iraq are tearing up the Koran and shouting no Arabism and no Islam and must support Nasser in his struggle against the red dragon.[91]

Concerning the disputes between the UAR and other states in the Arab League, this group of newspapers criticized those members who abstained from meetings, or were opposed to the UAR explicitly or implicitly.[92] All pro-UAR publications supported Cairo in its war of words with certain Lebanese politicians. Pierre Jumayyil, for instance, was attacked bitterly for opposing a possible cultural and political boycott of France as a consequence of its policy in Algeria. Also, he was depicted as 'being behind every movement to undermine Arab nationalism and [to] support Western, especially French, imperialism'.[93]

Economic relations

The UAR held the key to Lebanon's trade with the Near East, as Syria was the only open door for transit of goods to other Arab states – Lebanon's borders with Israel had been closed since 1948. The UAR market was the most important to Lebanon for geographical, economic and political reasons. Between 1953 and 1960 Lebanon's exports to Syria constituted 33 per cent of all exports to Arab countries. Egypt accounted for 13 per cent. Thus the UAR, in total, accounted for 46 per cent of all Lebanon's exports to the Arab world. Moreover, a staggering 61 per cent of Lebanon's imports from the Arab states were provided by Syria.[94]

Although Lebanon negotiated and signed economic agreements with the central government of the UAR, sections of such agreements relating to the Syrian region were not implemented wholly, or indeed even partially. Syria retained the right to pursue an economic policy regarding Lebanon, determined by economic differences between the two countries, which pre-dated the formation of the UAR in February 1958.[95]

Egyptian promises

In early 1959, Lebanon was at pains to strengthen its economy by, among other things, increasing trade with Egypt, which had been disrupted during 1958. This involved exporting fruit and vegetables to Egypt, while importing rice, potatoes and cotton. In addition, Lebanon's developed service sector was ideal for encouraging tourists to visit Lebanon. By 1961, the economic relationship between the two countries had marginally improved, reflecting an upturn in the political understanding between them.

Nasser gave the new Lebanese administration only a vague promise concerning the import of Lebanese apples in return for Egyptian rice. Al-Ahram made considerable political capital out of this issue, stating that the UAR was willing to help Lebanon by importing apples worth L£200,000 and exporting 3,000 tons of rice, despite the ban on the export of this vital commodity.[96] The Lebanese prime minister, Rashid Karami, laid the foundations of improved economic relations during his visit to Cairo on 3 January 1959. The Egyptian government promised to import more than 6,000 tons of apples at favourable prices. Secondly, Egypt promised to export 3,000 tons of rice at the favourable price of $145 instead of $153 per ton. Thirdly, Karami was promised the release of blocked funds for tourism worth E£492,000 scheduled at E£90,000 per month. Each year the Egyptian government undertook to subsidize Egyptian tourists wishing to travel to Lebanon.[97] Later, the Egyptian government offered one more concession, whereby Lebanese investors in Egypt were allowed to repatriate revenues accrued, while leaving capital investment intact.[98]

However, while Egypt exported its produce easily, Lebanese exports, especially apples, faced difficulties despite the agreement. In fact, by spring 1959 Egypt had exported about 1,600 tons of rice and 3,200 tons of potatoes, while outlining a plan to export 9,000 tons of rice to Lebanon, as part of a total volume of 12,000 tons.[99] The Egyptian market was an important one for Lebanese apples, since some Western governments, particularly Britain, refused to grant Lebanon fixed quotas. Britain's position was determined by the lobbying of British apple farmers, and London tried to deny any coolness towards the new government in Beirut. Therefore it explained to NATO members that Lebanon ought to improve competitiveness in Western markets, and not rely on fixed quotas. In fact, Lebanon was even encouraged to clinch the best bargain it could get from the UAR concerning transit dues.[100]

A delegation of apple producers from north Lebanon visited Prime Minister Karami on 24 March 1959, on the eve of the Shihab–Nasser summit, to press their demands to export their produce to Egypt, thereby fulfilling the terms of the trade accord. Karami placed the blame squarely with Egyptian traders and promised to 'investigate the matter'. This was perhaps more a means of appeasing the producers than a clear declaration of intent. Despite the repeated requests from Lebanon for Egypt to fulfil its role in the trade agreement, and Lebanon's adherence to the stipulation that its produce should be of high quality and sold at favourable prices, Egypt failed to import any Lebanese apples during the whole of 1959.[101] More Egyptian promises were made in 1960 and 1961, which produced some results. In 1960, for instance, Egypt imported apples from Lebanon worth L£483,391.[102] However, the structure of Egypt's imports from Lebanon altered to the extent that the fruit and vegetable component had decreased from 58.6 per cent in 1958, to a mere 39.4 per cent by 1960.[103]

Tourism was perhaps the second most important economic issue between the two countries. On 24 May 1959, an agreement was signed whereby citizens of the southern region of the UAR (Egypt) who wished to spend summer vacations in Lebanon were allowed to take currency up to a value of E£100 per head. Moreover, the Lebanese government promised to exchange it at the favourable rate of L£7.5 for each Egyptian pound. This was meant to encourage the estimated 25,000 Egyptians wishing to visit Lebanon, especially given the UAR's travel ban imposed on its citizens due to economic difficulties.[104] Moreover, Lebanon abolished its historical requirement of entry visas for Egyptian citizens on 24 June 1959. The accord on tourism was renewed in 1960 on similar terms as the previous year, allowing Lebanon to act as the most accessible resort for Egyptian travellers.[105]

Nevertheless, the fact remained that Egypt exported far more than it imported from Lebanon, and this immensely increased Lebanon's trade deficit with Egypt during this period. Egyptian exports to Lebanon almost tripled from 1959 (L£12.07 million) to 1960 (L£32.15 million), and almost doubled again in 1961 (L£51.68 million). Thus the share of the Lebanese market for Egyptian exports rose from 1.72 per cent in 1959 to nearly 5 per cent in 1961 (see Table 4a).[106] Lebanese exports to Egypt, however, failed to increase and stood at the boundary of L£2 million a year, while their share of the Egyptian market decreased to about half a per cent (see Table 4b).

Economic relations with Syria

Lebanon's relations with the Syrian region of the UAR was considered of prime importance by the Lebanese government in early 1959. Syria was able to exercise political, commercial and demographic pressures over Lebanon, as had happened in 1958. Syria constituted the 'transit gate' through which Lebanon's commerce with the Near East had to pass. Thus, it was the aim of the Lebanese government to settle economic issues with regard to this region by exploiting Egypt's hegemony over Syria.

During the first half of 1959, the Lebanese government was involved in fruitless negotiations with UAR officials to settle the Lebanese–Syrian import–export agreement; the circulation of people between the two countries; custom levies; and most important of all transit trade to other Arab states beyond Syria. The Syrians, not the Egyptians, created difficulties regarding the implementation of transit trade agreements. In Lebanon, problems with transit trade and Syria added to concerns in government circles over proposed projects for the development of the port of Latakia in Syria. It was thought that if such a project were to go ahead, it would pose a major threat to Beirut's position as the centre for Middle East trade and a major source of foreign exchange.[107]

A new agreement was signed in Cairo on 7 June 1959 aimed at settling the poor economic relations between Lebanon and Syria. This agreement provided for the halving of taxes on Syrians travelling to Lebanon; granting Lebanese businessmen, who acted as representatives for foreign companies in Syria, a period of five years postponement before being required to conform to Syrian law; and the removal of restrictions on free zone purchases. Lebanon regarded the last point as the most important since it provided an opportunity for Beirut to consolidate its paramount position as the centre for Middle East trade.[108] However, the Syrian business community considered the agreement as a concession given by Egyptian officials to Lebanon at Syria's expense, for purely Egyptian political purposes. Apart from the reduction of the exit tax paid by Syrians travelling to Lebanon, all items were perceived as harmful to Syrian interests.[109]

Despite grave misgivings, the Syrians co-operated with the 7 June agreement by reducing exit visa charges. However, custom regulations were applied strictly, as never before, making border crossing difficult between Syria and Lebanon. This action minimized benefits gained from travelling to Lebanon.[110] Also, the authorities in Syria allowed Saudi Arabian freight trucks to enter Lebanon but prohibited Jordanian and Iraqi cars.[111] Later, the Syrians asked Lebanon not to permit UAR visitors to travel to third countries unless they were provided with Syrian exit permits. Lebanon rejected this on the grounds that it was not compatible with normal international practice.[112] Therefore the Syrians imposed their own travel restrictions on Syrian nationals visiting Lebanon, justifying it as 'merely an economic restriction with no political tinge whatsoever', according to the UAR ambassador to Beirut, Abdul Hamid Ghalib.[113]

The Lebanese government attempted to use Egyptian political influence through Marshall 'Amer, Nasser's deputy, to force the

Syrians to implement the 7 June agreement. The Syrians 'nullified' the agreement by not only curbing travel to Lebanon, but also by not issuing licences to Syrian merchants who wanted to import from the Beirut free zone, and maintaining a restriction on transit trade. This was done in spite of Marshall 'Amer's order to exempt Lebanese fruit trucks from these regulations.[114] In sum, by manipulating the relationship between Syrian and Egypt, Lebanon aimed to settle its economic problems with Syria, which dated back to the pre-UAR period, but achieved limited success.

Damascus as the key to Lebanese trade

Syria, Lebanon and Jordan signed a commercial agreement on 9 December 1959, which was interpreted as a 'conciliatory gesture by Syria towards her two neighbours', but in fact was sign of more direct Egyptian control within the UAR. The Lebanese government naturally welcomed this agreement, as it was the first transit agreement to be reached since 1953, when Lebanese trucks were forced to unload their goods at the frontier on to Syrian carriers.[115] With the UAR's consent, Lebanon lobbied Jordan, Saudi Arabia and Iraq to implement the terms of the agreement.[116] However, no concrete results were achieved, despite the UAR's promises, due to Syria's reluctance to comply.[117]

The issue of Iraqi tourists who wished to spend their summer vacation in Lebanon proved to be a thorny one. It was estimated that in the summer of 1959, some 4,000 Iraqis wished to travel to Lebanon. This issue was to create tension between Lebanon and the UAR, due to the fact it had significant implications for the economic relationships between the three countries involved. Syria (the northern region of the UAR) had used the issue of tourism for political purposes, in an attempt to secure the economic and political isolation of Iraq. Lebanon secured from the outset official Iraqi approval for tourists who wished to visit Lebanon. However, in order not to create diplomatic problems between itself and the UAR, Lebanon applied conditions on the Iraqi tourists, such as forbidding their participation in political activities while on Lebanese soil. Moreover, Lebanon backed up its position by banning a 'popular Iraqi delegation' from visiting Beirut, in order not to fuel the rivalry between the delegation's hosts, the Lebanese Communist Party, and their pro-UAR rivals.[118]

Nevertheless, the UAR authorities in the northern region were unwilling to comply with a Lebanese request for the free passage of Iraqi tourists through Syria, arguing that the travelling of passengers in the Syrian territories is a 'political issue needing more consideration'.[119] Lebanon tried to circumvent the apparent deadlock by asking Iraq to increase the number of air travellers to Beirut. Iraq refused to agree to such a measure, underlining its preference for overland transit through Syria on the grounds that it was safer and, more importantly, cheaper. Iraq requested that Iraqi air travellers be given similar financial concessions by Lebanon to those offered to citizens of the UAR's southern region (Egypt). This meant that the Lebanese government should undertake to pay L£150 for every Iraqi air-traveller tourist, thus accounting for the difference between air and land fares to Lebanon. Moreover, the Iraqi government requested 25 per cent discount in air fares between Beirut and Baghdad in order to increase the number of limited income tourists, and to lift the ban on the entry of some Iraqi political activists – i.e. anti-UAR instigators.[120] These demands were met, in turn, by more conditions from the UAR, which requested that the Lebanese government should submit lists of potential Iraqi passengers a week before their departure via Syria, to ensure that no 'enemy elements' were included among them. As a result, the Lebanese government failed to secure an unconditional transit for Iraqi tourists via Syria due to the political nature of the Iraqi–UAR dispute.[121]

On 6 July 1960, the Lebanese government was able to extract an agreement from the UAR for that year's tourist season, which secured the free passage of Iraqi tourists through Syrian territory to Lebanon. This agreement stipulated that Iraqi tourists should travel to and from Lebanon by land on certain days (e.g. Monday, Wednesday and Friday) and use specific border crossing posts.[122] Despite this agreement, the political differences and rivalry between Nasser and Qassim meant that the free passage of Iraqi tourists was subject to the will of Syrian border officials and the prevailing political temperature of the area.

Conclusion

The Nasser–Shihab summit of 26 March 1959 laid the basis of a
new relationship between the Lebanese and Egyptian governments. The Shihab regime took special care, on the whole, to
avoid antagonizing President Nasser personally or to take sides
against the Egyptian government in its disputes with the Iraqi and
Jordanian governments in particular. As a result, Lebanon enjoyed
a period of internal stability, which was helped by the acquiescence of pro-UAR Lebanese groups. The Lebanese government
tried to overcome economic differences with Syria, which pre-
ceded the formation of the UAR, by seeking the help of Egyptian
officials in Cairo. But it was proven that mutual agreements lacked
the will of the Syrian side to comply, in spite of Egyptian political
pressures.

CHAPTER 5

Lebanon between Nasser and Arab Radicals

The superpowers' Cold War

The Cold War between the USA and the Soviet Union intensified during this period. Each endeavoured to advance its interests, while avoiding a direct military confrontation with the other. The Cuban missile crisis of October 1962 showed the dangers of confrontation and initiated a period of détente. The US objective in the Middle East was to contain the Arab–Israeli dispute by encouraging Arab states to concentrate on internal economic development. The ultimate purpose was to safeguard US interests in the region such as oil, Israel's security and the use of military facilities.

The Kennedy administration perceived Nasser as a regionally based bulwark against communism, offering him economic aid 'without strings'. William B. Quandt suggests that both the USA and Egypt seemed to understand that 'moderation towards Israel was expected of Nasser'.[1] America was capable of maintaining its good relationship with Nasser, despite Egypt's conflict with the USA's regional ally, Saudi Arabia. The crux of the matter concerned Yemen, following Egypt's role in the coup of 26 September 1962 there.[2]

The Soviet Union continued to support General Qassim of Iraq as a challenger to Nasser and his brand of Arab socialism until Qassim's fall on 8 February 1963. His demise dealt a severe blow to communism in Iraq, and the Middle East generally, followed as it was by a draconian policy in Iraq aimed at eliminating the communist movement.[3] In terms of regional politics, both the USA and Egypt were the beneficiaries of the resultant decline of Soviet prestige and leverage in the region.

However, the succession of President Johnson to the White House, on 22 November 1963, heralded the beginning of a major change in US policy towards the Egyptian regime, which was to be exploited by the Soviet Union. Three factors were significant in provoking this shift. First, the US government had become disillusioned with the policy of granting aid to Egypt, while Egyptian military involvement in the Yemen intensified. Secondly, the US policy of arming Israel raised fears in the Arab world and fuelled the burgeoning arms race in the region, despite the US government's claim that it was an 'important means of forestalling Israeli development of nuclear weapons'. Thirdly, the US administration lost interest in solving the Arab refugee problem and shifted its attention to Vietnam. Thus, UAR–US relations deteriorated rapidly, especially after economic aid to Egypt became scarce from 1965. This forced the Egyptian government to develop a closer relationship with the Soviet Union.[4]

The Arabs' Cold War

The Syrian army's coup d'état of 28 September 1961 put an end to the first experiment in Arab unity after the Second World War. Despite the setback to Nasser's prestige as well as to Egypt's pan-Arab role caused by the Syrian secession, Egypt remained at the centre of Arab politics. Nasser reorganized his regime through the adoption of the National Charter of 21 May 1962. He opted for radical policies inside Egypt through implementing a brand of 'Arab socialism' to curb the social and political powers of feudalism. Equally, Egyptian foreign policy was radicalized to fight reactionary as well as progressive competitor regimes in the Arab world.[5] Thus, Arab politics underwent three subsequent phases in this period: the intense ideological conflict of different regimes until the end of 1963, the Arab summits phase of 1964–65, and the battle of the Islamic Pact, from early 1966 until May 1967.

During the first phase, Egypt was at the centre of quarrels with almost every Arab state, save Lebanon. The dispute with the new Syrian regime intensified over the form of a possible reunion, and exploded after Egyptian implication in a coup attempt in April 1962. This led the Syrian government to lodge a complaint to the Arab League, and then to Egypt boycotting the Arab League for the following year. The fall of Qassim of Iraq on 8 February 1963 and the Syrian regime in Damascus on 8 March paved the way for the Egyptian government to regain its influence in the Arab East. The leaders of the new Syrian and Iraqi regimes rushed immediately to Cairo and held lengthy negotiations with Nasser, which culminated in the signing of a new union treaty on 17 April 1963. However, the deep mistrust between Nasser and the Ba'athists of Syria in particular undermined this treaty in the summer of 1963.[6]

The coup d'état in North Yemen on 26 September 1962, which overthrew the rule of the Zaidi Imams, provided Egypt with an opportunity to aid the new regime and make a strategic gain by simultaneously establishing a foothold on the Arabian peninsula. This developed, subsequently, into military intervention to 'protect the revolution' against the deposed Imam's forces backed by the Jordanian and Saudi Arabian governments. The battle between Egypt and these two states took the form of political, ideological and military confrontation in North Yemen, which lasted until June 1967.[7]

The second phase in Arab regional politics came when Nasser took the initiative to call for the first Arab summit in Cairo in response to an Israeli project to divert the waters of the River Jordan. Nasser suggested on 23 December 1963 that:

> In order to confront Israel, which challenged us last week when its chief-of-staff stood up and said 'we shall divert the water against the will of the Arabs, and the Arabs can do what they want', a meeting between Arab kings and Heads of State must take place as soon as possible, regardless of the conflicts and differences between them. Those with whom we are in conflict, we are prepared to meet; those with whom we have a quarrel, we are ready, for the sake of Palestine, to sit with.[8]

As a consequence, the first Arab summit took place on 13 January 1964, to be followed by another on 5 September of the same year. Moreover, Egypt took steps to improve its international diplomatic position by hosting an African summit in July 1964, as well as a non-aligned summit on 5 October 1964. Nasser's first aim was to maintain the atmosphere of Arab detente, while he worked to secure a dominant voice in the military and foreign affairs of the Arab countries. Moreover, he employed the Arab League and the new United Arab Command (UAC) to pre-empt the Israeli diversion plan with an Arab one. In doing so, he was able to transform the Israeli problem, for a while, from a divisive force among Arab countries to a rallying point – with Egypt in the lead.[9]

Nevertheless, this trend of 'successful' Arab summits came to an end in late 1965 over the question of how to defend Arab projects to divert the sources of the Jordan. It was at this juncture that the third phase came to the fore, characterized by the conflict between Saudi Arabia and Egypt. The call for an 'Islamic Alliance' by King Faisal found sympathy in Iran, Jordan, Pakistan and the Sudan. This strategy was linked to the US one of preventing communism from taking root in the Middle East. But Nasser perceived the project as an American ploy to remove him from power, and thus retaliated by resorting to his own version of 'revolutionary socialism'. In late 1966, the polarization between the 'progressive' camp led by Egypt and Syria, and the 'reactionary' camp led by Saudi Arabia, Jordan and Iran, reached its climax. The two camps were involved in a bitter ideological and military conflict in the Yemen, in addition to having different approaches over the most appropriate means of resolving the Palestinian issue.[10] This phase came to an end when Egypt rallied to defend Syria in May 1967. This resulted in major regional political shifts, which affected the progressive as well as the reactionary Arab states equally.

Stability in Lebanon

Despite the fact that the Middle East was racked with instability, Lebanon enjoyed a period of relative tranquillity throughout this period, both politically and economically. The Syrian secession from the UAR was a major factor in bringing down Sa'ib Salam's government in mid-October 1961, due to its indecision regarding the recognition of the new Syrian regime. Thus, President Shihab chose Rashid Karami to be his prime minister. The latter headed a strong government, which stayed in office from October 1961 until February 1964 – earning the distinction of being the longest serving cabinet to date.[11]

The attempted coup of 31 December 1961 by the Syrian Socialist Nationalist Party (SSNP) constituted a serious threat to the Lebanese regime. This led to accusations that Britain and Jordan instigated the coup since both states were perceived as traditional supporters of the party and its project for the political union of the Fertile Crescent states.[12] But the Lebanese government exposed the internal elements of the plot, and played down the supposed external ones in order, perhaps, not to be drawn into regional conflicts.

The election of Charles Hilu, who succeeded Shihab on 24 September 1964, was seen as a political continuation of the Shihabist regime. Hilu relied on the army, a loyalist chamber and successive prime ministers ('Uwayni, Karami and al-Yafi) to implement policy.[13] Thus, Shihab and Hilu succeeded during this period in pursuing policies which achieved some stability in Lebanon's internal affairs.

Relations after Syria's secession

Syria's secession from the UAR on 28 September 1961 caused a deep dilemma for the Lebanese government of Rashid Karami, as both Syria and Egypt competed to win over Lebanon. While Lebanese economic interests lay with Syria, Egypt enjoyed the support of the 'Muslim Street' and some Muslim ministers in the Lebanese government. The open conflict between Syria and Egypt over Lebanon involved the use of propaganda, conspiracy and diplomacy.[14]

Lebanon was subjected to Syrian pressure after October 1961 to move away from the Egyptian orbit in its foreign policy. But General Shihab refused to antagonize Egypt and continued to act upon the same guidelines agreed and laid down with Nasser on 26 March 1959. There were several reasons for this. First, Egypt continued to be the strongest Arab state, conducting an aggressive foreign policy using Arab nationalism and challenging other Arab regimes. In fact, Egypt was the only Arab state which could make or break any potential union projects in the Arab world. Secondly, Egypt continued to enjoy wide support from the Lebanese Muslim community, which constituted a significant constraint on any Lebanese government wishing to act contrary to Egypt's interests. As a result, Lebanon represented an ideal arena for Nasser to conduct his Arab battles, whether by means of propaganda, intelligence or conspiracies.

The Lebanese government acted in a sympathetic manner towards Egypt, and was, at the same time, hostile to Syria. The Lebanese army opened its camps to 7,000 Egyptian citizens expelled from Syria just after the break-up of the UAR.[15] In addition, Syria accused Lebanon of providing a base for Egyptian conspiracies against the new regime in Damascus, including arms smuggling by Egyptian agents into Syria, aided by General Ghalib, Egypt's ambassador to Beirut.[16] Moreover, the Lebanese government not only delayed but also evaded the recognition of the new Syrian regime. Indeed, some Lebanese ministers expressed openly their displeasure with the new regime in Damascus, and supported President Nasser. A clear example was Kamal Jumblatt, Minister of the Interior, who attacked the new regime in Damascus in his own daily, al-Anba'.[17] As a result, Syria resorted to imposing economic restrictions on Lebanon, and made it clear that Lebanon should co-ordinate policies with Syria as a pre-condition for an improvement in their relations.[18]

The Egyptian government perceived the coup attempt by the Syrian nationalists in Lebanon on 31 December 1961 as an attempt by regional players, especially Great Britain and Jordan, to create the Fertile Crescent project, which aimed at including Iraq, Jordan, Syria, Lebanon, Palestine and Cyprus into one single political unit. It was feared that this plan would diminish Egyptian influence in the Arab east, and restrict Egypt's influence to Africa only. Since Lebanon was 'sympathetic' to Egypt after its debacle in Syria, the attempted coup was, as stated by Haikal, designed also to remove General Shihab and replace him with ex-President Sham'un and the SSNP.[19] The Egyptian government seized the opportunity to expose the alleged external and internal plotters, and to cement its relationship with the Lebanese government. A leader was written in *La Bourse Egyptienne* by Muhammad H. Haikal in which he stated that:

> The coup attempt revealed three factors. First, those who kept accusing us in the past of plotting against Lebanon are themselves the plotters. Second, those who have accused us of being the enemies of democracy for a long time are themselves the partisans of violence and terror. Third, those who never stopped lobbying Lebanon to act against us, and to make Lebanon believe that we [Egypt] do not support its neutrality, are themselves the enemies of Lebanon's neutrality and independence.[20]

Also, Cairo encouraged the Lebanese government to resort to the UN Security Council to complain about alleged British involvement.[21] But the Lebanese government decided to bury the story of alleged foreign complicity, and opted instead to expose the internal side of the plot. The Lebanese Minister of Justice, Fu'ad Butrus, refused to name any foreign power suspected of aiding the plotters, in order to 'safeguard the judicial inquiry'. By contrast, Charles Hilu, a chief aide to President Shihab, said that over half of those arrested (4,000 people) were foreigners, the majority of whom were Palestinians, Jordanians and Syrians. This was due, perhaps, to a desire by the Lebanese government not to be too closely affiliated with Egypt and, furthermore, to distance itself from the problems associated with regional polarization.[22]

In mid-1962, Lebanon was subjected to great pressure from Egypt's regional rivals to change what they perceived as a sympathetic policy towards Egypt. Lebanon's foreign minister, Philip Takla, pleaded with Arab countries to leave the Lebanon out of their differences and not to 'try to impose moral or material pressure on her'.[23] This pressure took the form of threats from Syria, Iraq, Jordan and Saudi Arabia to impose an embargo on their imports through the port of Beirut. Syria lobbied Iraq and Saudi Arabia to divert their transit trade through the port of Latakia in Syria, while Jordan imposed 10 per cent extra tax on its imports which came via Beirut.[24] Each of these states, for different reasons, perceived Lebanese foreign policy as being biased against them and favourable to Egypt. The Iraqi government withdrew its ambassador from Lebanon on 11 May 1962, prevented Iraqi tourists from visiting Lebanon and stopped all imports of Lebanese agricultural produce. This step was taken in response to Lebanon's recognition of the newly independent state of Kuwait, in spite of Iraq's persistent territorial claim. Saudi Arabia withdrew its ambassador from Beirut on 23 May 1962, in protest against the failure of the Lebanese government to stop the campaigns of the pro-Egyptian section of the Lebanese press against the Saudi leadership.[25]

The Syrian position proved, by far, to be the most extreme among these states. Syria accused Lebanon of intentionally ignoring pro-Egyptian infiltration across the Syrian–Lebanese border at a time when the political situation inside Syria was still fragile as a result of the attempted coup of early April 1962. The Lebanese foreign minister, Philip Takla, visited Damascus on 7 July 1962 thereby becoming the first Lebanese official to visit Syria since it departed from the UAR, and 'promised' more control over Egyptian activities.[26] A clear example of Syrian pressure on Lebanon is illustrated by the statement of the then Syrian politician, Khalid al-'Azm, when he approached President

Shihab in July 1962 to demand the curtailing of Egyptian activities. Al-'Azm claimed to have told Shihab:

> We do not ask you to expel Abdul-Hamid Ghalib [the Egyptian ambassador to Beirut] and sever your relations with Egypt: but we would prefer if you do not support the Nasserists against us, and do not allow them to use Lebanon as a base for their conspiracies.[27]

According to al-'Azm, Shihab refused to close down pro-Egyptian publications and refrained from pressurizing pro-Egyptian politicians, on the grounds that it might affect the stability of Lebanon. It was clear to al-'Azm that Shihab preferred to appease the pro-Nasser constituency inside Lebanon and was not interested in joining the anti-Nasser trend.[28]

The Shtura Conference debacle

The Arab League conference of 22 August 1962 in Shtura, Lebanon, proved to be an embarrassment for the Egyptian and Lebanese governments. The conference was requested by the Syrian government to examine allegations of Egyptian interference in its internal affairs. The Syrian government accused the Lebanese foreign minister, Philip Takla, of conspiring with the Egyptian ambassador, General Ghalib, to undermine the conference. The aim was to convene the meeting in a remote area, away from publicity, and to restrict it to one hotel in order to keep away Syrian journalists. Furthermore, the Lebanese interior minister, Kamal Jumblatt, who took an uncompromising pro-Nasser stance, was accused of imposing restrictions on the entry of Syrian delegates. Al-'Azm claimed that Egyptian and Lebanese tactics had backfired since the people of Shtura and neighbouring Zahle were Christians, and therefore harboured anti-Nasser feelings created by the 1958 crisis. This made them sympathetic towards the Syrian delegation and supportive of its complaint.[29]

Despite Egyptian attempts to confine the conference to the heads of delegations, in order to reduce the propaganda gains of their Arab adversaries, the conference turned into a slanging match putting Egypt on the defensive. Egyptian press attaché, Anwar Al-Jamal, who attended the conference, gave an example of Egyptian tactics to remove Cairo's opponents from the conference hall. When a Jordanian delegate, Wasfi al-Tal, launched a stern attack on Egypt, the head of the Egyptian delegation, Mahmud Fawzi, suggested that the meeting should be restricted to the heads of delegations. This suggestion was implemented and al-Tal 'was thrown out to get rid of his troubles'.[30] In counter measure, the Syrian press and radio undertook, in conjunction with the anti-Nasser section of the Lebanese press, to publish and broadcast the proceedings of the conference, notwithstanding the decision to hold the meeting in camera. Moreover, the Syrian delegation's attacks were not, according to Khalid al-'Azm, restricted to the charge of interfering in Syria's internal affairs, but exposed Egyptian idleness towards Israeli shipping activities across the Gulf of Aqaba.[31]

The defection of the Egyptian military attaché to Beirut, Lieutenant-Colonel Zaghlul Abdul Rahman, played directly into the hands of the anti-Egypt camp. Abdul Rahman revealed, after being presented by the Syrian delegation to the Arab League meeting, that subversive activities had been launched from Beirut against Syria and other Arab states. Anwar al-Jamal stated that the Egyptian attaché defected for two reasons. First, the pressure brought to bear on him from his relative, Ahmad Abu al-Fatih, who had been conducting activities against the regime in Cairo, was so great. Secondly, the attaché was implicated in a gambling scandal involving Egyptian Embassy funds amounting to some E£200,000.[32]

Eventually, the conference was suspended following the decision of the Egyptian government to withdraw its delegation and leave the Arab League altogether, in protest against what it considered a barrage of Syrian insults directed at Egypt and at President Nasser personally. This episode placed the Lebanese government in an extremely difficult position, as it could not deny or confirm Syrian accusations against Egypt, fearing internal and external repercussions. In a political and diplomatic move, as much for its own sake as Egypt's, the Lebanese delegation manoeuvred to bring the proceedings, and the row, to a close once it had reached deadlock. Thus, the Lebanese delegation denied Egypt's critics the opportunity to reach a concrete decision condemning Egyptian actions. This move simultaneously exposed the Lebanese government to the charge of partisanship. Khalid al-'Azm claimed that most Arab delegates approved implicitly of the essence of Syrian charges, save the Lebanese foreign minister, Philip Takla, but were afraid of Nasser's revenge, if a decision against Egypt was adopted.[33]

Nevertheless, Shihab did not take specific steps to alter Lebanese foreign policy in the Arab domain. Instead, he sent a letter to Nasser calling on him to review his decision to leave the Arab League, as the League would 'lose any value without Egypt in view of the fact that it represents the biggest and strongest of all Arab countries'. Nasser promised Shihab a freeze on the Egyptian government's decision to withdraw from the League, but suspended, instead, all activities until the League's Council repudiated the slanders against 'Egypt's dignity'.[34] It was clear that the Lebanese government favoured the presence of Egypt in the League to balance the other Arab states in the area, but was unable to reorganize another League meeting in order to satisfy Egyptian conditions. Therefore the Egyptian government did not resume its activities in the Arab League until 10 March 1963, after the Syrian regime had been overthrown by a coup on 8 March.[35]

Lebanon was subjected, in the meantime, to stern economic measures by the Syrian government of Khalid al-'Azm, reaching their peak in January 1963. These measures included the barring of Lebanese and Egyptian citizens from entering Syria, in reaction to disturbances in Syria plotted by Egyptian groups using Lebanon as a base. It was said that Lebanon allowed the entry of Abdul-Hamid al-Sarraj, former head of the Syrian security services during the union with Egypt, twice from Cairo in order to conspire with Syrian exiles to overthrow the existing regime by paying them more than L£5 million. This action led to disturbances in Syria in January 1963, but Lebanon's role was exposed due to the fact that Sarraj was allowed to act freely.[36] Moreover, the Syrian government approached Jordan, Iraq and Saudi Arabia to conduct a collective embargo on transit trade from Beirut, in order to force Lebanon to adopt a neutral position in the Egyptian–Syrian conflict. Khalid al-'Azm stated the conditions which would need to be met if Lebanon was to avert the implementation of an embargo:

1. Impose a ban on the political activity of Egypt's ambassador to Beirut, Abdul-Hamid Ghalib.

2. Inform the Syrian government of the amounts which the ambassador used from Lebanese banks to pay his agents to conspire against Syria.

3. Submit a weekly report to the Syrian government giving details of names of Syrians and Egyptians who travelled to and from Egypt and ban those whom the Syrian government considered conspirators.

4. Change Lebanese foreign policy towards a neutral line.[37]

The Lebanese government refused the Syrian requests and played for time by issuing a statement expressing its readiness to clear the atmosphere. But the Iraqi coup d'état of 8 February 1963 undermined the Syrian call for an embargo on Lebanon, and the issue was put to rest after the Syrian regime itself fell on 8 March 1963. The new regimes of Syria and Iraq rushed to Egypt to conclude 'the Arab Union' for which the Lebanese government did not show enthusiasm.[38] However, relations between Egypt and Lebanon were not affected. As Nasser was directing polemics against his pan-Arab rivals, Lebanon stood on the sidelines.

The River Jordan diversion project

Relations between Egypt and Lebanon were seriously tested when Arab states attempted to respond to the new Israeli challenges. It was clear that Lebanon was unable and unwilling to participate in, or implement, any collective Arab measures, fearing either Israeli military reprisals or Arab interference in its internal affairs, or both.

On 26 December 1963, the UAR called for a meeting of the Arab League at summit level in order to co-ordinate a strategy to prevent Israel's near completion of the project to exploit the Jordan waters. The Lebanese government sustained pressure internally from the right-wing Christian element in the Lebanese parliament, which sought to exclude Lebanon from involvement in Arab plans. Philip Takla favoured leaving the matter to the Security Council, thus avoiding any action which might appear to challenge Israel.[39]

Therefore President Shihab stayed away from the Arab summit that took place in Cairo on 13 to 17 January, 1964. He justified his absence on the grounds of ill health, in an obvious attempt to avoid direct pressure from the Arab states and thereby gain room to manoeuvre politically. Despite the fact that the prime minister, Rashid Karami, headed the Lebanese delegation, the Egyptian government was offended. Cairo considered this to be 'under-representation', which might have a negative impact on the general perception of its role as host and the prestige of President Nasser. The Lebanese government did not reply to these protests, but highlighted the fact that the Egyptian president received

Karami in his home for a long time, and that Takla was included in the recommendations committee.[40]

The Lebanese delegation kept a low profile at the summit while sharp arguments raged between the Egyptian and Syrian leaders in particular. But the Lebanese government had no choice but to agree with the results of the summit which served to put Egypt at the centre of Arab politics by establishing the United Arab Command (AUC), to be headed by the Egyptian general Ali 'Amir and based in Cairo. This body was defensive in nature and was supposed to prepare a military plan, financed by the oil-rich Arab states, to protect the Arab project for the diversion of Jordan waters.[41]

Subsequently, the Egyptian government urged Lebanon, through the AUC, to expand its army and to purchase Soviet military equipment, offering to act as a go-between. However, the Lebanese government was wary of the Egyptian offer, since it would increase Nasser's leverage inside Lebanon and also enhance Egyptian ability to stage clandestine activities against the rival regime in Syria. This worried the US government, who therefore decided to make an offer of their own. A CIA document revealed that:

> The Lebanese, like the Jordanians, also prefer getting Western arms and equipment, but have said they must acquire new arms under any circumstances. The US has agreed, under certain conditions, to sell Lebanon 16 F.8A supersonic aircraft. The Egyptian offer to serve as a go-between for the purchase of Soviet weapons still stands, however, and may yet give Nasser added leverage in Lebanon. It is doubtful, however, that the administration of President Hilu will reconsider the Lebanese decision to purchase from the US.[42]

President Hilu, in fact, avoided Egyptian and US manipulation by opting to conclude a deal with France, Lebanon's traditional supplier, to purchase 12 Mirage-3 fighter jets in February 1966. However, the Lebanese government stated officially that Lebanon and France had merely signed an agreement for French 'technical assistance' in the military field. This was meant to ward off Egyptian and Arab criticism since Dassault, the Mirage manufacturer, was put on the Arab blacklist because of its links with Israel.[43] Hilu stated that the AUC favoured the purchase of the Soviet MIG fighters over the French Mirage, on the grounds that the MIG deal was cheaper. But he succeeded in bringing the AUC to pay for the Mirage deal, citing technical and training advantages relating to Lebanon's traditional links with France.[44]

Quarrels in Alexandria

The second Arab summit, which was held in Alexandria on 5 September 1964, was intended to follow up plans for the diversion of the Jordan waters. The conference presented Lebanon with many difficulties, both in form and substance. President Shihab declined to participate in this summit and opted, instead, to send his successor, Charles Hilu, to represent the Lebanese government.[45] Hilu states that Shihab was unwilling to involve himself in official undertakings, since his term was due to expire on 23 September 1964. This convinced Hilu to agree to attend the summit as the president's representative.[46] The compromise meant that while avoiding giving offence to Nasser personally, it was also a short-term tactic – the Lebanese delegate avoided the need to take important decisions. Haikal gave the story a 'secret' dimension by stating that Shihab sent an intelligence officer to meet Nasser to inform him about foreign activities in Beirut using Lebanese public figures and newspapers. Moreover, the officer reported that these foreign agents had penetrated the Lebanese security police. Haikal quoted this officer as saying that President Shihab did not wish to involve himself in this matter, especially as his term had almost expired, and Charles Hilu would replace him.[47] The important factor in Haikal's story is not only its substance, but also its agreement with Hilu's account that Shihab wished at all costs to avoid visiting Cairo.

President-elect Hilu stated at the summit Lebanon's reservations over the Jordan waters plan presented to the AUC by its chairman, General Ali 'Amir of Egypt. First, the Lebanese government objected to 'Amir being granted considerable autonomy in the overall control of the AUC, since this clashed with Lebanese sovereignty. Secondly, the Lebanese delegation found it impossible to accept the suggestion that General 'Amir should have the authority to deploy Arab forces according to 'strategic pre-requisites'. Thirdly, the Lebanese delegation objected to Arab forces, especially from Syria, being stationed on Lebanese territory. It was considered that this would invite Israeli intervention. Fourthly, the inadequacy of the military measures implemented since the first summit to defend the Jordan waters plan jeopardized the whole project. Lastly, the process of implementing any plan would take time, due to constitutional and power-sharing arrangements in Lebanon between the president, cabinet and parliament.[48] Furthermore, Hilu's unspoken objection was the fear that any Arab force stationed in Lebanon might tilt the Christian–Muslim balance in favour of the Muslims.[49]

According to President Hilu, Nasser was keen to get results in his dealings with him, which made Nasser overlook the 'constitutional and psychological problems' mentioned above. Nasser's deputy, Marshall 'Amir, suggested sending an Egyptian brigade to help protect Lebanon in order to calm Lebanese sensitivity to an apparent Syrian offer of troops. Moreover, 'Amir guaranteed the protection of Lebanon against Israel by the Egyptian air force. President Hilu declined the Egyptian offer of 'protection', as he regarded it not so much as a defence against Israel, but as an attempt by Egypt to outbid Syria's radicalism in the eyes of Arab public opinion. Hilu says that he held an hour-long meeting with Nasser before the start of the summit. He mentions that Nasser was ready to compromise over the Lebanese objection to the entry of Syrian forces into Lebanon. But Nasser and 'Amir urged him first to accept the decision to start the Arab diversion project of the River Jordan immediately.[50]

The Lebanese refusal to allow the military presence of Arab forces on Lebanese territory opened the way for the other delegates to accuse Lebanon of opportunism. The charge was that Lebanon was ready to 'support Arab measures from which it benefits, such as the boycott of Israel, while refusing to do anything from which it might suffer'.[51] Hilu said that when Nasser suggested granting him a four-month period in order to drop his objections, he answered by saying:

> I don't know which period is suitable for me, whether it is going to be short or long. I think that every matter is related to the effectiveness of the military assistance, which is going to be offered to us, especially that of the air protection cover [in order to guard the works in Lebanon from possible Israeli attack].[52]

President 'Arif of Iraq, Nasser's ally at this juncture, threatened to embarrass Hilu publicly by suggesting that Lebanon represented a barrier to collective Arab projects. This could have undermined the Arab credentials of the Lebanese government, and possibly incited the Lebanese Muslim community against Hilu.[53]

However, Hilu and Nasser opted for a compromise after diplomatic tactics on both sides were exhausted. Nasser offered Hilu a four-month period to prepare a plan to protect the water diversion project and to clear this issue constitutionally in Lebanon. Moreover, Nasser accepted Hilu's suggestion that the leader of the AUC must seek Lebanese approval before ordering the initiation of the diversion works, regardless of the AUC leader's objection. Thus, the decision of the summit required the immediate start of the diversion plan, while documenting Lebanese reservations in the minutes.[54] Nasser, in fact, succeeded in obtaining Lebanese public approval for the decisions taken at the summit. The Egyptian president thereby secured a consensus among Arab leaders over the outcome of the summit, although Lebanese arguments were shelved.

Different tactics

Once the Lebanese and Egyptian governments had made their positions clear to one another at the Alexandria summit, both countries pursued different tactics to further their interests. The Egyptian government, for instance, adopted both diplomatic and confrontational methods to bend Lebanese objections, ranging from economic concessions to sustained media attacks. Lebanon unintentionally satisfied Cairo's thirst for propaganda by the high profile character of President Hilu and other Lebanese officials who shuttled to and from Cairo – though without making any substantial concessions.

The Egyptian government continued to repeat its offer to send Egyptian troops to Lebanon, despite the initial Lebanese refusal at the Alexandria summit. Muhammad H. Haikal, for instance, wrote in *al-Ahram* on 25 September 1964, that Egypt possessed the best equipped and most effective deterrent against Israel among frontline Arab states. Therefore it was unwise for Arab states, especially Lebanon, to reject the Egyptian offer to send troops under the AUC auspices.[55] Furthermore, Nasser promised Hilu, while attending the non-aligned summit in Cairo on 8 October 1964, to review the Egyptian position over mutual economic issues. This went as far as declaring the intention to purchase Lebanese apples worth E£500,000 and to execute compensation settlements for Lebanese citizens whose property was sequestrated in Egypt in 1961.[56]

The Lebanese government resisted these overtures and affirmed its views on two counts. First, it favoured installing the planned water piping station to divert one of the Jordan River sources (al-Wazzani) in Syria, instead of Lebanon where the river originated. The obvious reason behind this was to avoid inviting Arab troops to protect this project from Israel, whose border with Lebanon was only 2 km away. Secondly, the Lebanese government suggested delaying the establishment of the Kawkaba tunnel inside Lebanese territory until other stages of the Arab project went well ahead.[57]

This attitude led to an Egyptian media campaign against the Lebanese government, which intensified on the eve of the Conference of Arab Prime Ministers held in Cairo on 9 January 1965. The Lebanese government reacted immediately by launching a 'clarification campaign', which aimed to prove that Lebanon had fulfilled its financial, technical, administrative and military commitments towards various Arab causes. The Lebanese government published statistics detailing its contributions to Arab causes: E£224,985 paid to Egypt's central bank for the Arab Diversion Project of the Jordan River; E£167,520 paid towards Arab military effort; E£17,999 paid towards the establishment of the Arab Unified Command; E£8,999 paid to meet the expenses of the AUC. Moreover, Lebanon's contributions towards meeting the expenses of the PLO and the Palestine Liberation Army were already presented in a bill to be approved by the Lebanese parliament.[58]

The Lebanese delegation sought throughout the conference to counter Egyptian pressure by arguing that all Arab fronts should be activated in case Israel decided to attack Lebanon. This argument was supported by Jordan and Saudi Arabia, and aimed at exposing Egyptian intentions. The implication was that while the Egyptian government pushed other Arab states to a possible confrontation with Israel, Egypt itself was hiding behind UN forces in Gaza and the Strait of Aqaba.[59]

Eventually, the Lebanese delegation succeeded in bringing the Cairo conference to accept Lebanese terms relating to the diversion plan in Lebanese territory. Therefore while the Lebanese government undertook to install the proposed water piping station on the Wazzni source, it held the sole responsibility for operating and protecting it. In addition, the AUC had no right to interfere in this matter unless asked by the Lebanese military command and after resolutions taken by the Lebanese government and parliament.[60] Furthermore, the Lebanese parliament adopted unanimously the government line by issuing a decree on 21 January 1965, which stated that:

> The Lebanese parliament ... has unanimously decided to support the attitude of the Lebanese delegation at the above mentioned Conference as regards the project to exploit the tributaries of the Jordan River. It has also decided to empower the Council of Ministers, after due consultation with the Lebanese Army General Staff, to allow Arab troops to enter Lebanon in case of an attack which threatens national security or in case of emergency military situations which demand rapid measures.[61]

Thus, Lebanese national interests were protected by this position which served, according to Hilu, to defend Lebanon 'from [Egyptian or Arab] demagogy and Israeli aggression'.[62] The Egyptian government reacted on 16 January 1965 by freezing its earlier economic concessions, made during the Alexandria summit in early September 1964, and also by cancelling its offer regarding Lebanese exports to Egypt – apples in particular.[63]

Hilu's compromise

Nevertheless, the Lebanese government could not afford to alienate Egypt completely, since the latter possessed enough Arab credentials to protect Lebanon from more radical states, namely Syria and Iraq. To this end, President Hilu accepted an offer to pay an official visit to Cairo on 1 May 1965 amid Egyptian–Tunisian polemics. These were caused by President Burguiba's initiative, announced on 15 March 1965, calling on the Arab states to be realistic and make peace with Israel. Hilu chose Cairo as the first capital to visit, followed directly by official visits to Paris and the Vatican on 5 and 10 May 1965 respectively. This was a clear move to symbolize Lebanon's 'balanced' attachment to both the Arab world represented by Egypt, and the West. Hilu says that his visit to Cairo was timed to begin on 2 May, but Nasser wished the visit to begin on 1 May 1965. While Hilu refrains from giving the exact reason for this change, al-Hayat suggests that Nasser wanted to exploit Hilu's presence during Nasser's 1 May speech, which was expected to focus on attacking the Tunisian president – especially after the UAR withdrew its ambassador from Tunisia. In other words, Hilu would feel obliged to denounce Burguiba, an act he surely wanted to avoid, as a gesture of solidarity with Nasser.[64]

According to Hilu, he was given a 'popular' reception on 1 May 1965, in which he addressed the 'Egyptian masses' on the occasion of Labour Day. In return, his name and his state's name were chanted repeatedly.[65] Nasser, in turn, declared the UAR's unconditional solidarity with Lebanon and offered assistance against any possible attack. Nasser said:

> We know very well that Lebanon constitutes one target, which is prone to be subjected to [Israeli] aggression. Therefore, O Your Excellency [Hilu], I want you to know that the UAR is predisposed to prevent such aggression from achieving any of its objectives whether in Lebanon or in any other Arab country. I want to confirm this to you from the first day of your visit here, and before we start our talks.[66]

During the same visit, President Hilu reiterated Lebanon's position on the Arab project to divert the Jordan waters as being 'a development project rather than a war plan'. Moreover, Hilu argued that diversion work in Lebanon had to wait until the completion of the al-Nabattya Dam. Then, the Lebanese government might be able to argue that the diversion project was a purely agrarian plan and was vital for Lebanon's economy. This denial of political ill will was geared to foil any clash with Israel. Nasser, in return, assured Hilu that 'any aggression on Lebanon would be considered as an aggression against Egypt'. Hilu interpreted this remark as a symbolic gesture, but he was more interested in employing Nasser's influence to restrain Arab radicals from dragging Lebanon into war with Israel. It was also hoped that this rendered the need for military assistance from Egypt unnecessary.[67]

Consequently the joint communiqué was termed by Hilu as 'classical', in that it mentioned all the common-ground points, such as Palestine, and avoided those which were contentious such as the Arab diversion project and economic relations. The mooted invitation for Nasser to visit Lebanon was omitted from the communiqué, under a request from Hilu who, in private, opposed such a visit in order to avoid protests from right-wing Christian leaders.[68]

Later, the Arab summit convened in Casablanca on 13 September 1965 indicated a decrease in Egyptian pressure on

Lebanon. The inter-Arab conflict took a new turn with differences emerging over the water diversion plan, Palestine and the Yemen. The Lebanese government reiterated its opposition to the entry of any Arab force into Lebanon, unless authorized by the Lebanese government and parliament, to the illegal entry of Palestinians into Lebanon, and to the introduction of conscription to its army. It was agreed that every country had the freedom to implement the diversion plan according to 'its list of priorities'.[69]

According to President Hilu, Nasser helped him, in his capacity as the chairman of the session, to allocate special time to discuss the military situation on the Lebanese front, thus not lumping it with the Syrian front. This enabled Hilu to win the argument with the AUC commander, and also to ward off any Syrian attempt to interfere in Lebanese affairs under the guise of 'helping to defend Lebanon against Israel'.[70] Eventually, by 1965, Israel had succeeded in inaugurating its diversion plan, while attacking Syrian mechanical equipment working on the Arab diversion. This brought complete cessation of the work in July 1966 despite Syrian protests of being left alone by Egypt. Lebanon took the hint that Egypt was not going to war 'for the sake of few bulldozers' and confined its work to its modest plan.[71] Lebanese–Egyptian relations had survived a serious test due to the fact that Nasser and Hilu were, in fact, not willing to go along with the radicals' agenda.

The Islamic Pact challenge

King Faisal of Saudi Arabia initiated a movement to challenge the regional leadership of Nasser and his brand of Arab nationalism, in December 1965. To this end, Saudi Arabia concluded a comprehensive understanding with Iran on 8 December 1965 to establish an Islamic Pact. The Lebanese government immediately declared a position of neutrality in this new phase of regional confrontation. Prime minister-designate, 'Abdallah al-Yafi, stated on 6 April 1966 that because of the religious nature of its population, Lebanon could not join 'any Islamic or Christian pact'.[72] This professed neutrality was interpreted by the Islamic Pact states to be Lebanon's reluctance, once more, to adopt publicly a challenging stance to Egyptian policies.

The Lebanese government's tactical action in Egypt's favour was the expulsion of the Iranian ambassador to Beirut, Ali

Fattuhi, on 19 January 1966 for attacking President Nasser during a press conference. In return, the Iranian government asked Lebanon to recall its ambassador but stopped short of severing diplomatic relations. This was a clear indication to the members of the Islamic Pact that the Lebanese government would not, or could not, tolerate any anti-Egyptian activities.[73]

On 15 June 1966, Nasser declared his departure from the policies of Arab collective action and Arab summits, while Saudi Arabia adopted the opposite line. The Lebanese government at first paid lip service to Arab summits and attempted to mediate between Egypt and Saudi Arabia. However, it toed the Egyptian line when Beirut supported a proposal to postpone the fourth Arab summit in Algiers scheduled for 5 September 1966. This happened in spite of Saudi Arabia's objection and its subsequent decision to freeze its commitments towards the Arab summit institutions. In return, the Egyptian government supported a conciliatory Lebanese suggestion, made to the Arab League, to hold the ordinary session of the Arab League Council and the Arab Joint Defence Council on 10 September 1966.[74]

The Lebanese delegation to the session supported pro-Egyptian resolutions on Arab affairs, despite a Saudi attempt on 8 September 1966 to request that Lebanon should resort to neutrality in inter-Arab disputes. The foreign minister, 'Umar al-Saqqaf, visited Beirut on the eve of the session to protest at Lebanon's departure from its traditional policies and its treating Saudi requests with 'ignorance or inaction.[75] Moreover, the Tunisian government expressed complaints concerning the Lebanese delegation's voting in support of an Egyptian resolution condemning President Burguiba's initiative on Palestine. It argued that it would have been better if the Lebanese government expressed reservations 'like the Saudis'.[76]

The Intra Bank crisis, which emerged on 15 October 1966, shook the Lebanese economy and was interpreted as a measure marking Saudi disapproval of Lebanon's pro-Egyptian stance under the government of 'Abdallah al-Yafi. Moreover, the withdrawal of deposits by Saudi Arabian investors from Lebanon's biggest private bank was considered as an economic weapon, intended to bring about a change of policy, or at least to soften Lebanon's position concerning the Islamic Pact project and to tame the pro-Nasser press in Beirut.[77]

However, the Lebanese government did not find it politically prudent to change its policies, despite the fact that Egypt was unable to offer any substantial economic assistance. The Egyptian government dispatched an economic delegation to meet the Lebanese president, Charles Hilu. Only a token level of help was offered to assist the Bank Misr-Lubnan (the Egypt–Lebanon Bank) with 'large amounts of hard currency', but this did not extend to other banks.[78] The new Lebanese prime minister, Rashid Karami, who was appointed to solve the economic crisis, took a vigorous line against the Islamic Pact. He launched a bitter attack on the pact when he stated on 14 January 1967, that 'no Lebanese citizen could believe that such suspicious pacts are the only means of restoring Palestine'.[79] This clear attack on Saudi Arabia, coupled with a reluctance to recognize or act upon any anti-Saudi activities on Lebanese territory – which were sponsored by Egypt – caused a state of open crisis in Lebanese–Saudi relations. The Saudi government protested, in particular, at the press conference held by the pro-Egyptian Yemeni ambassador to Beirut, Adul Rahman al-Baydhani, on 11 January 1966, in which he accused that government of 'serving the designs of colonialism'.[80]

Consequently, on 1 March 1967 the Saudi Minister for Foreign Affairs, 'Umar al-Saqqaf, requested Lebanon to make a clear choice between alignment with either Saudi Arabia or Egypt. He drew the Lebanese government's attention to the benefits of 'good relations' with Saudi Arabia. Al-Saqqaf claimed that Saudi Arabia had sent huge numbers of tourists to Lebanon with relatively large amounts of disposable income. In addition, Saudi Arabia provided Lebanon with substantial amounts of investment capital. Also, Saudi Arabia's oil pipelines traversed Lebanon, thus generating revenues to the Lebanese state. Al-Saqqaf pointed out that Egypt had prevented its tourists from visiting Lebanon and had sequestrated Lebanese property.[81]

The Saudi–Egyptian conflict over Lebanese foreign policy intensified, which gave rise, among other things, to Muslim–Christian tension inside Lebanon. While some leaders of the Muslim community supported Egypt without question, Christian right-wing leaders stepped up their pressure on the government to cease its pro-Egyptian policies and ally itself with Saudi Arabia – for advantageous economic reasons. In addition to Saudi official representations, Lebanese ex-patriots in Saudi Arabia were made to present petitions to President Hilu, requesting him to rectify Lebanese foreign policy.[82]

Egyptian influence after secession

Syria's secession from the UAR conveyed two different messages to Lebanese groups. The Christian right-wing leaders of Lebanon were relieved to see a reduction of Egyptian influence in the Arab world, removing the perceived threat of annexation of Lebanon by the UAR. The Muslim and Arab nationalist groups, on the other hand, continued to perceive Nasser as the champion of Arab nationalism. The UAR persisted in making approaches to both groups during this period in order to maintain and strengthen the support of the Muslim groups and to neutralize Christian groups.

Muslim and Arab nationalist groups

The informal political pacts which Nasser had maintained with Muslim and Arab nationalist groups since 1958 were backed by a complex intelligence network to ensure total support for Egyptian policies – notwithstanding the internal differences and competition among these groups.[83] The Egyptian Embassy and its long-serving ambassador, General Ghalib, played an important role in co-ordinating this support. As discussed in Chapters 3 and 4, General Ghalib worked with the Muslim political leaders, the *zu'ama*, who patronized the local bosses, the *qabadays*, to ensure the support of the masses through the patron–client network. The continuing allegiance of the Arab nationalist groups and intellectuals ensured the overwhelming support of the Muslim and Arab nationalist 'street' which became known as the 'Nasserist forces'. This support proved valuable to Nasser in the challenges during the period.

Syria's secession from the UAR did not affect Nasser's constituency in Lebanon. On the contrary, 'popular' support was expressed through huge demonstrations in Beirut, Sidon and Tripoli. Also, delegations flocked to the Egyptian Embassy to express support for Nasser's leadership of the Arab nationalist movement and for the UAR. Political leaders condemned the Syrian move as a blow to Arab nationalism and pledged their support for Nasser to wipe out the effects of this separatist movement. Kamal Jumblatt, leader of the Progressive Socialist Party, founded an umbrella organization consisting of parties and individuals collectively called the 'Progressive Arab Front' to challenge the Syrian move and support Nasser. The front included the Progressive Socialist Party, the Arab Nationalist Movement, Ma'ruf Sa'ad MP, Issam al-Hajjar MP, Wafiq al-Tibi, Ahmad Suwayd, Faruq Barbir, Jamil Kibbi, Khalid Saghiah, Suhail Idris, As'ad al-Muqaddim and Georges Rajji.[84] The outspoken opposition to the new regime in Syria imposed a check on the Lebanese government, which was reluctant to recognize it, thereby souring the relations between the two countries. A report from the British ambassador to Beirut, Moore Crossthwaite, states that 'a month and a half after the coup, the new Karame [sic] Government has still to make the first really friendly move towards Syria, and it is clear that the Moslem [sic] members of the government are reluctant to engage themselves personally'.[85]

The Muslim community's allegiance to Nasser proved strong, despite Syrian attempts to challenge it. Khalid al-'Azm, Syria's prime minister, tried in vain to convince Muslim political leaders not to side with Egypt against Syria. To this end, al-'Azm offered Lebanon improved economic relations, taking advantage of the negative impact of Egyptian socialist policies on Lebanese trade and Lebanese residents in Egypt. However, al-'Azm eventually admitted failure, due to 'the strong stature of Nasser in the hearts of the Muslim community in Lebanon'.[86] Another British document states that on 18 October 1961, a delegation of Lebanese industrialists and merchants called on the Syrian prime minister and the minister of finance and had talks with industrialists in Syria. This delegation proved to be largely Christian, since nine out of the twelve Muslims who had agreed to go made 'some excuse at the last moment.'[87] The support for Nasser from the Lebanese Muslim community and Arab nationalist groups was expressed in all inter-Arab political conflicts in which Nasser's regime was involved. For example, all pro-Nasser political groups supported, whether by demonstrations or public statements, the Iraqi coup of 8 February 1963, which toppled Nasser's bitter enemy, General Qassim.[88]

In the spring of 1965, the pro-Egyptian groups opposed the Lebanese government on two foreign policy issues: the Burguiba visit to Lebanon and the reluctance to withdraw the Lebanese ambassador from West Germany. These groups, led by Rashid Karami and Kamal Jumblatt, boycotted several receptions organized in honour of President Burguiba during his visit to Lebanon in early March 1965. This signalled clear displeasure at the Tunisian president's public statements, which called on the Arabs to compromise over Palestine. Karami and Jumblatt stated that their boycotts were carried out in concert with the Egyptian ambassador who attended only one reception.[89]

These groups deplored the Lebanese government's indecision regarding the severing of relations with West Germany, due to its recognition of Israel. They also called for the recognition of East Germany, thus emulating the UAR's move. The threat of a campaign in parliament and in 'the street' worked in favour of pro-Cairo groups. The Lebanese delegation to the Arab League did not express reservations on 14 March 1965 over the decision to withdraw Arab ambassadors from Bonn. As a result, the Lebanese ambassador was withdrawn from Bonn, and diplomatic relations were severed as soon as West Germany recognized Israel on 13 May 1965. While taking this step, the Lebanese government refused to follow suit totally by recognizing East Germany.[90]

Nasser invited the Sunni Muslim communal leader, Sa'ib Salam, to Cairo on 21 March 1965 to examine Salam's complaints concerning difficulties in his dealings with Lebanese pro-Nasser elements and Egypt's ambassador, General Ghalib. Salam's exclusion from office by Shihab since October 1961, and the appointment of his Nasserist rivals in Beirut such as 'Uthman al-Dana, forced him to shift to the right on the Lebanese political spectrum. This, coupled with his alignment with Saudi Arabia, Egypt's rival, signalled his cooling of relations with Cairo.[91] Salam tried to mend fences with Nasser by aiming to prove that he did not support the idea of the Islamic Pact. Instead, Salam offered to act as mediator between the Egyptian and Saudi governments through his special relationship with Saudi defence minister, Prince Sultan. Salam relayed to Nasser Saudi readiness to accept him as chairman of the committee which would call for an Islamic conference to discuss the idea of an Islamic Pact.[92] But his attempt failed to give any positive results.

The Egyptian regime co-operated with two newspaper publishers who were involved in politics despite being regarded as outside the ranks of the Lebanese political establishment. First,

'Adnan al-Hakim, the leader of the Najjadah Party and publisher of *Sawt al-'Uruba*, continued to enjoy Nasser's patronage. This was related to al-Hakim's continuous and vigorous demands for social and political equality for Lebanese Muslims and to his unquestioned support for Nasser in his public statements. In spite of these factors, or perhaps because of them, al-Hakim was not included in President Hilu's delegation on his visit to Cairo on 1 May 1965. However, al-Hakim was invited separately by the regime in Cairo to be present at Hilu's official reception, thus signalling to Hilu Nasser's support for al-Hakim. During his stay in Cairo, Hilu accepted an invitation to lay the foundation stone of a Lebanese youth hostel for which al-Hakim took the credit as the initiator of the scheme.[93]

Secondly, Muhsin Ibrahim, the head of the organization of Arab nationalists and editor-in-chief of *al-Hurriyah*, was granted special access to high official sources in Egypt in order to 'fight battles against imperialism'. The case of Egyptian journalist Mustafa Amin, who was arrested and charged for working for the CIA in July 1965, illustrates how Ibrahim was instructed to exploit this issue against the West. Muhammad H. Haikal stated that Nasser's secretary for information, Sami Sharaf, sent a telegram to the Egyptian ambassador to Beirut, General Ghalib, just after Amin's arrest. The telegram summed up the case against Amin and instructed Ghalib to inform Muhsin Ibrahim to publish the case widely on the same day. Then Ibrahim was invited to visit Cairo immediately to be presented with more details of the affair and thereby further embarrass the West and its so-called agents.[94]

The Islamic Pact project did not earn any support among Lebanese Muslim groups, since President Nasser opposed it from the outset. Kamal Jumblatt orchestrated a campaign to fight the pact in early February 1966, utilizing the support he commanded from the Lebanese left-wing groups.[95] The strength of this campaign was shown when the publisher of *al-Hayat*, Kamil Mruweh, was assassinated on 16 May 1966, for his support of Saudi policy regarding the Islamic Pact. The pro-Egyptian press in Beirut defended the assassination on the grounds that it was motivated politically, and therefore should not be tried by the courts as a 'mere criminal act'.[96] For instance, Salim al-Lawzi, publisher of *al-Hawadiss* magazine, attacked the prosecution lawyers and branded them as supporters of the Islamic Pact. Despite the fact that al-Lawzi was tried over the harshness of his verbal accusations, he continued to defend the 'noble intention of the crime' until the main accused, Ibrahim Qulailat, was acquitted in March 1968.[97]

By early 1967, the paramount Saudi–Egyptian conflict polarized even the 'moderate' groups in the Lebanese Muslim community who flocked to Cairo in order to express their support for Egypt's policies. Kamil al-As'ad, a former Speaker of the Parliament, stated during a visit to Cairo on 15 February 1967, that 'it falls to Arabs alone to solve the Palestine cause', which meant implicitly the rejection of the Islamic Pact in this respect.[98] 'Uthman al-Dana, an MP for Beirut, also attacked the Islamic Pact in a press conference held in Cairo on 14 March 1967, describing it as 'an attempt by the reactionary elements aimed at the restoration of imperialistic domination over the Arab countries'.[99] The Lebanese Mufti's support for Nasser proved by far Cairo's most effective weapon with which to challenge Saudi Arabia's version of political Islam. The Mufti, Sheikh Hassan Khalid, employed 'progressive' rhetoric in rejecting 'any pact or alliance based on enhancing the influence of imperialism and the enemies harbouring wicked intentions towards Islam and Arabism'.[100] Moreover, Sheikh Khalid hailed the UAR's efforts on behalf of Islam and refuted deviation charges propagated by Saudi Arabia against Egypt and its 'socialist' ideology. He declared on 6 March 1967 that:

> Egypt fosters fields of Islamic studies all over the world. Her exertions on behalf of the glory of Islam are our pride. ... As Muslims in Lebanon we feel close attachment to Egypt. We support Egypt in all her stands. We are Egypt's sons and soldiers, who are entrusted with realizing her mission.[101]

This clear Lebanese Muslim support for Nasser against King Faisal was expressed by Sunni politicians and, to a lesser extent, Shi'a leaders. Despite pressure brought upon Lebanese Shi'a leaders by the Shah of Iran, this group was not prepared to support publicly the proposed Islamic Pact. A consequence of the polarization was the disaffection of right-wing Christians, who felt that Lebanese Muslim allegiance to Cairo was reflected in Lebanese government policy, thus bringing Saudi economic pressure to rectify this position. Moreover, it was impossible for the Lebanese Christians to adopt King Faisal as a patron to counter Nasser in

Arab conflicts, especially over the move to form an Islamic Pact, as Faisal represented the 'strictest form of Islam'.[102]

Lebanese Christian leaders

Although the break-up of the UAR relieved Lebanese Christian leaders of the perceived threat to Lebanon's sovereignty, they refused to join openly in political alliances against Egypt. Khalid al-ʿAzm, Syria's veteran politician, stated in his memoirs that he contacted Pierre Jumayyil, the leader of the Phalange Party, immediately after the secession to co-ordinate efforts against President Nasser, especially as Lebanese Muslims refused to abandon Nasser's leadership. Al-ʿAzm offered a similar political alliance to the Maronite Patriarch playing on the Christian fear of Arab nationalism. This indicated his desperation to find political allies against Egypt. However, these efforts failed, according to al-ʿAzm, to produce any tangible results due to President Shihab's power of veto over Christian leaders in any challenge to Nasser which might destabilize Lebanon's fragile national unity. Moreover, al-ʿAzm suspected that Pierre Jumayyil was deceived by Nasser's promises of support as a candidate for the post of president.[103]

Lebanon's Christian leaders refused to join Nasser's bandwagon, but they maintained remoteness from any anti-Nasser alliances. Therefore when some Christian Maronite leaders objected to Egyptian-inspired campaigns against Saudi Arabia and Jordan in the Lebanese press in May 1961, they were accused of inflaming sectarianism. The pro-Egyptian journalist Salim al-Lawzi rebuked these leaders in his magazine, *al-Hawadiss*, on 11 May 1962, stating that:

> The fact that President Nasser commands immense influence over Lebanese Muslims should be appreciated, and benefited from, by all Maronite leaders who wish to see Lebanon strong and united, instead of leaving Lebanese Muslim representatives to exploit this factor for their own selfish motives. ... President Nasser is recognized as a pan-Arab leader in all corners of the Arab world, so why do we [the Lebanese] insist on portraying Nasser as a sectarian leader [of the Muslim community]. ... We call upon all sincere Lebanese who are keen ... to keep Lebanese national unity out of Cold War dangers, to use Nasser's influence over Lebanese Muslims in the service of the national unity of Lebanon.[104]

Although the UAR favoured the election of General Shihab for a second term as president, it declined to endorse anyone publicly once Shihab decided not to stand, for this carried the probability of antagonizing Christian Maronite leaders. Some tactics, such as hinting that a new Coptic Egyptian ambassador would be appointed after the elections, were used in order perhaps to pacify Christian hard-liners.[105] The Egyptian regime supported implicitly the election of Charles Hilu in agreement with Shihab and the Vatican, as he was perceived as not belonging to the Christian hard-line camp.[106]

However, the right-wing press in Lebanon took it upon itself to reply to Egyptian propaganda attacks. *Al-'Amal*, for instance, reprimanded Egypt for pressurizing Lebanese officials to offer concessions on the Jordan River project when it said in its editorial of 12 January 1965 that:

> We would have preferred that the attention of *al-Ahram* and *al-Akhbar* newspapers, as well as other organs of the institutionalized press, radio and television [in the UAR] was directed towards the promised Egyptian presidential campaign in March. This would have been better than to attack Lebanon, mistreat its prime minister and ignore the basic rules of protocol in receiving the Lebanese delegation. ... It would have been better if the media paid more attention to convincing the [Egyptian] people that the meat and bread are plentiful [in Egypt].[107]

Nevertheless, Nasser took the initiative on 28 March 1965, to reconcile relations with Christian right-wing leaders, by inviting the Maronite leader, Sulaiman Franjieh, to Cairo. Nasser listened to Franjieh's complaints regarding Egyptian and pro-Egyptian groups in Lebanon and their intimidation of Christian groups.[108] Also, the Egyptian government sent an emissary to the Maronite Patriarch on 16 April 1965 to smooth the way for mutual visits between Christian and Egyptian leaders, which was to start with a visit by the Speaker of Parliament, Anwar Sadat, and culminate in a visit by Nasser himself in 1966.[109]

However, this gesture was met with a refusal from Christian leaders such as Sham'un, Jumayyil and Eddy who opposed the principle of Nasser visiting Lebanon. The reply was expressed privately by President Charles Hilu to Nasser during his visit to Egypt on 1 May 1965.[110] In fact, these leaders perceived the Egyptian–Lebanese relationship as imbalanced and working to serve Egyptian interests only. On 6 May 1965, the right-wing newspaper *al-Safa'* attacked the communiqué emanating from the Nasser–Hilu summit because it neglected Lebanese interests. The newspaper argued that the Egyptian government failed, on the one hand, to address Lebanese requests relating to compensation for confiscated Lebanese property in Egypt since 1961. Also Cairo was not serious in either solving the problem which blocked Egyptian tourists from visiting Beirut, or facilitating the import of Lebanese apples. Moreover, Lebanese publications were not allowed freely into Egypt, while Lebanon's doors were wide open to the Egyptian press. The Lebanese government, on the other hand, supported Egypt unreservedly on foreign policy issues such as condemning imperialism and sympathizing with national liberation movements in Asia and Africa.[111]

Furthermore, the Christian leaders shunned an Egyptian invitation to challenge the Islamic Pact project to avoid antagonizing Saudi Arabia in particular. Pierre Jumayyil, for instance, repeated on 6 May 1966 his statements of neutrality on inter-Arab conflicts and refused to join Nasser's crusade, since 'we did not witness any Saudi interference in Lebanese affairs'.[112] At the same time, former president Camille Sham'un and the Maronite Patriarch, Butrus Ma'ushi, were busy establishing political links with King Faisal of Saudi Arabia, which ultimately they wanted to use against Nasserism in Lebanon. This was clearly an appropriate means of achieving the respective political aims of both parties. A delegation of three Christian members of parliament, Joseph Mughabghab, Sami al-Bustani and Salim Lahhud, visited Saudi Arabia on 14 May 1965 to deliver a letter from ex-President Sham'un, and an oral message from the Maronite Patriarch to King Faisal.[113]

In early 1967, as Egypt pulled the Lebanese government and the Lebanese Muslim community to its side, a parallel Christian campaign was orchestrated to protest against Lebanon's alignment with Egypt. Sham'un, Jumayyil and Eddy pressed Hilu, on 28 March 1967, to rectify Lebanon's foreign policy and to stop the Egyptian Embassy's interference in Lebanese internal and external affairs. Pierre Jumayyil cited two examples to indicate the bias of Lebanese foreign policy towards Egypt. First, while the Lebanese government expelled the Iranian ambassador in January 1966 for attacking Nasser personally, it refrained from adopting the same method with the Yemeni ambassador (pro-Egyptian) for attacking

Saudi Arabia. Secondly, the Lebanese government supported the PLO leader, Ahmad al-Shuqayri, against Jordan in the Arab League because this was dictated by Cairo.[114] President Nasser invited these leaders to visit Cairo in order to listen to their grievances, though their campaign had an element of internal political purpose. *The Economist*, commented on this issue on 15 April 1967:

> President Nasser has been careful to say the right things about Leba-non; and recently invited Maronite leaders to Cairo to hear personally his views of Egyptian–Lebanese relations. It is to be hoped that they will have the courage to go. Playing on the confessional nerve may be good electioneering, and nobody can forget that parliamentary elec-tions are due next year. But to put the interests of the Maronite community ahead of national unity is, in a sense, to abdicate the right to leadership.[115]

Thus, relations between the Egyptian government and Lebanese Christian leaders remained poor, despite Cairo's endeavours to build bridges and put to rest Lebanese Christian fears.

Little change in trade

Egyptian leverage over Lebanon's economy receded after Sep-tember 1961, when Syria seceded from the UAR, thus confining economic relations to those with Egypt only. The Lebanese economy grew steadily during the 1960s, due to the injection of unprecedented levels of foreign capital, mainly from the Gulf states; the significance of economic relations with Egypt thereby diminished. According to Mahmud Riad, this worked in Leba-non's favour, freeing it to pursue its own economic policies.[116] However, the Lebanese government was at pains to convince the Egyptian government to honour promises made in relation to three main economic spheres: Lebanese exports to Egypt, tourism to Lebanon from Egypt, and compensation for the property of Lebanese nationals expropriated by the regime in Cairo in July 1961.

The Egyptian position on trade with Lebanon, according to Mahmud Riad, was that it did not need any essential products from Lebanon for its domestic market. But when Lebanon faced an export crisis, especially in apples, Egypt tried to help by increasing its apple imports, despite Egypt's own economic difficulties.[117]

Therefore when the Iraqi government announced its abrupt decision to stop the importation of Lebanese apples on 8 October 1964, Nasser 'compensated' Lebanon by declaring Cairo's intention to import apples worth E£500,000.[118] However, the domestic economic difficulties of Egypt prevented this from happening. In addition, it could be argued that the emergence of differences between the two states concerning the River Jordan diversion project in January 1965 took its toll. The Lebanese government concluded annual agreements to secure the export of apples, the value of which increased from E£300,000 in 1962 to E£500,000 in 1965. However, the actual figures were far lower than those agreed between the two governments. Thus, while Egypt imported 3,244 tons of apples during the 1963/64 season (approximately 5 per cent of total apple exports), it ceased its imports completely during the 1964/65 season. Moreover, no concrete agreements were concluded after 1965; instead they were replaced by general and vague promises to purchase Lebanese imports when economic conditions in Egypt permitted.[119]

Egyptian tourism to Lebanon was regulated by mutual agreements ratified annually. Lebanon offered concessions in the form of a preferential exchange rate to Egyptian tourists. The number of tourists fluctuated around the figure of 10,000 in the mid-1960s. Egyptian tourists accounted for approximately 2 per cent of all tourists arriving in Lebanon. Despite this relatively small number, Egypt had accumulated a debt of L£10 million by 1965 as a result of its inability to cover the cost of tourism to Lebanon.[120]

The balance of trade continued to tilt in Egypt's favour during this period. Although Lebanese imports from Egypt matched Lebanese exports to Egypt in terms of percentage of trade (around 1 per cent), there was a huge difference in real value. Lebanese trade with Egypt was constantly in deficit from 1962: L£6.5 million in that year and L£10 million in 1966 (see Tables 5a and 5b).

Difficulties in compensation

The issue of compensation for confiscated property belonging to Lebanese nationals in Egypt after nationalization proved to be a thorny and persistent problem between the two governments. In mid-1962, lengthy negotiations resulted in the formation of a joint committee to conclude a settlement. However, a resolution failed to materialize because of sharp disagreement over the number of claimants to be included and the level of compensation to be awarded. Lebanese estimates put the number of claimants at 50 and the required level of compensation at E£14 million in total.[121] A new 'accord de principle' between the two governments was rejected in December 1963 by the Lebanese government because of unfavourable Egyptian terms. The new proposals reduced the compensation figure to E£8 million and distributed payments over a ten-year period.[122]

Eventually, the Lebanese government accepted the Egyptian terms and endorsed a compensation agreement on 24 December 1964, which the Lebanese ambassador to Cairo, Joseph Abu Khatir, had concluded on 18 November 1964. This compensation agreement comprised four main points. First, Egypt undertook to compensate 65 per cent of the real value of the property (E£7 million = L£49 million) and pay yearly a sum of no less than E£400,000 to the Lebanese government, which took responsibility for its distribution to its citizens. Secondly, the Lebanese government guaranteed to spend 50 per cent of this annual sum on sending Lebanese tourists to Egypt. Thirdly, the remaining portion was to be used to fund 20 per cent of Egyptian exports to Lebanon, with the exception of cotton, rice and petrol. Lastly, the Lebanese government pledged not to re-export the imported Egyptian products to a third country. This aimed at forcing Lebanon to import a more diverse range of products to the benefit of the Egyptian economy.[123] In addition, the stipulation that goods purchased from Egypt should not be re-exported from Lebanon was an attempt by the Egyptian government to prevent Lebanon from benefiting financially from Egyptian exports or to interfere with Egypt's established markets.

Rashid Karami's government was instrumental in seeing this agreement through parliament on 4 May 1965, in spite of strong objections from some Lebanese claimants and pro-Sham'un deputies inside the chamber. First, the Lebanese government accepted without question the valuations of the judicial authorities in Egypt, which resulted in reducing the claims to a mere E£7 million. Secondly, the agreement reduced the compensation payment from E£1 million to only E£400,000 per year. Thirdly, the claimants who were entitled to benefit were those who had held Lebanese citizenship between July 1961 and November 1964. Also, any claimant who held dual nationality (i.e. Egyptian and Lebanese) would lose his claim altogether.[124] Karami attempted to quell the furore inside the chamber. Excusing Egypt's approach, he stated that 'every Arab sister state possesses the right to nationalize property, and it is considered an internal affair and, therefore, this policy was not directed against Lebanon alone'.[125]

However, the Egyptian government delayed the implementation of the accord and offered what were, in essence, token concessions. For instance, in early 1967, the Egyptian government permitted Lebanese citizens, who revoked their Egyptian nationality, to leave Egypt with a maximum of E£5,000 per person.[126] The June war of 1967 further postponed the implementation of the agreement, leaving the Lebanese government to appease the claimants with assurances that the matter would be resolved at a later date. By August 1969, Egypt's payments totalled L£10 million, estimated at approximately 20 per cent of the total sum agreed.[127] Mahmud Riad explained the delay as stemming from the lack of hard currency in Egypt, rather than an 'intention not to pay'.[128] Hamdi al-Tahiri, an Egyptian diplomat who served in Beirut in the mid-1960s, concurs with this assertion and adds that Lebanon 'benefited immensely from smuggled Egyptian capital after 1961', which underlines perhaps the resentment felt by Cairo towards Lebanon's laissez-faire economic system.[129]

In short, despite the economic problems and the failure to implement numerous economic and financial agreements between the two states, successive Lebanese governments preferred not to press these issues to excess in public. Economic disputes and negotiations were, however, conducted behind closed doors to a large extent.

Conclusion

Egyptian–Lebanese relations were, in general, to the satisfaction of both parties. President Shihab adhered to the understanding reached with Nasser in their summit of March 1959, despite Syrian and Arab political and economic pressure to undermine the relationship. This ensured the support of the Lebanese government by pro-Egyptian groups, which underpinned internal political stability. President Charles Hilu followed the same policy guidelines, although tension emerged with Cairo concerning

Lebanon's role in Arab collective projects. Despite the fact that the economic relationship between the two states worked, by and large, in Egypt's favour, Lebanese governments chose to overlook this matter, which in turn won an Egyptian indifference to Lebanon's laissez-faire economic system.

CHAPTER 6

Lebanon and the Cairo Accord

Setback for the Soviet Union in 1967

The June war of 1967 was the product of a complex regional chain of events, coupled with the involvement of the USA and the Soviet Union, which has left many questions unanswered to this day. A clear result of the war was the victory of the pro-Western Israel and the defeat of the pro-Soviet Egypt and Syria in addition to Jordan. It meant that Soviet credibility to defend its regional allies or to intervene in order to change the course of events suffered a severe setback. It was argued that the Soviet leadership declined to offer military support to the Arabs on the grounds that the attack was carried out by Israel alone, and that the USA was not involved as claimed by some Arab leaders. Instead, the Soviet leaders preferred to press for a ceasefire, which came into effect only after Israel achieved its goals. This trend was not confined to the Middle East region only, but also impinged on other Cold War battle arenas such as the Far East where, from 1966, America bombed North Vietnam, another Soviet ally, with impunity.[1]

The UN Security Council Resolution 242 of 22 November 1967 formed the guidelines for a possible peace settlement in the Middle East. It was agreed upon by both superpowers. However, the resolution reflected the strategic advantages which America enjoyed in the Middle East, and its conditions for an acceptable peace settlement. The USA achieved the defeat of pro-Soviet Arab states without risking a military confrontation with the Soviet Union or becoming embroiled in a clash with a regional state as had happened in Vietnam. Moreover, America held the key to any potential political settlement to the Arab–Israeli dispute since it was able to extract concessions from its ally Israel. The conditions included the free navigation of international waters, a solution to the Palestinian refugee problem, the recognition of the right of all states, including Israel, to live in peace within secure and recognized boundaries, and the withdrawal of Israeli forces from Arab territories occupied during the war. The last point, concerning the Israeli withdrawal from 'the occupied territories' was intentionally left vague at US insistence.[2]

While UN envoy Gunnar Jarring was shuttling between Middle East capitals in 1968 in what amounted to a useless exercise to implement the 242 Resolution, superpower rivalry increased, thus transforming the region into a major Cold War battleground. The US government, under President Lyndon Johnson, applied negligible pressure on Israel to co-operate with the UN peace initiative and simultaneously continued arms shipments to Tel Aviv to strengthen its military capability. Similarly, the Soviet government embarked on a campaign of political, economic and military aid for its allies, Syria and Egypt, in an attempt to regain its shattered prestige in the Middle East. In turn, America launched a diplomatic offensive in the summer of 1970 which became known as the 'Rogers Plan', which was accepted by Egypt and Israel, and resulted in a ceasefire agreement.[3] This measure provided regional stability, as perceived by the USA, and enabled Washington to regain the initiative on the diplomatic front, thereby further marginalizing the Soviet Union.

And defeat for the Arabs

The military clash between Israel and Syria on 7 April 1967 started a series of dramatic events which culminated in the Israeli military strike on Egypt, Syria and Jordan on 5 June 1967, and the resultant Israeli occupation of the Sinai Peninsula, the Golan Heights, the West Bank and the Gaza Strip. Sir Anthony Nutting and Malcolm Kerr have argued that Nasser was reluctant to challenge Israel, but was forced to respond to the challenges of Israeli 'hawks' on the one hand, and Syrian and Jordanian Arab leadership rivalries on the other. This had the effect of making him the most popular Arab leader in modern history, but made war with Israel inevitable. Nasser's miscalculations were to dispatch his army to Sinai on 15 May 1967, to request the UN to withdraw its forces from the Egyptian–Israeli border, and his closure of the Gulf of Aqaba on 22 May 1967.[4] Ali al-Din Hillal agrees with this

view of affairs, but goes further to suggest that the US government exploited the crisis in order to weaken Arab 'revolutionary'
elements as a pretext to control the Arab political order.[5]

The Arab summit at Khartoum, held on 29 August 1967, was
aimed at dealing with the problem of Israel's supremacy in the
Middle East. It made a number of important resolutions. First, the
ending of the 'Arab Cold War', as it was termed by Malcolm Kerr,
was achieved between regimes of 'revolutionaries' and 'reaction-
aries', since both camps now joined forces to wipe out the after-
effects of the June war. As a result, Egypt agreed to withdraw its
forces from North Yemen in a move calculated to appease Saudi
Arabia. Secondly, the oil-rich Arab states of Saudi Arabia, Kuwait
and Libya undertook to support the economies of Egypt and
Jordan in order to compensate them for their war losses in
economic and military terms. Thirdly, while adopting the radical
principle towards Israel of 'no peace, no negotiation, and no
recognition', the summit endorsed the use of political and diplomatic means to regain Arab occupied territory.[6]

Consequently, Egypt and Jordan endorsed UN Resolution 242
of 22 November 1967, which established the first framework for a
settlement of the Arab–Israeli conflict. However, Syria, Algeria,
Iraq and the PLO rejected the UN resolution on the grounds that
it failed to address the Palestine issue. Kerr argues that Nasser and
King Hussein formed an axis in an attempt to regain their territories (not least because both states had lost economically strategic
areas of territory) through diplomatic means. Syria, on the other
hand, preferred not to take up the opportunity of a diplomatic
effort as it could afford to bide its time over the Golan Heights,
since they were of no significant economic value.[7] Thereafter, the
Palestinian resistance movement emerged as a new factor in the
Arab–Israeli conflict, benefiting from the vacuum created by the
Arab inability to 'liberate' Palestine. Guerrilla operations in 1968
and 1969, especially those staged from Jordanian and Lebanese
soil, earned heavy Israeli retaliation, which threatened the status
quo in these two states.

President Nasser began his 'war of attrition' along the Suez
Canal in March 1969, to break the deadlock in the UN peace-
making efforts. When the US Secretary of State, William Rogers,
launched his peace initiative in early summer 1970, Egypt and
Jordan accepted this initiative which antagonized the Palestinian
guerrilla movement and led to armed conflict with the Jordanian

army in the summer of 1970. Nasser played the role of mediator and tried in vain to halt the crisis. His death, on 28 September 1970, meant that he had been unable to achieve either peace or victory.[8]

Lebanon escapes the war

Lebanon was the only Arab country bordering Israel which was not involved in the June war of 1967. It thus escaped the devastation of its small armed forces and the occupation of its territory. The short-term effects of the June war were beneficial to Lebanon's stability. First, a weakened Lebanese economy, caused by the banking crisis of 1966, was able to recover after the June war. An increase in Arab investment in addition to booming trade helped Lebanon to retain its position as the gateway to the Arab hinterland. Secondly, the decline in Christian–Muslim rivalry, which had intensified prior to the June war, stemmed from the Arab states' defeat and resulted in the erosion of Arab nationalist pressure to co-ordinate military affairs with the Unified Arab Command (see Chapter 5). Therefore the Christian community was relieved of the possible nightmare of stationing Arab armies in southern Lebanon and the concern over upsetting the political balance in favour of the Muslim community. This signalled a slide towards the political centre, which gave the country 'the stability of indecision'. Thirdly, the detente between King Faisal and President Nasser at Khartoum was reflected in a toning down in the ideological war which their countries conducted through their respective agents in the Lebanese printed media.[9]

However, by the end of 1968, the long-term effects of the June war began to take their toll on Lebanon as it was gradually pulled into the Arab–Israeli conflict. On 12 May 1968, the first attack on Israeli settlements near the Lebanese border was carried out by Lebanon-based Palestinian guerrillas. This invited swift Israeli retaliation against suspected bases inside the Lebanese border villages, which, at times, embroiled the Lebanese army. The Israeli air raid on Beirut airport on 28 December 1968 resulted in the destruction of 13 Lebanese civilian aircraft and escalated the internal political crisis surrounding the role of Lebanon itself in the Arab–Israeli conflict.[10]

The Lebanese army's violent suppression of a pro-guerrilla student demonstration on 23 April 1969 caused many casualties in major Lebanese cities, and led to the resignation of Rashid Karami's government. Consequently, Lebanon was left without a government for six months, since no Sunni Muslim politician would agree to head a government while the Lebanese army was trying to suppress the Palestinian guerrillas. Hilu was forced to compromise in October 1969, when Syria was on the verge of interfering militarily to give support to Palestinian guerrillas.[11] The Egyptian government then brokered what became known as the 'Cairo Accord', which was ostensibly designed to organize Palestinian affairs in Lebanon, but in fact resulted in the relinquishing of Lebanese sovereignty over a section of territory to the guerrillas for the sake of re-establishing internal order.

Endorsement of Lebanese dithering

The Lebanese government had supported Egypt in its political confrontation with Israel and the West from the beginnings of the crisis in mid-May 1967. When Nasser dispatched his troops to Sinai on 17 May 1967, the Lebanese government announced precautionary defensive measures in concert with Egypt and other Arab states bordering Israel. Moreover, a planned visit by some warships from the US Sixth Fleet to Beirut was postponed in order to indicate support for the Arab cause and to avoid being seen as pro-Western just as regional tensions were intensifying.[12] The Lebanese prime minister, Rashid Karami, gave unequivocal support to the Egyptian government's decision to close the Gulf of Aqaba to Israeli shipping on 24 May 1967, declaring that:

> It is impossible for anyone to deny the UAR's right and sovereignty over the Gulf of Aqaba. ... Our support for President Nasser's stance stems from our belief in the justice of our [Arab] cause, and our readiness to defend it until the achievement of our noble goal. Therefore there is no way to hesitate when the challenge rises, and we will not give up our clear and unambiguous right and sovereignty.[13]

The Lebanese foreign minister, Georges Hakim, toed too the Egyptian line in rejecting on 27 May 1967 either a UN naval force or a joint US–UK task force to open the Tiran straits for international shipping, branding the proposal as a 'unilateral intervention'.[14] Later, Hakim offered to boost Egyptian diplomatic efforts by co-ordinating a concerted campaign to win over some West European and Latin American states to the Arab cause.[15]

The Israeli attack on Egypt on 5 June 1967, posed a deep dilemma for the Lebanese government, specifically as to whether or not to live up to its rhetoric and engage the Israeli army on the Lebanese front. The prime minister, Rashid Karami, expressed his support for Egypt by declaring in parliament on the first day of the war that:

> What we expected has taken place. Israel began the battle by attacking the UAR this morning. It is natural for all Arab fronts to move, since there is only one armistice line and the battle is supposed to be joint and decisive. ... Lebanon is united with the Arab states and is committed to fulfil its pledges. Lebanon should prove in these difficult days that it is capable of playing an effective role in the decisive battle.[16]

However, President Hilu and the commander of the Lebanese army, General Bustani, objected to any military activity against Israel, especially after it became clear that Tel Aviv had already won the war. In fact, the enormity of the Arab defeat made it unfeasible for Egypt or any other frontline state to question Lebanon for its absence from the war, since any Lebanese involvement would not have altered the outcome.[17]

In order to avoid alienating either the West or Egypt and other Arab states, Lebanon made cautious policy decisions in an attempt to balance these competing forces. The Lebanese government opted to follow Egypt into taking political action against the West for its alleged direct military support of Israel during the June war. The British and US ambassadors were asked to leave Beirut on 8 June 1967. However, the Lebanese government stopped short of severing Lebanon's diplomatic relations with these two states.[18] Furthermore, Hilu and Prime Minister Karami showed their solidarity with Nasser, following Egypt's defeat, by requesting that the Egyptian leader withdraw his resignation from the UAR presidency and return 'to assume the leadership of the Arab march'.[19]

The Lebanese government did not, in fact, take any unilateral diplomatic steps to disengage from the implications of the Arab–Israeli conflict, until Egypt itself adopted a pragmatic approach at the Khartoum summit on 31 August 1967. The Egyptian foreign minister, Mahmud Riad, said at a later stage that:

Although Egypt had severed relations with the US and maintained this policy, Nasser did not ask the other Arab states to take the same step, especially those countries which enjoyed a traditional friendship with the US, Nasser's aim was to keep an Arab door open for dialogue with the US.[20]

The Lebanese government acted immediately and returned its ambassadors to London and Washington in order to 'serve the Arab cause in the diplomatic and information fields'.[21] Moreover, a 'sympathetic' tone was maintained towards Egypt's terms concerning the UN-sponsored political settlement to the Arab–Israeli conflict.[22] In short, the Lebanese government maintained cordial relations with Egypt before and after the June war, thus enabling it to avoid being charged of lacking any 'Arab credentials' as had occurred in 1956 (see Chapter 2).

Mediating between Lebanon and PLO

The Israeli raid on Beirut Airport on 28 December 1968 pulled Lebanon into the quagmire of the Arab–Israeli conflict. The resulting internal political debate concerning the responsibility of the Lebanese army in defending the airport signalled the beginning of a crisis over Lebanon's role in the Arab strategy regarding Israel. The Egyptian government entered the fray immediately through its semi-official spokesman, Muhammad H. Haikal, who allocated the blame not to the Lebanese army as such, but to the orientation of Lebanese policy, which relied on the 'myth' of Western protection. Moreover, Haikal defended the Palestinian 'resistance' movement against Lebanese accusations of inciting the Israeli attack, by accusing the Lebanese regime of turning a blind eye on 'the activities of many hostile forces, which had used Lebanon unconditionally as a stage to attack the Arab nation'.[23]

The Egyptian media criticized the Lebanese regime's tendency to preserve Lebanon's special status by isolating itself from the Arab world, and for contemplating the suggestion of a neutral Lebanon sustained by permanent UN forces on its border with Israel. Egyptian criticisms came at a time when UN peace efforts had reached a position of deadlock, and when Egypt was frustrated with American efforts to force a regional peace settlement based on 'Israeli terms'.[24]

The problem over Lebanon's involvement in the Arab–Israeli dispute re-surfaced when clashes between the Lebanese army and

Palestinian guerrillas occurred on 23 April 1969, developing into wider civil disorder and a new internal political crisis. President Hilu called upon Nasser on 7 May to mediate between the Lebanese authorities and the Palestinian guerrillas. Nasser accepted and dispatched his special envoy, Dr Hassan Sabri al-Khuli, who started his efforts immediately.[25]

The reasons for the Lebanese government's preference for Egyptian mediation in this internal conflict were numerous. First, Nasser commanded great respect not only among the Palestinian guerrillas but also among the Lebanese Muslim community who, in the main, gave their support to the Palestinian guerrillas at this juncture. Thus, it was useful to invoke Nasser's role as the guarantor of Lebanese national unity, as had been established with President Shihab in 1959.[26] Secondly, the Egyptian government possessed outstanding Arab nationalist credentials which were necessary to balance the radical Iraqi and Syrian political currents in Lebanon. These two regimes were backing the guerrillas with funds and arms. Thus, the Egyptian role presented an 'Arab cover' to the Lebanese regime, which was eager to avoid the deadly charge of being associated with Israeli policies. Thirdly, the Lebanese government desired an 'Arab solution' through Egypt, in order to avoid a repeat of the 1958 crisis with possible Arab or foreign intervention.[27]

The Egyptian government, for its part, accepted the Lebanese request so as to enable a moderate and non-rival Arab regime to restore internal stability. This factor was important for Egyptian foreign policy, which was desperate for more frontline support to its peace strategy. The Lebanese government had, in fact, been the first Arab government to voice support for the Egyptian–Jordanian peace initiative presented by King Hussein on 10 April 1969.[28]

By sending its envoy to Beirut, the Egyptian government sought to suppress a Lebanese request for the holding of a summit of frontline Arab states, in order to co-ordinate a common policy towards the guerrillas. The real Egyptian motivation was to avoid playing into the hands of Syria and the guerrillas at a time when Egypt was busy pursuing a pragmatic approach to work out a settlement based on UN Resolution 242.[29]

The Egyptian envoy, Dr Hassan Sabri al-Khuli, sought, first, to stop Syrian support for the guerrillas. He then embarked on an effort to find a formula to end the crisis between the Lebanese government and the Palestinian guerrillas. Dr Khuli was initially sympathetic to the Lebanese government's views on restricting the freedom of movement of the guerrillas, in order to 'preserve south Lebanon from possible Israeli occupation'.[30] But the guerrillas' refusal to compromise put an end to his mission after only three days. Thus, he claimed that he would return to Cairo to relay the results to President Nasser. This signalled, in effect, an Egyptian reluctance to antagonize any party which may have led to a continuation of the crisis.[31]

The Lebanese president approached Nasser again by sending him a letter with the Egyptian ambassador to Beirut on 23 May 1969. Hilu requested Nasser's assistance in finding a solution to the guerrilla problem on Lebanese territory.[32] However, Nasser showed reluctance to grant political sanctuary to a Lebanese regime eager to crush the guerrillas. Therefore he prevented his ambassador from returning to Beirut. Cairo was reluctant to deliver a deal similar to that of 1959 between Nasser and Shihab, and this in effect prevented President Hilu from gaining the co-operation of Lebanese leaders loyal to Nasser.[33] Nevertheless, the Lebanese government still hoped for an Arab summit, with Egyptian help, to lift the issue out of the Lebanese political arena through the adoption of a common Arab policy. Nasser adopted two contradictory guidelines: first, 'we must not ask of any Arab country more than it can give'; secondly, 'we shall judge every Arab government by the way it deals with the guerrillas'.[34]

The Egyptian decision to escalate the war of attrition with Israel after 19 July 1969 was intended to create a political momentum which would ultimately bring an end to the stalemate in the Arab–Israeli conflict. Thus, the Egyptian government shifted its priorities and dropped its balance of the above two guidelines in favour of the second option. This effectively meant opposing any 'isolation' of the Lebanese front with Israel. Consequently, when the Egyptian foreign minister, Mahmud Riad, proposed a recommendation to grant freedom of action to Palestinian guerrillas at the Arab League foreign ministers' meeting at the end of August 1969, Lebanon was the only country to express reservations.[35] This signalled that the Lebanese government had lost the argument on the inter-Arab political scene, because of a change of tactics on the part of the Egyptian leadership. Therefore the Lebanese army's attempt to crush the guerrillas in October

1969 met with Egyptian and Arab opposition. This was expressed through diplomatic and political channels, as well as by Syrian military threats. On 22 October 1969 President Nasser appealed personally to President Hilu to stop the fighting, stating that:

> The reports emanating from Lebanon on military clashes between the Lebanese army and the Palestinian resistance forces cause us the strongest and deepest anxiety. We feel grieved that at a critical time of our nation's struggle, we find that Arab bullets are fired at the wrong target, whatever the justifications and reason given. ... We cannot imagine what the [Palestinian] resistance faces in Lebanon, while at the same time it suffers from the enemy's [Israel's] fire and violence.[36]

As a consequence of this, the Lebanese regime was put on the defensive and was isolated in the Arab world. It was perceived as encircling the Palestinian guerrillas in south Lebanon, adjacent to the Israeli border. On 23 October, Hilu replied to Nasser's letter to explain the situation and to stress his commitment to the Palestinian cause:

> I cannot help but express my regret for the absence of clarity of facts presented to the Arab public opinion regarding the events ... [and] I am fully ready to work with all my efforts to explain the reality of the events to the Arab sister states, whether collectively or individually. ... We declare that Lebanon still – as always – considers the Palestine issue its prime cause. And [Lebanon] believes that the sacred struggle of the Arabs imposes on every Arab state the duty to pool efforts, unite and contribute to a common plan to win the battle [against the enemy].[37]

The Cairo Accord

Ultimately, the Lebanese government had no alternative but to accept Egyptian mediation terms, which consisted of two complementary elements. First, the Egyptian envoy, Dr Khuli, sought to tone down Syrian military and political measures against Lebanon. Secondly, on 28 October 1969, Cairo hosted negotiations between Palestinian guerrilla leaders and a Lebanese government delegation, with a view to working out a compromise. After securing concessions from the Lebanese delegation, the Egyptian government invited the Palestinian guerrilla leaders to work out the details of the co-ordination process on 24 October

1969.[38] What resulted from these efforts became known as the 'Cairo Accord', which represented a form of co-existence between the Lebanese government and the Palestinian guerrillas. In fact it granted the guerrillas freedom to operate from Lebanese territory in the area bordering Israel under some token restrictions.[39]

Despite much hesitation over the issue of sovereignty, the Lebanese government endorsed the accord, whose exact details were kept secret for some time, in order to extract some benefits internally and externally. First, the Cairo Accord offered a new lease of life to the Lebanese regime, averting a possible civil war between Christians and Muslims similar to that of 1958. It also cleared the way for the prime minister-designate, Rashid Karami, to form a new government with Egyptian blessing. Thus, Egypt appeared to constitute the 'guarantor' of Lebanese national unity at times of crisis. Lebanon's signing of the Cairo Accord, therefore, had a similar impact, in effect, as the Nasser–Shihab summit of 'understanding' of 26 March 1959.[40] Secondly, the Lebanese government reluctantly entered the realm of Arab–Israeli conflict, under Egyptian auspices. This was deemed politically more prudent than entering into an arrangement with Syria. The Lebanese regime hoped to gain financial assistance from the Arab League with Egyptian backing, without being openly counted as a member of the frontline states or the proposed eastern front (Syria, Iraq and Jordan).[41] Thirdly, Egypt undertook to bring the guerrillas into line with the accord, in so doing allowing the Lebanese government a breathing space until such time as more favourable political circumstances prevailed regionally. Thus, Lebanese officials kept visiting Cairo to 'clarify' the accord and its appendices, and to ask President Nasser to press the guerrillas for its implementation.[42]

Consequently, the Lebanese government supported Nasser's acceptance of the Rogers initiative on 25 July 1970 in the hope that it would bring about a settlement to the question of Israeli occupation of Arab territories. But the real aim was to welcome any attempt to settle the problems with Palestinians inside Lebanon. Prime Minister Rashid Karami stated in Cairo on 3 August 1970 that:

> President Nasser's leadership of the Arab March is a basic insurance to achieve the desired goals of the Arabs. President Nasser's 'yes' to the American initiative is an expression of bravery. Cairo's stance was a surprise for the enemies, and [I suppose] what happened in some

Arab capitals as a reaction to it was mere spontaneity which comes out in difficult times from those who follow these emotions and passion, but they will return to the right path.[43]

Lebanon's position ran counter to and clashed with that of Iraqi, Syrian, and hard-line Palestinian groups, who accused the government of distancing itself from the Arab–Israeli conflict in conjunction with Egyptian policy.[44] However, both the routing of Palestinian guerrillas by the Jordanian army in September 1970 and Nasser's sudden death on 28 September 1970 shifted the focus of inter-Arab rivalry from the Lebanese arena. Under the new regimes of Anwar Sadat and Sulaiman Franjieh, the terms which underpinned relations between the Lebanese and Egyptian governments were transformed.

Muslim groups stay loyal

The Egyptian defeat in the June war affected its relations with the various Lebanese groups. Despite its resignation from the 'Arab Cold War' and its total absorption in the Arab–Israeli conflict, Egypt retained a strong presence in the Lebanese domestic political arena, at least until the death of Nasser on 28 September 1970.

President Nasser enjoyed the support of a majority of the 'Muslim street' and its leadership, as well as of most Arab nationalist groups before and after his defeat in the June war. Former premier Sa'ib Salam, for instance, visited Cairo on 1 June 1967 to 'support and bless the steps taken by the UAR for the sake of Palestine and Arab dignity'.[45] Lebanese cities, with an overwhelmingly Muslim population, declared a general strike on 10 June 1967, and thousands of demonstrators marched in the streets requesting that Nasser revoke his decision to resign as president of the UAR. Moreover, political and religious leaders flocked to the UAR Embassy in Beirut to declare their allegiance to President Nasser and request his return to 'the leadership of the Arabs'. Kamal Jumblatt, the leader of the Progressive Socialist Party, stated emotionally that:

> Abd al-Nasser has taught us to be always above the events and defeats, and taught us, also, to convert the defeat into victory since these are qualities of leaders and true men. We will march with Nasser until the end, and we will always achieve victory with God's will.[46]

In parliament, Muslim deputies took the initiative in convening a special session to echo the cries of the 'street' in favour of Nasser's return to the presidency. A statement was issued just after Nasser's return to the UAR's presidency stating that:

> While the Lebanese parliament was convening to discuss issuing an appeal to President Nasser to revoke his resignation, the parliament took notice of Nasser's positive answer to Arab wishes [i.e. Nasser's withdrawal of his resignation]. ... He [Nasser] will continue at the helm of the leadership [of the Arabs] enjoying their confidence. It [the parliament] declares its satisfaction for this new step, which President Nasser took in the path of bitter struggle against aggression and conspiracy.[47]

The Lebanese internal crisis, which resulted from clashes between the Lebanese army and the Palestinian guerrillas on 23 April 1969, presented the Egyptian government with a difficult dilemma. Despite being invited by the Lebanese government to mediate, the Egyptian government needed to give primacy to protecting its Muslim constituency, and it did so by adopting two lines. First, it refused to back the Lebanese government's move to crack down on the guerrillas, for this was certain to harm Egypt's popular support in the 'Muslim street'. This was due to the newly formed alliance between Lebanese Muslim groups and Palestinian guerrillas.[48] Secondly, the Egyptian government kept a close watch on contenders for the post of prime minister. Hilu was desperate to select a prime minister who would co-operate with the president's office, while Egyptian policy was intended to prevent the emergence of a unified Lebanese administration capable of using the military option against the Palestinian guerrillas or inviting foreign troops on to Lebanese soil. It was reported that the Egyptian envoy refused President Hilu's request to force the prime minister-designate, Rashid Karami, to co-operate in forming a new government in order to end the political stalemate. However, Karami was unwilling to accept unless he received an Egyptian guarantee of support for any government he formed in order to strengthen his arm against Hilu and protect him from the 'Muslim street'.[49] As a result, Muslim political leaders followed Egyptian proposals to solve the crisis, because the alternative would have carried the potential of political suicide.[50]

The Cairo Accord enhanced the Egyptian position with both the 'Muslim street' and its leadership. First, it provided the traditional leadership, zu'ama, with a formula to rejoin the Leba-

nese regime, which had effectively been left in the hands of the
Christian president for more than six months. Thus, Cairo had
showed the Muslim political leadership that it would protect their
interests in Lebanon. As a result, Rashid Karami re-embarked on
the task of forming a government 'to implement the Cairo
Accord'.[51] The Egyptian ambassador to Beirut, General Ghalib,
helped Karami in his mission when the latter was blocked by the
pro-Cairo Kamal Jumblatt's conditions over his inclusion in the
new government.[52] Secondly, the accord boosted Cairo's pan-Arab
credentials with the Lebanese 'Muslim street', for it was seen as
protecting Palestinian guerrillas against the Lebanese regime. In
addition, it committed Lebanon to playing its own part in the
Arab–Israeli confrontation by co-ordinating efforts with other
Arab states towards serving the Palestinian cause in particular. In
other words, the accord not only strengthened Lebanese Muslims'
allegiance to Nasser, but also enhanced their long-term political
interests in Lebanon. This was done through the Muslim community's alliance with the Palestinians as opposed to the right-wing
element within the Christian community.[53]

As a consequence, the Muslim community and its leadership
refused to join the Arab rejection front and extremist Palestinian
guerrillas, in their denunciation of Nasser's acceptance of the
Rogers Plan in July 1970. In fact, the 'street' supported Nasser
over inter-Arab issues by displaying pro-Nasser placards and
staging demonstrations in Beirut and Tripoli.[54] The purpose was
to counter anti-Nasser demonstrations staged by pro-Iraqi and
pro-Syrian groups, who denounced Nasser's acceptance of the
Rogers Plan, depicting it as his retirement from the 'Arab struggle
against Israel'. The loyalty to Nasser and his political line continued until his death and beyond.[55]

Christian leaders co-opted

Although Christian leaders were concerned with the crisis between Egypt and Israel, only ex-President Sham'un, paradoxically,
aired his support for the Egyptian case over the Gulf of Aqaba –
notwithstanding his estrangement from President Nasser since
1958.[56] The Arab defeat in the June war created a sense of relief
among right-wing Christians in Lebanon, as this weakened the
Arab nationalist tide which, it was feared, might engulf Lebanon

in an Arab unity project. Consequently, the *al-Hilf* bloc, which included the three prominent Maronite leaders Pierre Jumayyil, Raymond Eddy and Camille Sham'un, increased its pressure on the Lebanese government to distance itself from the growing anti-Western trend in Arab politics.[57]

The political ascendancy of *al-Hilf*, expressed in the elections of March 1968, alerted the Egyptian government, which feared possible repercussions for Lebanese foreign policy.[58] In the aftermath of Israel's attack on Beirut Airport on 28 December 1968, *al-Hilf* came under fire from Egypt for propagating the idea of a neutral Lebanon protected by a UN force.[59] However, Egyptian dissatisfaction proved short-lived. Fearing a rise in hostility from Christian leaders, Nasser opted to refrain from meddling in Lebanese internal affairs. Moreover, decorations were sent to two members of *al-Hilf* as goodwill gestures, and Pierre Eddy, a brother of Raymond Eddy, was invited to Cairo to smooth differences on 15 February 1969.[60]

Thereafter, Egyptian tactics sought to gain favour with Christian political figures by giving implicit promises of political support to candidates running for the presidential elections of August 1970. Despite the Egyptian preference for *al-Nahj* (a cluster of political groups who supported ex-President Shihab's leadership), contacts were maintained with *al-Hilf* as a way to check the former, which was in power, especially regarding its tough policy towards the Palestinian guerrillas.[61] Thus, Egyptian mediation efforts in the April 1969 crisis were appreciated openly by both groups. This was proven when a statement issued by *al-Hilf*, complaining of 'Egyptian intervention in Lebanese affairs', was withdrawn from publication just one hour after its release.[62] Furthermore, ex-President Sham'un declared his support openly for President Nasser's call for an Arab summit to co-ordinate efforts against Israel, in order 'not to leave the UAR in the battle alone'. This stance was a clear political manoeuvre intended to mend fences with Nasser at a time when President Hilu was adopting an uncompromising position against the guerrillas.[63]

Many Lebanese Christian groups perceived the Cairo Accord as favourable to the Palestinians and harmful to Lebanese sovereignty. While Raymond Eddy opposed the new accord publicly, ex-President Sham'un kept his options open. However, the leader of the Phalange, Pierre Jumayyil, Sulaiman Franjieh and others joined the new Lebanese government to implement the accord for two tactical reasons. First, Nasser stood as the best guarantor of Lebanese stability in the short-term, at least, in the face of more radical states such as Syria and Iraq. Secondly, each Christian leader sought to prove his 'Arab credentials' as a necessary move to gain Nasser's support. This, it was hoped, would enable any Christian Maronite candidate to win the votes of Muslim deputies in the approaching presidential elections.[64]

The removal of the Lebanese army chief, General Emile Bustani, from office was perceived mainly as a measure by President Hilu to appease a dissatisfied Christian political elite who felt betrayed by him and Bustani. General Bustani had, in fact, signed the Cairo Accord, and was said to have gained President Nasser's confidence and backing as a contender for the Lebanese presidency.[65]

As the Lebanese presidential elections neared, Nasser's preference was said to be for the return of former president Shihab who continued to enjoy Cairo's blessing. He possessed the will to provide internal stability and was considered compliant with Egyptian foreign policy guidelines. But when Shihab announced his decision not to run as a candidate, pro-Egyptian Lebanese groups were split. While some supported Elias Sarkis of the *al-Nahj* bloc, others turned to Sulaiman Franjieh. While Franjieh was not openly hostile towards Egyptian policy, he had shifted towards the right of the political spectrum.[66] The Sulaiman Franjieh presidency, beginning on 23 September 1970, coincided with President Nasser's death. Both events signalled a new phase in the foreign policies of both states.

Change in Egyptian media policy

A positive aspect of Egypt's defeat in the June war, according to Adeed Dawisha, was the stimulation of domestic public debate and analysis concerning the causes of the 'disaster' through the critical evaluation of basic Arab values and attitudes. Muhammad Haikel, in *al-Ahram* of 20 June 1967, started this concerted campaign of 'self-criticism' when he examined the emotional and intellectual deficiencies in the Arab character.[67] Later, other official media organs echoed the new tendency toward 'realism'. Ahmad Baha al-Din, for instance, called for changing the political propaganda directed towards local and foreign audiences. A new tactic propagated the view that magic solutions for the destruction of Israel were not valid any more.[68] Muhammad 'Aruq was appointed as the new head of the 'Voice of Arabs' to apply the 'scientific method' in programmes addressing the Arab masses.[69]

This new strategy was reflected clearly in Egyptian media reporting of Lebanese affairs, while the pro-Egyptian media in Lebanon found it difficult to apply the same line.

Coverage of Lebanese affairs

Despite the change of strategy in the Egyptian media, it remained nationalized and therefore continued to express the official line of the political regime. Thus, any action by the Lebanese government or any political group was praised or condemned according to its impact on Egyptian national interests. After June 1967, Lebanese affairs did not occupy a great deal of the Egyptian media's attention because they had no impact on the Arab–Israeli conflict. Despite criticizing the shift towards the right in the 1968 elections, and the labelling of al-Hilf as an 'ally of foreign powers', the general tendency was to ignore Lebanese internal affairs. Moreover, lip service was paid to the regime of Hilu as the guardian of Lebanese stability and national unity.[70]

However, a change occurred in early January 1969, with the waging of a propaganda campaign against the Lebanese regime and right-wing political parties who argued for a 'neutral' Lebanon after Israel's raid on Beirut Airport. Al-Ahram, for instance, criticized the idea of stationing UN forces on the Lebanese–Israeli border, and went further to attack the political line of the Lebanese regime by publishing an article on 13 January 1969, saying that:

> The stationing of international forces on the Lebanese borders is a bankrupt policy, and it is necessary to review the goals of the Lebanese body politik fundamentally. Until 28 December 1968, those who believed in this theory [the stationing of UN forces] thought that they would not have to give an account to the Lebanese people, thinking that they were capable of maintaining the special status of Lebanon and therefore isolating it from the Arab world. Many Lebanese question the reasons for not recognizing the red China government ... and what really prevented Lebanon from obtaining military equipment and aircraft from the Soviets?[71]

This campaign subsided only when the pro-Sham'un ministers resigned from the newly formed government in late January 1969, and more 'moderate' Maronite leaders were appointed. Cairo perceived this as undermining the monopoly of representation of the Maronite community by the tripartite alliance, *al-Hilf*.[72]

The Egyptian media shifted to a more balanced and representative view of political currents in Lebanon after the clashes of April 1969 between the Lebanese army and the Palestinian guerrillas. Egyptian diplomacy sought to solve the crisis, and not adopt the traditional bias against right-wing Christian leaders.[73] The crisis was depicted as a 'conspiracy' conducted by America in order to achieve two goals: the vigorous suppression of the Palestinian guerrillas and the isolation of the Lebanese from the wider Arab world.[74] This stress on the external aspects of the crisis helped to portray the Christian–Muslim rift in Lebanon as a product of colonialism and not of the Arab nationalist movement. Egypt, it was claimed, possessed an admirable pedigree regarding Christian–Muslim relations, since it was Ibrahim Pasha (the ruler of Egypt) who had granted complete equality between Christians and Muslims during the nineteenth century.[75]

Furthermore, the dispatch of President Nasser's son, Khalid, on a sports tour of Lebanon during the crisis represented a diplomatic exercise to stress Egypt's non-partisan stance. Khalid 'Abdul Nasser spent more than two weeks in Lebanon playing sport, and was hosted by several political groups. He visited the right-wing leader Pierre Jumayyil in his party headquarters, *al-Kata'ib*, and the left-wing leader Kamal Jumblatt in his hometown of al-Mukhtara.[76]

After the Cairo Accord, the aim was to protect south Lebanon from Israel and to continue to allow Palestinian freedom of action in the same area. In addition, more attention was paid to the Lebanese Shi'a community which constituted the majority of the population in south Lebanon, in order to win it over to support Palestinian operations against Israel. Therefore extensive interviews were published with Imam Mussa al-Sadr, the spiritual leader of the Shi'a community in Lebanon, who professed his desire to close ranks among Muslim sects and support the Palestinian cause.[77]

In sum, Egyptian media interest in Lebanese affairs declined after the June war. The crisis over Lebanon's foreign policy direction in early 1969 marked an important restarting point for media attention. This lasted until the end of 1970, especially after Lebanon was forced into the quagmire of the Arab–Israeli conflict.

Fighting Cairo's battles in Beirut

The June war destroyed Egypt's military power as well as detrimentally affecting its economic and political position in the Arab world. It became necessary for Egypt to preserve its prestige by using its strong propaganda machine in Beirut in order to influence Lebanese, Egyptian and Arab public opinion. This was done through the pro-Egyptian media based in Beirut, which had supported Nasser and his regime. Equally, it was important to attack his Arab and international rivals, using whatever tactics were necessary. Nicholas Herbert succinctly described the situation in the London *Times* newspaper of 7 October 1968 as follows:

> Egyptian-subsidized papers in Beirut may be saying something slightly different for the benefit of a non-Egyptian readership, or to combat some equally inspired Saudi Arabian or Iraqi mouthpiece, which is busily imparting King Faisal's or President Bakr's version of the truth to press attachés and foreign correspondents milling about the Lebanese capital, in a vain effort to divine the overall picture of events. As a press, which lives on subsidy or sufferance, the Arab press holds the mirror up to a governmental view of life rather than to public opinion; but in the course of time the two become confused.[78]

In other words, media wars between Egypt and other Arab regimes continued to develop through the Beirut arena, despite the Arab detente at the Khartoum summit in late August 1967. It is useful to contrast the tone of two Beirut publications of the period: the Nasserist weekly *al-Hawadiss*, which had defended Egyptian foreign policy since October 1956 (see Chapter 2), and the pro-Saudi daily *al-Hayat*.

Al-Hayat attributed the responsibility for the June 'disaster' to Egypt and other 'revolutionary' regimes as early as 8 July 1967, calling for Saudi Arabia to take over leadership of the Arab world.[79] *Al-Hawadiss*, on the other hand, accused the Syrian regime of inciting Israel into a confrontation and then dragging Egypt into the war. Moreover, it laid responsibility for the defeat of the

Arab armies on all Arab regimes collectively, and called for support to be offered to Nasser in his drive to correct the 'path of the Arab revolution'.[80]

Al-Hayat interpreted and publicized news of popular dissent in Egypt, such as the demonstrations of 22 February and 27 November 1968, as a statement of no confidence in the regime.[81] Al-Hawadiss, for its part, repeated the Egyptian government account of events, and went further, praising any internal political initiatives on how to proceed. For instance, in its issue of 30 March 1968, al-Hawadiss commented on Nasser's referendum on a new internal political programme by saying that:

> The Egyptian regime's initiative to open the way for the masses to freedom of expression, recognition of its [the masses] complete revolutionary freedom and granting a pact for action outlining mutual responsibilities with the leadership is a proof of strength, proof of confidence and proof of discovering the real revolutionary path, which requires the people to act as a guide and leader. ... That is how we [al-Hawadiss] understood the referendum yesterday in Egypt. ... Al-Hawadiss says yes for revolutionary democracy ... yes O 'Abdul Nasser.[82]

Al-Hayat was generally critical of Egyptian foreign policy. An example of al-Hayat's line was its approach towards Egypt's position on the UN regional peace initiative of early autumn 1968. An editorial in al-Hayat dismissed with cynicism the call of Dr Boutros Boutros-Ghali in al-Ahram, for the sacking of all staff of Egyptian diplomatic missions for their inefficiency, and substituting them with Swedish staff.[83] Al-Hawadiss, on the other hand, echoed the Egyptian line, allocating the blame for Arab diplomatic failures to the Arab League, and counting any success as an Egyptian 'diplomatic victory'.[84]

The close relationship between the 'Muslim street' and the Palestinian guerrilla movement, which intensified from April 1969, was reflected in the Beirut press. In this climate, Lebanese journalist Sulaiman al-Firzili argued that his former editor, Salim al-Lawzi, had shifted his allegiance from President Nasser to the Palestinian guerrilla movement.[85] However, the move was not total. The balanced approach of al-Hawadiss was illustrated over Nasser's decision to accept the Rogers Plan in July 1970. This earned conciliatory praise from an editorial, arguing that 'it is right for the Palestinian revolution to oppose the Rogers Plan, but in accordance with Egypt's consent'.[86]

Nevertheless, as Egypt's material capability declined and was, therefore, no longer able to extend the same levels of financial support, this role was gradually substituted by Gulf petro-dollars. *Al-Hawadiss* magazine invited direct investment in 1970 from Sheikh Jabir al-Ahmad, the Kuwaiti Crown Prince.[87] The change in the publication's source of funding was reflected directly in the first issue after the new injection of funds: in its editorial, its administration and even its appearance. By way of a re-launch of the 'new *al-Hawadiss*' on 17 October 1969, the editor, Salim al-Lawzi, made the following statement:

> After the June defeat I recognized that the period of the aimless roaming of [my] newspaper has come to an end. ... One person owned *al-Hawadiss* and it has to change to become a corporate enterprise. *Al-Hawadiss* used to favour lifting [Arab] morale instead of providing the facts. But now it must put facts before morale lifting.[88]

In sum, the Egyptian government continued to use Beirut as a media battleground after the June war of 1967, to propagate its policies and challenge other Arab foes. Nasser's political stature remained intact with his traditional allies in the media. However, by 1969 the Egyptian government's ability to control these allies was undermined by the greater financial capability of new competitors in the Beirut media.

Balance in trade at last

Lebanese–Egyptian trade was affected to some extent by the June war, but continued to function more or less upon the same basis as in previous years. Egypt continued to be a minor trading partner of Lebanon. During the period 1966–67, Lebanese trade with the oil-rich Arab states, notably Saudi Arabia and Iraq, continued to produce a favourable balance of trade.[89]

The issue of Lebanese apple exports continued to dominate economic relations as Egypt failed to comply with the trade protocol of 1966, obliging Cairo to import $500,000 worth of apples per season. Despite repeated requests by the Lebanese government in 1967–68, the Egyptian authorities failed to import any substantial quantity.[90] A new trade protocol was signed in January 1970 whereby Egypt undertook to import $250,000 worth of apples, which represented a reduction of 50 per cent on the previous trade agreement.[91] By the end of 1970, Egyptian imports of Lebanese apples and citrus fruits failed to reach any substantial quantity.[92]

The trade balance continued to grow in Egypt's favour until 1969 when it reached L£12 million (see Tables 6a and 6b). In 1970, and for the first time since the early 1950s, Lebanese exports to Egypt were greater than imports from the same country. While the margin was about $500,000 in Lebanon's favour in 1970, it soared in 1971 to a record level of $2.9 million (see Tables 6a and 6b).

Conclusion

The decision of the Lebanese government not to participate in the 1967 June war did not have a damaging effect on relations with the Egyptian government. Egyptian foreign policy aims of the post-war period required the support of the Lebanese government in its negotiations during the UN and US peace initiatives. The Cairo Accord of 1969 represented the Egyptian will to settle differences between the Lebanese government and the Palestinian guerrilla movement at a minimum cost to Egyptian regional policy. Nasser was aware that supporting either side against the other would have undermined his status inside Lebanon as well as in the other Arab states.

CHAPTER 7

Decrease of Egyptian Influence since 1971

US supremacy in the Middle East

Egypt's expulsion of thousands of Soviet experts in July 1972 caused a great deal of damage to Moscow's reputation and influence in the Middle East. As a result, Soviet attention was directed towards Syria and Iraq in order to safeguard their presence in the area. The detente between the two superpowers made some Arab leaders feel that it was difficult to win back lost territories through peaceful means. However, the Soviet Union was reluctant to see Egypt and Syria suffer military defeat at the hands of Israel in October 1973. But Moscow's extensive help to its allies was countered by US arms shipments to Israel. Although the Arabs did not win the war, they succeeded in changing the status quo and convinced the UN to hold the Geneva conference to search for a comprehensive solution to the Arab–Israeli conflict.

The Camp David Accords of 1979 represented the peak of US hegemony in the area, thus confining Moscow to the role of mere observer on the diplomatic front. However, these accords did not lead to a comprehensive peace; instead they crippled Egypt's regional role. Thus, Israel found it so easy to invade Lebanon in June 1982 in the absence of any credible Arab challenge. The USA arrived later on the scene under the guise of a multinational force to assist the Lebanese government, thus avoiding the UN and the Soviet Union altogether. Moscow countered this US move by strengthening ties with its Syrian ally and providing Damascus with new weapons. Consequently, Moscow succeeded in aborting the Reagan initiative, and regained some of its lost ground in the Middle East.[1]

President Gorbachev's policy from 1985 showed a tendency to co-operate with Washington and to improve Soviet relations with conservative Arab states such as Egypt, Jordan and Oman. It is ironic that the defeat of Iraq in 1991 by the US-led coalition offered the latter an opportunity to call for a conference on the Middle East. The Soviet Union agreed to be a joint patron of the Madrid conference with the USA, though Russia took over this task, however limited, after Soviet disintegration.[2] Later, America ignored the Madrid formula and pushed the peace process towards bilateral deals between Israel and its neighbours, leaving Syria and Lebanon in the cold by 1999.

Civil war in Lebanon

In the early 1970s Arab conservative states assisted the administration of President Sulaiman Franjieh in its efforts to contain the activities of Palestinian guerrillas in Lebanon. Despite the fact that these states backed the PLO financially, they feared radical forces aiming at undermining the status quo. This factor played some part in discouraging Christian extremists from seeking a compromise with Lebanese factions sympathetic to the Palestinians. Thus, the PLO along with Lebanese left-wing and Sunni Muslim parties lost favour in some Arab capitals, which made Syrian intervention inevitable. This inter-Arab dispute saw Iraq backing the anti-Syrian forces, while Libya and Egypt opted for diplomatic pressure and mediation.[3]

President Elias Sarkis succeeded in restoring order in 1977, but the crisis exploded again in mid-1978 when Syrian forces fought with right-wing Christians. Thereafter, Lebanon evolved into an arena of conflict between local, regional and international players. President Amin Jumayyil was not able to hold the state together during his rule of 1982 to 1988, and the Muslim–Christian rift spread widely into the government and the army. Eventually, Jumayyil fired a departing shot by appointing General Michel Aoun as head of a military government until such time as elections could be held. Despite Aoun's opposition, regional and international factors converged into putting the Taif Accord into practice in 1990. As a result President Elias Hrawi forced Aoun out of power with Syrian backing. The new regime disarmed militias and put an end to civil war; and by 1999 the Taif formula was still holding, despite strong objections to its partial implementation.

Continuity with Sadat until 1974

In early 1971, the Lebanese government co-operated with UN peace efforts, through Jarring's shuttle diplomacy, and refused Israeli overtures to embark on secret negotiations. Moreover, Beirut expressed its support for Egypt's flexible approach on the grounds that 'it resulted in unmasking Israel's expansionist policy in front of international opinion'. Lebanon's foreign minister, Khalil Abu Hamad, responded positively to an Egyptian offer to co-ordinate a position on the Rogers initiative, and visited Cairo on 27 April 1971. Sadat was pleased that Beirut toed the Egyptian line, though it was done, implicitly, in return for excluding Lebanon from a military strategy against Israel.[4]

This Egyptian–Lebanese co-ordination was implemented in UN General Assembly sessions and meetings of the Arab Defence Council and Arab foreign ministers. After Egypt and Syria declared war on Israel on 6 October 1973, the Lebanese government sought to achieve two goals: first, never to give Israel the pretext to attack Lebanon militarily, for it was feared that south Lebanon and its water resources would certainly be lost; secondly, to implement some defensive measures to pre-empt any attempt by Israel to attack the Syrian army's rear via Lebanon, in addition to offering Damascus some kind of logistic support. In fact, Lebanese officials hoped that this would strengthen their hand in rejecting Syrian requests to send troops into Lebanese territory, as it was certain to push Lebanon into the war.[5]

Furthermore, the Lebanese government tried to secure Egyptian understanding of the argument that serving Lebanese interests would lead ultimately to serving Arab interests. This was figured clearly in the response of Prime Minister Taquieddine al-Sulh, to those who pleaded that Lebanon ought to fight side by side with its Arab brothers:

> I am very careful not to let emotions push me to depart from my norm to embark on delivering passionate rhetoric. However, I wish to stress that Egypt has a noble place in my heart as well as in Lebanese hearts. This stems from a long history between our two countries and Egypt's distinctive roles in our Arab world. In fact, Egypt has played civic, cultural, revolutionary, progressive and, later,

military roles ... all these factors make it imperative that our big sister should occupy such a noble status. ... As for President Sadat, I say that I am impressed by his abilities ... for he acts wisely and reasonably, in a way that does not compromise his sincere intention nor his deep conviction and belief in Egyptian rights and interests, as well as those of the Arabs.[6]

Therefore the Lebanese government felt comfortable in restricting its support for Egypt to the diplomatic domain, in order to avoid Israeli punishment. But Palestinian guerrillas, based in Lebanon, pursued a different strategy aimed at launching cross-border raids on Israel. This situation imposed on the Egyptian government the difficult balancing act of choosing between the logic of the state and the logic of revolution. In other words, Cairo worked to cement the Arab regional order without allowing radical forces to enact an open confrontation with Israel. As for Lebanon, its government was willing but unable to close borders with Israel fearing the deadly accusation of protecting 'the enemy'. Instead, Beirut sought to restrict Palestinian activities at a time when other Arab fronts with Israel were virtually closed. Here, Egypt did play a mediating role between the Palestinian and Lebanese sides. Mahmud Riad, the Arab League General Secretary, was dispatched to Beirut in September 1972 to defuse tension after the attack on the Israeli Olympic team in Munich. Riad obtained a new set of guarantees and promises from Palestinian movements to respect the terms of the Cairo Accord of 1969.[7]

Afterwards, whenever relations deteriorated between the Lebanese army and Palestinian guerrillas, Cairo interfered to restore calm on the basis of 'not allowing Israel to exploit differences among brothers'. For example, the Egyptian parliament dispatched a telegram on 10 December 1972 to the Lebanese parliament to seek help in 'protecting the Palestine revolution and not allowing Lebanon to be turned into a slaughterhouse for the guerrillas'.[8] When Syria tried to help Palestinian fighters in May 1973 by applying a degree of military pressure on Lebanon by closing the border, the Egyptian government sent hurriedly a special envoy to mediate between Beirut and Damascus.[9] Furthermore, whenever Israel launched punitive raids on Palestinian camps in Lebanon, as was the case in mid-May 1974 following the Ma'alout operation, the Egyptian government denounced Israel publicly, without hinting at Palestinian responsibility.[10] In sum, the

Lebanese government maintained its co-ordination with the Egyptian government towards the Arab–Israeli conflict and accepted Egyptian mediation to contain the excesses of Palestinian fighters in Lebanon.

Egypt and the civil war

The Lebanese civil war brought about the disintegration of central government in Beirut and the emergence of various militias representing political parties and sects. This situation forced regional and international mediators to deal not only with official bodies but also with warring factions. Egypt was no exception. Arab League General Secretary, Mahmud Riad, heeded Cairo's call, and negotiated a ceasefire agreement between Palestinian fighters and the Phalange militia – just two days after the start of the civil war.[11]

Regional competition between Syria and Egypt, and Israel to some extent, intensified with every stage of civil strife in Lebanon. While Syria focused on promoting its own initiative, the Egyptian government resorted to calling for an 'Arab solution' to the crisis under the pretext of pre-empting Israeli meddling in south Lebanon. But in reality, Cairo aimed at blocking Syria's near hegemony over Lebanon. Thus, Syria boycotted a meeting of Arab foreign ministers held in Cairo on 15 October 1975, though its sole aim was to debate the Lebanese crisis.[12]

The Egyptian perception of the Lebanese crisis was that it incorporated a Lebanese–Palestinian problem and had a purely internal dimension. Regarding the first part, Egypt called on both sides to implement the Cairo Accord of 1969, while urging the Lebanese to embark on a dialogue to preserve national unity. A statement issued by the Egyptian government on 1 December 1975 summed up its aims as follows:

> Egypt requests the monitoring of weapons in Lebanese cities. Egypt stresses the necessity of resorting to dialogue, not arms, as the right medium to settle differences in a country known to be an example in this respect. Egypt condemns irresponsible acts committed by members of the Phalange party. Egypt equally condemns the pro-Syrian Sa'iqa organization and its overt as well as its covert activities against both Muslims and Christians. Egypt strongly opposes dividing Lebanon and regards those who propagate this as traitors. Egypt considers any attempt to internationalize the Lebanese conflict as capital treachery.[13]

In early 1976, the Egyptian government condemned the use of the Lebanese army to subjugate Palestinian guerrillas and called on the Arab League to live up to its responsibilities and protect Palestinian resistance. But the Lebanese government snubbed Egyptian moves to 'arabize' the crisis, preferring instead to deal with the Syrian initiative. The latter bore fruit on 6 February 1976, when Presidents Assad and Franjieh initiated a reform plan for the Lebanese constitution, while Syria undertook to guarantee Palestinian adherence to the Cairo Accord and its appendices. This development intensified Egyptian–Syrian rivalry. But Egypt confined its role to that of calling for the protection of Palestinian fighters from the Lebanese army, right-wing Christians and Syria.[14]

Furthermore, on 28 March 1976, Sadat suggested the dispatch of Arab forces to restore peace in Lebanon and warned the Soviet Union not to interfere in the civil war. But when President Franjieh ignored Egyptian overtures, Sadat backed a Lebanese opposition request that Franjieh should resign for being responsible for prolonging the civil war. Moreover, Sadat called upon France to mediate between warring factions despite Cairo's early objection to any foreign meddling in Arab affairs. This was perhaps to embarrass Syria for its military squeeze of the PLO and its Lebanese allies in the spring of 1976. In fact, the Egyptian government condemned Syrian intervention publicly and called on the Arab League to hold an urgent session devoted to 'protecting the Palestine revolution instead of stabbing it in the back'.[15]

Nonetheless, the Egyptian government was unable to change the course of events or even protect its traditional allies. It was only after Saudi Arabia sponsored a Syrian–Egyptian reconciliation in late June 1976 that Cairo was able to play a symbolic role in establishing an Arab force led by Egyptian General Mohammed Hassan Ghoneim – albeit without Egyptian soldiers. Moreover, Egyptian special envoy, Hassan Sabri al-Khuli, was dispatched to Beirut to mediate, though under the banner of the Arab League this time. It is important to note that Egyptian efforts were restricted to the humanitarian and diplomatic spheres, rather than to active political or military participation. This included securing medical aid for besieged Palestinian camps, and facilitating the withdrawal of PLO fighters and their Lebanese allies from the advancing Syrian and right-wing forces. Despite al-Khuli's shuttle diplomacy between Beirut and Damascus in the summer of 1976,

Syrian forces crushed all resistance and approached the outskirts of Beirut, while Christian militias occupied all Palestinian camps located in their enclave.[16]

Elias Sarkis's assumption of power on 23 September 1976 paved the way for Cairo to re-open contacts with the new regime in Beirut. In fact, Sarkis had earlier visited Cairo and met Sadat to seek his help in tackling the last hurdles in the crisis. Johnny Abdo, ex-head of Lebanese Intelligence, said later that Sarkis was eager to see an end to the Egyptian–Syrian dispute 'because it was expressed in one form or another in our country'.[17]

Egypt took part in the mini-summit held in Riyadh in mid-October 1976 alongside Saudi Arabia, Kuwait and Syria, then hosted a full summit on 25 October to endorse the decisions taken at the first one. It was agreed to implement an 'Arab solution' to the crisis and to submerge the Arab Peacekeeping Force into a newly created Arab Deterrence Force. However, Egypt did not dispatch any military units to Lebanon, thus leaving Syria to form the backbone of the new force. In fact, Egypt was included as a member in the supervising committee, headed by President Sarkis, whose tasks included wiping out the legacy of civil war and forcing the PLO to implement their part of the Cairo Accord.[18]

Peace for Egypt and war for Lebanon

President Sadat's visit to Jerusalem in November 1977 caused severe paralysis to Lebanese government efforts aimed at reasserting its control over the whole country. Not only was Arab consensus on Israel shattered but also Syria and the PLO became allies, which made it impossible for the Syrian-dominated Arab deterrence force to tame Palestine fighters in Lebanon. As a result, the PLO launched attacks on Israel from Lebanese territory in the hope that retaliation would abort the fledgling peace process between Cairo and Tel Aviv. This resulted in the re-eruption of the civil war as right-wing Christians objected to this strategy, in the belief that it would certainly lead to Palestinian domination of Lebanon.[19]

Egypt's strategy focused on containing military clashes between Israel and other Arab states, in order to allow the peace process to gain ground. Thus, when Israel launched 'the Litani operation' on 14 March 1978 in revenge for a Palestinian attack

on the Haifa–Tel-Aviv highway, Egypt's foreign minister, Mohammed Ibrahim Kamil, was the first to condemn it for 'violating
Lebanese sovereignty'. Moreover, Kamil stressed that stability was
necessary in south Lebanon even if this led to the dispatch of UN
troops to 'protect Lebanese territory from Israeli greed until such
a time when the Lebanese army is capable of protecting [Leba-
nese] territory'.[20] Furthermore, the Egyptian government
supported the renewal of the Arab Deterrence Force's mission in
Lebanon, during an Arab League Council meeting held in Cairo in
late March 1978, in spite of Syria's abstention.[21] Thus, it was ironic
that Egypt favoured the preservation of the status quo in Lebanon, albeit under Syrian tutelage, in order to concentrate on peace
negotiations with Israel.

The Camp David Accords left the Lebanese government with
no choice but to side with the majority of Arab states who
opposed Cairo. Sarkis and his prime minister, Salim al-Huss,
attended the Arab summit held in Baghdad on 1 November 1978
to debate the situation, after ostracizing Egypt. Al-Huss headed a
delegation dispatched by the summit to Cairo in the hope of
convincing Sadat to back-track on his policy. However, the
Egyptian president did not care much for Lebanon's mediating
role, and snubbed al-Huss and his delegation publicly. As result,
the summit rewarded Lebanon by adopting its four requests. First,
it stressed the need for full implementation of the previous Riyadh
and Cairo summits, especially the issue of disarming Palestinian
fighters. Secondly, it offered financial aid to help reconstruction
efforts after the civil war. Thirdly, it assisted the Lebanese government to regain sovereignty of the whole area of south Lebanon
as referred to in UN Resolutions 425 and 426. Lastly, while the
summit stressed its rejection in principle of settling Palestinian
refugees in countries of residence, it refrained from mentioning
Lebanon by name.[22]

Later, the Lebanese government endorsed the resolutions of
the second Baghdad summit, held in late March 1979, which
called for a withdrawal of ambassadors from Cairo, severing
diplomatic ties with Egypt, freezing the latter's membership in the
Arab League and moving its headquarters to Tunisia. Consequently, the Lebanese government severed ties with Cairo on 25
April 1979.[23] For the next three years, Egyptian influence in Beirut

was eradicated, while Cairo was busy pursuing the issue of regaining the Sinai peninsula from Israel.

The Israeli invasion of Lebanon in early June 1982 posed a dilemma for Egypt as to how to respond. It was clear that Egyptian opposition to Israeli actions was merely rhetorical and lacked any military dimension. Egypt's former foreign minister, Mohammed Ibrahim Kamil, believed that his country would have been able to alter the course of events had it not signed the Camp David Accords.[24] Instead, the Egyptian government tried to exploit the opportunity in the diplomatic domain in order to break its isolation. First, it stressed its strong opposition to Israel's invasion of Lebanon as it might have serious implications on the peace achieved with Tel Aviv. Secondly, Cairo sought to enhance its reputation by aiming to protect the Palestinian presence in Lebanon from Israeli onslaught. Lastly, it wished to exploit Syrian weakness to thereby persuade the Lebanese government to follow Egypt's path and sign a peace treaty with Israel.

Therefore Kamal Hassan Ali, the Egyptian foreign minister, visited Washington less than a week after the Israeli attacks to inform President Reagan that the situation was 'unacceptable'. He also suggested, in mid-July 1982, holding an Arab summit devoted solely to debate the situation in Lebanon, but his offer was snubbed by everyone save Jordan and the Sudan. In late July, the Egyptian government co-sponsored with France a draft resolution in the UN Security Council, which called for settling the Lebanese crisis by diplomatic means and mutual recognition between Israel and the PLO. In fact, Cairo went further in its protest and boycotted the self-determination talks, which were attached to the Camp David Accords, until Israel withdrew its troops from Lebanon and the USA recognized the PLO. Moreover, the Egyptian ambassador was recalled from Tel Aviv in the aftermath of the Sabra and Shatilla massacres, as a sign of disgruntlement with Israeli complacency. More importantly, Dr Boutros Boutros-Ghali, Egyptian Minister for Foreign Affairs, visited Beirut on 7 December 1982 to encourage President Amin Jumayyil to sign a peace treaty with Israel – notwithstanding the fact that diplomatic relations between Cairo and Beirut had been severed since 1979. Later, Egypt sought to urge the USA to pressurize Israel to leave Lebanon, while helping to mute Arab opposition to Lebanon signing the agreement of 17 May 1983. However, Syria and its

Lebanese allies succeeded in aborting this plan, thus causing Egypt to lose a potentially valuable ally in the region.[25]

Subsequently, Syria moved to reduce Yasser Arafat's influence among Palestinians in Lebanon by backing his foes within the PLO. This development reduced the room for manoeuvre available to the Lebanese government to co-ordinate policy with Cairo, at a time when Egyptian–Syrian rivalry was rekindled.[26] For instance, Amin Jumayyil resorted to holding secret talks with President Mubarak, while his plane was being re-fuelled at Cairo airport.[27] However, the situation changed following Syria's approval of the Amman Summit resolution, issued on 10 November 1987, which called for the restoration of diplomatic ties with Egypt and the latter's return to the Arab League on 12 May 1989. Consequently, diplomatic relations were restored between Egypt and Lebanon on 28 June 1989, ten years after Camp David.[28]

From the Taif Agreement until 1999

Although Egypt did not play an active part in concluding the Taif Agreement in 1989, the outcome was not averse to Cairo's vision of improving the status of Lebanese Muslims. It is important to note that the Egyptian government accepted the legitimacy of President Elias Hrawi in his contest with Iraqi-backed challenger, Michel Aoun, though unenthusiastically. But Lebanon's stance during the Kuwait crisis of 1990–91 was in tandem with the Egyptian policy, as a result of Arab near-consensus over how to deal with Baghdad. The Madrid Conference and the ensuing peace process put Arab differences on how to deal with Israel on hold for some time. As a result, Lebanon, along with Syria, Jordan and the PLO, embarked on a policy of co-ordination with Egypt, especially since the latter played the role of indirect mediator between them and Israel.[29]

It seemed that Egypt's focus since 1993 was directed towards helping the PLO and Israel to reach a deal, but this irritated the Lebanese government who repeated its preference for a collective Arab approach towards Tel Aviv. Therefore the Oslo Declaration increased Lebanese fears of not only being left behind but also of schemes to settle Palestinian refugees in Lebanon. It was clear that Lebanon's decision to tie its position to Syria's bore benefits and punishments for Beirut. However, Lebanese officials sought

Egyptian help to mitigate Israeli bombardments of south Lebanon, which caused heavy casualties and destroyed Lebanese infrastructure. For instance, Nabih Birri, the Speaker of the Lebanese Parliament, during a visit to Cairo in the summer of 1994, declared:

> We recognize fully that Arab victories are not imminent, but all we are seeking is to reduce our losses. That is why I come here to inform our big sister, Egypt, on the real situation in South Lebanon and the Israeli aggression on civilians, territory and all UN resolutions. We consider what happens in South Lebanon as an aggression on Egypt itself ... and while we are here we request that the Arabs pay their debt to Lebanon, which is about $700 million, especially since it is the only country which is still suffering [from Israel].[30]

However, Mubarak advised Lebanon to work out an appropriate mechanism, in conjunction with Syria, then seek Israel's full compliance with UN Resolution 425. But Rabin's assassination in the autumn of 1995 halted cautious moves on the Lebanese and Syrian tracks with Israel. When Cairo and Washington convened the Sharm Sheikh Conference, on 13 March 1996, to denounce terrorism in the wake of a series of suicide bombings on Israeli civilians, the Lebanese government opted to abstain along with Syria. Aware of the dangers of isolation, Lebanon's prime minister, Rafiq al-Hariri, and foreign minister, Faris Buwaiz, rushed immediately to Cairo to explain their country's need to distinguish between legitimate Lebanese resistance to Israeli occupation and terrorism. Hariri met political and media figures arguing his country's case, especially 'the unity of Syrian and Lebanese trucks', and tried to gain favour by inviting Egyptian business to participate in reconstruction projects in Lebanon. It was clear that President Mubarak urged Lebanon and Syria to keep faith in the peace process and show restraint in order not to disturb Perez's bid to return to power as Israeli elections were approaching.[31]

But Netanyahu defeated Perez and threw the whole peace process into stalemate. Although Israel eventually recognized UN Resolution 425 in April 1998, the Lebanese government hesitated first, then rejected Israeli offers to enter talks to implement it. As before, Prime Minister Hariri begged Cairo to understand his government's reasons for neglecting what it had been asking Tel Aviv to offer over the past years. Later, the Lebanese government gained Egyptian understanding of its position, benefiting from

Mubarak's mistrust of Netanyahu's policies, in addition to clinging to the concept of the unity between Lebanese and Syrian tracks.[32]

Loss of influence inside Lebanon

The policy of *Infitah* (openness) pursued by President Sadat led in one respect to a widening of contacts with Lebanese Christian parties. For instance, in February 1974, the Arab Socialist Union invited the leader of the Phalange party, Pierre Jumayyil, to visit Cairo where he was assured that 'Egyptian socialism is not for export'. While this newly found Egyptian moderation boosted the confidence of right-wing Christians, it caused irritation among Muslim parties and groups – Egypt's traditional allies. They feared losing a key protector vis-à-vis the Christians.[33]

Therefore the Egyptian government did not move to help its Muslim and pan-Arab allies in the early stages of the civil war. It is true there was a state of mutual suspicion before 13 April 1975, which flared up occasionally into press attacks on Cairo's inclination towards Washington. Also, Sadat's battle against Nasserist forces inside Egypt did not endear him to Arab nationalists in other Arab countries, Lebanon in particular. But the eruption of the civil war pushed these groups to request Egyptian assistance to counter-balance the foreign backing enjoyed by other parties. For instance, the leader of the 'Nasserist organization in Lebanon – the union of popular forces', Kamal Shatilla, pleaded his case in vain while visiting Cairo in August 1975:

> There is co-ordination between us and the Arab Socialist Union in Egypt on the level of political thought achieved through the comprehensive understanding of the [Egyptian] revolution, the necessity of liberation, the principles of Socialism, freedom and unity, the faith in the Arab nationalist movement, and above all implementing the principles of non-alignment in foreign policy. Here, we can distinguish between some anti-Arab and anti-Socialist utterances printed in a few [Egyptian] publications, and the nationalist, socialist and democratic path led by President Sadat. The fact is that when we criticize some negative aspects of the press, it does not prevent us from backing revolutionary Egypt ... for we cannot continue marching in the Arab unity path, without Egypt being in the lead.[34]

Nevertheless, Egyptian aloofness did not change until the end of 1975, when Lebanese Muslims and Palestinians faced a systematic campaign of massacres by Christian right-wing militias. As a result, the official Egyptian position summed up the war as an aggression by Maronite Christians against the Muslims and secular progressive groups, in order to divide Lebanon. This Egyptian revision sought to mend fences with former allies, especially the various Nasserist groups. An editorial in *Rose al-Yussuf* weekly summed up the Egyptian view by saying:

> It is clear that the Phalange party is keen to run a sectarian battle while declaring at the same time, along with its cronies, that the insti-gator is the [Palestinian] Resistance and international leftists. And the party continues playing its part in this sectarian design, while enjoying complete protection from Arab media [by claiming] that every Mus-lim has turned into a communist. The battle has not ended and will not end easily because the Phalangists and their allies aim to widen its scope by rejecting any dialogue on political reform. Also, there are those who call for the Lebanese question to be internationalized, thus evading the local or Arab solution.[35]

Yet Egyptian military and financial assistance was not forthcom-ing to Muslims or Nasserist organizations, as happened in 1958 (see Chapter 3). In fact, Libya and Iraq filled this vacuum, donat-ing millions of dollars to leftist and Palestinian organizations. Egypt's contribution was confined to uttering sympathetic statements in diplomatic circles and media spheres.[36] Therefore, when the Lebanese National Movement was subjected to Syrian military and political pressure in the early summer of 1976, Cairo resorted to calling on Arab states to adopt a clear stance regarding 'Syrian intervention in Lebanon'. In fact, the Lebanese National Movement wished that Egypt would send a token military force to boost morale and embarrass Syria. But Egyptian activities were restricted to the political and humanitarian spheres and channelled via the Arab League, in the hope of protecting Sadat's Arab credentials at home and abroad.[37]

Sadat's visit to Jerusalem in the autumn of 1977 shocked pro-Egyptian groups in Lebanon, and led them to join other Arab nationalists and leftists in declaring that the Egyptian president had betrayed Nasser's legacy. While these groups gave Nasser the benefit of the doubt in 1969 after he accepted the Rogers plan, Sadat's step of giving up the struggle against the enemy – the bedrock of Egyptian policy since 1956 – proved too difficult for them to swallow. Therefore Muslim and Nasserist groups had no choice but to look for new backers among the anti-Sadat camp, particularly Iraq, Libya, Syria, South Yemen and the PLO. This chasm deepened after the Egyptian government endorsed the Camp David Accords, with these groups calling for the isolation of Sadat's regime, stripping it of any legitimacy and breaking all contacts with Cairo. A statement by the Lebanese National Movement, an umbrella for most Nasserist and leftist parties, showed a complete U-turn in rhetoric, when it declared on 28 March 1979 that:

> It is completely true that we have to distinguish between Sadat's regime and the Egyptian people, but it is unwise to use this pretext to achieve a misguided goal. If we pursue a benevolent policy towards Sadat's regime in order not to hurt Egyptian interests, then we would in fact be doing a disservice to the real interests of the Egyptian people. Also, if we really care about these people, then we would better express it by inflicting severe punishment on Sadat's regime. Afterwards, we have to offer the best possible assistance to the Egyptian national movement, which is the real representative of the Egyptian people and the force able to lead the struggle to topple Sadat's regime and the so-called peace accord – which is surrender in reality.[38]

Israel's invasion of Lebanon in June 1982 and Sadat's earlier assassination reduced the bitterness between the two sides, as Egyptian official and popular sympathy was expressed over the suffering of Lebanese civilians. But the rapprochement process was slow at a time when the leaders of many Nasserist organizations and Sunni groups lost ground in the aftermath of the PLO departure from Beirut and Tripoli.

The replaying of religious cards

After the early 1990s, the demise of Arab nationalist ideology led to closer ties between Egyptian officials and the traditional Muslim establishment. In fact, there was a growing tendency among Sunnis and Shi'as to welcome Egyptian overtures in order to balance Iranian influence in Lebanon, since Tehran had already cemented its ties with radical Muslim clerics. As a result, Egyptian diplomats responded positively to national invitations despite some awkward clashes with fundamentalist clerics. For instance, Sheikh Mahir Hammud, a pro-Iranian Sunni activist, denounced the presence of the 'Camp David ambassador' during a religious event held on 4 March 1994 and withdrew. In return, the Egyptian ambassador, Sayyid Abu Zaid Umar, issued a strongly worded reply, stating that:

> Who is this Sheikh? We did not notice his presence in either the mosque or his departure? Nobody in the mosque really took notice of his protest; thus he jumped up to air it through the media. Who is he to misbehave and insult all attendees including the most respected clerics? Is this an Islamic virtue? We know that pretence, vulgarity, and sowing divisions in mosques are forbidden. It is good of him to leave and we also call upon him not to be present at any place we visit. Parroting nationalist and patriotic terminology has become a mere play well known to us, and our people will not be deceived; so he would be better to stop it.[39]

Although this incident was not repeated, its impact indicated that Egyptian policy was not isolated any more, at a time when Muslim and leftist parties were adopting gradually pragmatic views on regional and international affairs. This change affected Sunni and Shi'a clerics among the traditional establishment, as well as radicals turned officials in the Lebanese regime after Taif. Therefore the visit of the head of the Higher Shi'a Council, Sheikh Muhammed Mahdi Shamseddine, to Cairo in late May 1994 was justified on the grounds of 'seeking co-ordination between religious thinkers in Lebanon, Egypt, and Arab and Islamic worlds under the new world order'.[40] He rushed to Cairo again in February 1997 to halt official propaganda directed against a radical Egyptian organization, for the sole reason that its members belonged the Shi'a sect. It was clear that there was mutual desire to put an end to this problem, which symbolized occasional political discord between Cairo and Tehran, which was bound to spill over into Lebanon.[41] Likewise, the Coptic Patriarch, Anba Shnuda, kept a high profile while visiting Beirut and stressed the virtues of national unity and religious harmony in Egypt, Lebanon and the Arab world.[42]

By 1996, parliamentary, tourist and sporting ties were restored, thus pushing the process of normalization to a new depth.[43] Despite financial difficulties affecting the Egyptian religious mission in Lebanon, the Arab University of Beirut regained some of its vitality after a period of uncertainty. This was due to Sadat's threats to close it in the early 1980s after radical groups had used it to oppose his policies. Now this Egyptian-controlled institution was being propped up to offer reasonable education to a wider section of Lebanese and Arab students.[44] However, on the eve of its 40th anniversary, it is still prone to accusations that it favours Egyptians nationals over Lebanese in academic posts, lacks research capabilities and fills the market with poorly trained graduates.[45]

New promises in trade

The increase in Lebanon's trade with Arab Gulf states after the early 1970s, coupled with economic disruption during the civil war, reduced economic exchange with Egypt to a negligible amount. Moreover, the diplomatic boycott of Cairo after its signing of the Camp David Accords meant that official trade agreements and protocols were not renewed until the early 1990s. In fact, an agreement of economic co-ordination was signed in February 1992 – endorsed by the Lebanese and Egyptian parliaments – which sought to encourage bilateral trade by exempting certain products – 38 Lebanese and 58 Egyptian – from tariffs. Furthermore, the Lebanese tourist office was reopened in mid-August 1994 in the hope of regaining a near monopoly of Egyptian tourism, as had been the case in the 1950s and 1960s.[46]

Nevertheless, the value of total trade rose from $16 million in 1993 to only $39 million in 1994, thus incurring an Egyptian complaint at the slow pace of growth. Also, the Egyptian prime minister, Kamal al-Janzuri, requested that his country ought to have a slice of reconstruction deals, and that restrictions on employing Egyptian workers in Lebanon should be lifted. Although the Speaker of the Lebanese Parliament, Nabih Berri, had called upon Egyptian contractors to help rebuild south Lebanon in August 1994, the Lebanese government held back. As a matter of fact, it had been customary since 1993 to expel Egyptian workers who had entered Lebanon illegally. For instance, in late August 1994, 270 Egyptian workers were expelled to Damascus after Lebanese authorities claimed to have uncovered a racket charging $1,500 for every infiltrator entering via Turkey and Jordan.[47]

Despite the fact that Lebanese and Egyptian ministers signed three agreements on 18 March 1996, which included the setting up of a bilateral higher committee, safeguarding investments and reducing tariffs, the real aim was to encourage businessmen to indulge in joint ventures. In effect, Lebanese premier, Rafiq

Hariri, gave only vague promises to open Lebanese markets to more Egyptian products, and refused to allocate a certain share of deals to Egyptian companies – though he asked them to be more efficient and competitive.[48] In return for these Lebanese 'good intentions', the Egyptian government offered to help Lebanon by promising to import 20,000 tons of Lebanese apples and reduce taxes on them from 70 to 20 per cent.[49]

In early March 1997, a fully fledged crisis erupted between Lebanon and Egypt after the Lebanese Minister of Agriculture, Shawqi Fakhuri, forbade the import of Egyptian potatoes outside the limits specified in the agricultural protocol. This invited a spontaneous Egyptian retaliation which took the form of stopping all imports of Lebanese apples, calling off a visit by an official delegation, lodging a formal protest and recalling Ambassador Adil al-Khidairy from Beirut. Fakhuri justified his decision by saying that he had to respond to a protest from local potato farmers at the flooding of the Lebanese market with cheaper Egyptian potatoes. But the Egyptian ambassador claimed that Egyptian farmers and exporters had suffered as a result of this, leaving Cairo no choice but to bar the entry of 27 containers of Lebanese apples to Egyptian markets on the grounds that they 'were not accompanied with health certificates'.[50] In the ensuing war of words, it became clear that the apple–potato crisis represented the tip of the iceberg, and that the real issue was a failure to maintain a fair trade balance, which was tipped in Egypt's favour. Minister Fakhuri stated with a rare bitter tone that:

> We reject the harm inflicted on Lebanese interests and note that we imported in the last three months 33,000 tons of agricultural products form Egypt while they only accepted the entry of 2,000 tons of our produce. We are even restricted to export only apples [to the Egyptian market] while we import up to 49 agricultural products [from Egypt] and without restricting quantities. Whenever we send apples to Egypt, we face a set of bureaucratic difficulties such as paying tax and undertaking inspections which can take 10 to 20 days – thus rendering our apples to rot and becoming unattractive for the consumer. This happens at a time when we allow all Egyptian produce to enter the Lebanese market in 24 hours free from any taxes whatsoever. In short, all we are asking for is to be treated with fairness and apply reciprocity.[51]

Consequently, Lebanon's prime minister rushed to Cairo and held urgent talks with President Mubarak and his prime minister al-

Janzuri, in order to mend fences. Hariri stated that he was 'embarrassed' to dwell on this subject and tried to gloss it over. Eventually, Hariri struck a deal with Egyptian officials and the crisis withered away. As a result, the Lebanese government annulled its decision regarding Egyptian potatoes in return for importing 10,500 tons of apples as well as 'promising' to import 20,000 tons in the 1997–98 season.[52]

Egyptian attempts to gain more access to Lebanese markets were repeated in August 1997, when Premier al-Janzuri visited Beirut accompanied with official and business delegations. He demanded increasing trade exchanges by suggesting the setting up of a joint export house. Moreover, he tried to soothe Lebanese concerns over the persistence of subjecting Lebanese produce to unnecessary delay. Al-Janzuri explained that:

> Egypt has borne a bigger burden in the past and engaged in wars for the sake of Arab causes, and now it bears a bigger burden in the struggle for peace and it is ready to participate in the process of development. Global economic interests impose on us the necessity to move speedily towards [Arab] integration. It is sad that our mutual trade is estimated at $60 million, while the volume of our trade with the rest of the world runs at $29 billion. We will not be the side who opposes increasing trade with Lebanon and other Arab countries and particularly in investment. If there are problems regarding the quarantine of agricultural and animal products, then I want you to be sure that it is not directed against Lebanon specifically but at other countries as well. If there is a Lebanese wish for a freer trade in agriculture, industry, tourism and other domains, then we will welcome it, but we would not ask you to do more than you can afford to.[53]

By 1999, the two governments reached a broad understanding and signed 26 agreements involving public and private sectors with a 'new promise' to set up bilateral duty-free zones. Nevertheless, there was no hint on how to rectify the balance of trade, tipped in Egypt's favour, nor what specific measures would be taken to allow even a limited flow of Egyptian workers into Lebanon. Egyptian exports to Lebanon rocketed to $160 million in 1997, while the value of imported goods stood at just $60 million. This huge imbalance has proved difficult to rectify despite all the political and economic manoeuvring by both sides.[54]

Conclusion

Egyptian influence started to recede after Sadat proceeded with his peace strategy. While Syria's role in Lebanon was growing during the civil war, Egyptian efforts focused on humanitarian and diplomatic spheres under the umbrella of the Arab League. Sadat's visit to Jerusalem and his endorsement of the Camp David Accords squeezed Egyptian influence from the Levant in general, and Lebanon in particular. Therefore economic, diplomatic and political ties were severed with Egypt. In 1982, Cairo tried to regain some ground by 'helping' President Jumayyil's regime sign a peace treaty with Israel, but failed in this bid after Syria and its Lebanese allies gained the upper hand. In the early 1990s, regional and international developments played a great part in removing barriers which stood in the way of restoring economic and political ties between Cairo and Beirut. However, economic tensions erupted for a short time in the spring of 1997. Despite the apparent goodwill in signing bilateral agreements, it remains to be seen whether economic problems can be glossed over by political solutions or vice versa.

Conclusion

The relations between Lebanon and Egypt during the last 50 years have passed through phases of both conflict and co-operation. While Lebanon was a fringe state in both the Arab and the Middle East system, Egypt was a core state in both. The causes of conflict in the 1950s lay in the attempt by the Egyptian regime to prevent Lebanon joining the various regional pacts, in order to avert the isolation of Egypt. After 1958, the Egyptian regime succeeded in maintaining its hegemony over Lebanon as part of its strategy to lead the Arab world. This, however, withered away after Sadat and Mubarak aligned Egypt to the West and worked to preserve the status quo.

Egypt possessed few concrete capabilities to influence the policies of the Lebanese government. However, the Egyptian regime was able to compensate for this constraint by employing alternative methods. First, although Egypt was in no position to offer Lebanon economic assistance, since both countries were dependent on foreign aid, the Egyptian government imposed constraints regarding the timing and conditions of Lebanese aid requests to the West. Secondly, Lebanon's geographic position enabled it to be immune from direct Egyptian intervention. However, this proved not to be an absolute constraint since the Egyptian government was able to influence Lebanese politics through its contacts with Lebanese Muslims. Moreover, Egypt's union with Syria in 1958 removed this geographical constraint until October 1961. Thirdly, Arab nationalist ideology enabled Egypt to rally Lebanese Muslims to its side. The Lebanese regime did not adopt any official ideology. Fourthly, Lebanese governments adopted a self-defined notion of neutrality, intended to ward off pressure to side with any of the competing Arab camps. However, President Sham'un's close co-operation with the Baghdad Pact countries and his subscribing to the Eisenhower

Doctrine provided Nasser with an effective propaganda weapon. Lastly, although Israel was a possible power with whom the Lebanese government could have struck a political alliance to check Egyptian hegemony, Arab consensus (official lip service but more importantly popular opinion) killed such an option. Instead, the Lebanese regime always supported Arab League resolutions concerning the Arab–Israeli conflict.

When the Egyptian and Iraqi governments battled through the early 1950s over the domination of the Arab system and the issue of foreign pacts, the Lebanese regime tried to mediate between them. This represented a declaration of neutrality in inter-Arab conflict. The Lebanese government maintained its ability to manoeuvre after it signed the Point-Four economic assistance programme with America without incurring Egypt's fury (see Chapter 1).

The Suez debacle posed a dilemma for the Lebanese government. While it was acceptable to pay lip service to Egypt's cause before the hostilities broke out, it was extremely difficult for the Lebanese government to sustain this afterwards. The Lebanese regime not only chose to maintain its bonds with the West, but also accepted the Eisenhower Doctrine. This put it at loggerheads with Egypt and Syria who led the anti-Western drive. Nasser strengthened his nascent relations with Lebanese Muslims in order to check the Sham'un regime (see Chapter 2).

The union of Egypt and Syria in 1958 represented a nightmare scenario for the Lebanese regime. It was feared that Lebanon would be swallowed into an Arab–Muslim super state. President Nasser, the charismatic leader who had mobilized the majority of Lebanese Muslims into paying him allegiance, was now in control of Lebanon's lifeline with the Arab hinterland. The UAR backed the revolt of the Lebanese opposition to Sham'un through propaganda, cross-border intrusions, finance and weaponry. President Sham'un resorted to making complaints against UAR interference to the Arab League and the UN Security Council. Sham'un favoured direct US intervention which came on 15 July 1958, due to regional considerations. At this point, the UAR dispute with Lebanon took on not only a regional aspect but also an international one, since both superpowers were trying to assert their positions. Finally, the UAR accepted a compromise in the UN General Assembly, whereby President Nasser undertook to respect Lebanese sovereignty in return for a US withdrawal (see Chapter 3).

The Nasser–Shihab summit of 26 March 1958 laid the basis for a new relationship between the two countries. The Lebanese government promised to adopt a foreign policy compatible with Egyptian policy objectives in the Arab arena in particular. As a result, Lebanon enjoyed a period of internal stability due to the acquiescence of pro-UAR Lebanese groups (see Chapter 4).

After the break-up of the UAR, Shihab adhered to his previous understanding with Nasser – despite the absence of Egyptian power on the Lebanese borders. The Lebanese government resisted political and economic pressure from Syria, Iraq, Jordan and Saudi Arabia to join the anti-Nasser crusade. President Hilu followed the same policy after 1964, despite the occasional strain in relations concerning collective Arab projects. Furthermore, Lebanese governments handed Nasser a considerable political advantage by opposing Saudi policies in relation to the Islamic Pact, in spite of Saudi economic pressure (see Chapter 5).

Lebanon's non-participation in the June war of 1967 did not have a damaging effect on relations with the Egyptian government. The Lebanese government supported the aims of Egyptian foreign policy concerning UN and US peace initiatives. The Cairo Accord of 1969 represented an Egyptian will to mediate between the Lebanese government and Palestinian guerrillas at a minimum cost to Nasser's prestige (see Chapter 6).

While Syrian influence was growing in Lebanon during the civil war, Egyptian predominance diminished under the screen of humanitarian help under the banner of the Arab League. The Camp David Accords led to the break up of diplomatic and political ties. In 1983, Cairo's attempt to persuade Lebanon to sign a peace treaty with Israel was aborted by Syria and its Lebanese allies. Since 1990, bilateral ties were repaired and grew steadily especially during Rafiq Hariri's premiership of 1992–98. However, economic relations are the main source of discord in spite of all the 'final' agreements and goodwill statements (see Chapter 7).

In sum, Lebanese–Egyptian relations were marked by the following factors. First, Lebanon was forced to accept the leading role of Egypt in the Arab system between 1958 and 1970. Secondly, the appeasement of Lebanese Muslims, who lent their loyalty to President Nasser, was considered vital to Lebanese

internal stability after 1958. Egypt, in turn, assisted them symboli-
cally through education (e.g. the founding of the Arab University
in Beirut). Thirdly, the Lebanese regime acquired necessary Arab
credentials by paying lip service to Nasser's leadership, while
avoiding co-operating with or antagonizing Israel. Fourthly,
economic relations were on the whole in favour of Egypt, as
Egypt persisted in exporting more to Lebanon than it imported.
But Lebanese governments declined to use this issue against
Egypt since this would have caused Lebanon political losses
greater than possible economic gains. Fifthly, Egypt, as leader of
the Arab system, was useful to Lebanon: it paralysed Syrian
traditional ambitions to dominate Lebanon, though these reap-
peared in the form of Syrian military intervention in 1976.[1] Finally,
Egyptian strategy since 1990 was concentrated on preserving
economic advantage in the balance of trade. Despite many 'final
agreements' and the political will to involve the private sector in
both countries to rectify the situation, the gap is still very wide.

Notes

Introduction

[1] Bahgat Korany, 'Foreign Policy Models and their Empirical Relevance in Third World Actors: A Critique and Alternative', *International Social Science Journal*, No. 26, 1974, pp 70–94.

[2] Bahgat Korany and Ali E. Hillal Dessouki, *The Foreign Policies of Arab States* (Washington: Westview Press, 1991), p 11.

[3] *Ibid*. The authors note more shared characteristics in the Arab system, especially the effects of the creation of Israel on Arab states in the east in particular.

[4] Robert W. Macdonald, *The League of Arab States: A Study in the Dynamics of Regional Organisation* (New Jersey: Princeton University Press, 1965), pp 33–9. The participating delegations were from Lebanon, Egypt, Iraq, Syria and Jordan; observers from Saudi Arabia, Yemen, Libya, Morocco and Palestine were also present.

[5] Bassim al-Jisr, *Le Pacte Nationale Libanais*, Ph.D. thesis, University of Paris, 1978, pp 140–9.

[6] William Haddad, *Le Liban Entre la Politique de Neutralité et la Politique Arabe*, Ph.D. thesis, University of Paris, 1967, p 126.

[7] *Rose al-Yussuf*, Cairo, 4 February 1952. The cover of this magazine depicts Churchill and Eisenhower acting as cowboys trying to push Arab states, represented as cows, into the North Atlantic ranch. It is significant that Lebanon was portrayed in the forefront of the cattle, while Egypt was depicted as the last member willing to join.

[8] Paul Noble, 'The Arab System: Pressures, Constraints and Opportunities' in Dessouki and Korany, *The Foreign Policies of Arab States*, pp 60–1.

[9] *Ibid.*, pp 61–5. See also Adeed Dawisha, *Egypt in the Arab World: The Elements of Foreign Policy* (London: Macmillan, 1976), pp 159–80. Dawisha explains the political instruments used by the Egyptian regime in detail.

Chapter 1

[1] US/NARA, IR-SM. Dr Stephen Penrose, 'Comment on the Soviet Challenge in the Near East', Princeton, 2 June 1951, pp 1–3.

[2] US/NARA, IR-SM, 9 December 1952, pp 1–28.

[3] PRO, FO371/98241-E1023/7, 10 July 1952.

[4] *Foreign Relations of the United States, 1952–4*, Vol ix, Part 1 (Washington: US Government Printing Office), 1986, pp 525–8.

180   THE STRUGGLE FOR LEBANON

5 PRO, FO371/115473-V10338/7, 20 December 1955.

6 *CIA Reports*, Reel 1, 1951, pp 141–4.

7 *al-Hayat*, Beirut, 21 April 1954. A press conference given by the then prime minister of Egypt, Colonel Nasser.

8 PRO, FO371/104197-E1072/8, 24 December 1953. A senior British diplomat in London, P.S. Fella, objected to a suggestion made by the British ambassador to Baghdad to support the Iraqi prime minister, Fadhil al-Jamali, in his Arab unity projects. This was justified on the grounds that 'it remains our (private) view that the realization of Iraqi–Jordan union or some wider scheme would be detrimental to our interests'. Therefore Mr Fella recommended to 'adhere to declarations made in 1941 and 1943, which supported an Arab League, and not to do anything else'.

9 Muhammad H. Haikal, *Malaffat al-Suways* [The Suez Files] (Cairo: al-Ahram Publishing Co., 1986), pp 318–20. Haikal gives an account of a meeting he witnessed between Nasser and Iraq's prime minister, Nuri al-Sa'id, in which each leader tried in vain to convince the other of his views. While Nuri advocated joining the Turco-Pakistani Pact and gaining arms from the West to defend the region against the Soviet Union, Nasser identified Israel as the enemy and favoured Arab collective security based on the Arab League's Charter.

10 Dawisha, *Egypt in the Arab World: The Elements of Foreign Policy*, pp 11–12.

11 *Ibid.*, pp 12–13.

12 *al-Hayat*, Beirut, 18 and 19 September 1952.

13 US/NARA/C-WDC, Lebanon, 1952–4.

14 *al-Hayat*, Beirut, 7 January and 4 February 1953.

15 *Foreign Relations of the United States, 1952–4*, pp 1104–5.

16 PRO, FO371/98536-EL1052/3, 30 September 1952. The British ambassador to Beirut, Chapman-Andrews, said that Sham'un told him that 'so long as he was president ... the Lebanon would be completely at the disposal of Her Majesty's Government in the event of world war'. This, he added, would apply 'whether we have a written agreement or not'. Despite the fact that Sham'un wanted to rely on Great Britain for obtaining weapons on favourable terms, the British ambassador discouraged him from antagonizing the French (Britain's ally) as they perceived Lebanon as their special zone.

17 PRO, FO371/110958-VL1017/7, 25 October 1954.

18 US/NARA/C-WDC, Department of State, 8 October 1954.

19 PRO, FO371/110846-V2191/4, 26 October 1954. The British ambassador to Beirut, Chapman Andrews, wrote to Sir Anthony Eden that 'it's worth recording that this embassy maintains the closest liaison with the head of the [Lebanese] security police on measures against communism'.

20 PRO, FO371/121423-V1691/1, 9 January 1956.

21 PRO, FO371/98539-EL1071/1, 19 March 1952.

22 *La Bourse Egyptienne*, Cairo, 19 July, 9 and 19 August 1952. See also PRO, FO371/98524-EL1013/1, 9 January 1953.

23 *al-Hayat*, Beirut, 26 and 27 September, 5 October 1952.

24 PRO, FO371/104490-L1022/2, 31 March 1953.

25 *al-Ahram*, Cairo, 28 April 1953.

26 *Foreign Relations of the United States, 1952–4*, p 65.

27 *La Bourse Egyptienne*, Cairo, 21 October 1954.

[28] US/NARA, IR-SM, 25 February 1954.

[29] *al-Hayat*, Beirut, 30 March, 13–16 May 1954.

[30] PRO, FO371/110959-VL1022/3, 14 June 1954.

[31] *al-Hayat*, Beirut, 30 May 1954.

[32] Haikal, *Malaffat al-Suways*, pp 315–6. See also *al-Hayat*, Beirut, 3 and 4 July 1954.

[33] US/NARA, IR-SM, 8 October 1954.

[34] *al-Hayat*, Beirut, 28 November, 12 and 22 December 1954.

[35] *Summary of World Broadcasts* (Caversham: British Broadcasting Corporation), No. 536, 21 January 1955, p 44.

[36] *al-Hayat*, Beirut, 3 and 4 February 1955.

[37] *Summary of World Broadcasts*, No. 543, 15 February 1955, p 32.

[38] *al-Hayat*, Beirut, 15 and 17 February 1955. Visits by Iraqi and Pakistani officials to Lebanon took place in order to explore Lebanon's position on the pact.

[39] *Foreign Relations of the United States, 1955–57*, Vol xiii (Washington: US Government Printing Office, 1988), pp 170–3.

[40] *Summary of World Broadcasts*, No. 552, 18 March 1955, p 49.

[41] *al-Hayat*, Beirut, 3 and 9 April, 13 and 14 May 1955.

[42] PRO, FO371/115727-VL10316/2, 5 September 1955.

[43] PRO, FO371/115726-VL1022/1, 10 October 1955.

[44] *Foreign Relations of the United States, 1955–57*, p 178. British Foreign Secretary, Harold Macmillan, wanted to discuss with his US counterpart, Dulles, the need to offer Lebanon economic and military aid because 'the Lebanese president [was] under strong pressure [to] join [the] Syrian–Egyptian pact'. Macmillan also says that 'If one country which had refused to accept Egyptian policies received our backing, that would set [the] trend in [the] right direction'.

[45] PRO, FO371/115727-VL10316/4, 8 December 1955. A report on a seven-day visit by the Egyptian Minister of State, Anwar Sadat, to Lebanon. Sadat was quoted as saying that 'Egypt was prepared to supply the Lebanon and all the Arab states with arms'.

[46] *al-Ahram*, Cairo, 3 July 1956.

[47] PRO, FO371/110958-VL1017/7, 25 October 1955.

[48] Ahmad Hamrush, *Abdel-Nasser wal-'Arab* [Nasser and the Arabs], Vol 3 (Beirut: al-Mu'assasa al-'Arabia li-Dirasat wal-Nashr, 1976), pp 21–2.

[49] *al-Hayat*, Beirut, 22 February 1955.

[50] *al-Hayat*, Beirut, 23 February 1955.

[51] *al-Ahram*, Cairo, 28 February 1955.

[52] *al-Hayat*, Beirut, 2 April 1955.

[53] *al-Hayat*, Beirut, 5 October 1955. Franjieh's speech was made during a parliamentary session to vote on a new government headed by Rashid Karami. This session was attended by the Egyptian Minister for Endowments, Sheikh Ahmad Hassan al-Baquri, and the Egyptian ambassador to Beirut, General Abdul Hamid Ghalib.

[54] PRO, FO371/115727-VL 10316/4, 8 December 1955.

[55] PRO, FO371/121609-VL10316/3, 11 July 1956. See also *al-Hayat*, Beirut, 30 March 1956. A row erupted between outgoing Premier, Rashid Karami, and his successor, 'Abdallah al-Yafi, over Arab policies and pacts.

[56] Ahmad Hamrush, *Shuhud Thawrat Yulyu* [The July Revolution's Witnesses] (Beirut: al-Mu'assasa al-'Arabia lil-Dirasat wal-Nashr, 1977), p 48.

[57] PRO, FO371/115727-VL10316/4, 8 December 1955.

[58] *Rose al-Yussuf*, Cairo, No. 1439–1445, January and February 1956. The Lebanese ambassador to Cairo, Khalil Taqieddine, reacted angrily to a barrage of questions by saying 'I do not like to be perceived as the accused … we do not need to be lectured about nationalism' (No. 1445).

[59] PRO, FO371/104197-E1072/6, 9 December 1953. *Al-Hayat*'s owner and editor, Kamil Mroueh, forewarned a British diplomat about his intention of launching a press campaign to promote political unity between Iraq and Jordan, for which he had Iraqi support.

[60] US/NARA, IR-SM, 18 May 1954. A report on the political activities of the publisher of the *al-Misri* newspaper, Ahmed Abu al-Fatih, who used Beirut as his base following his court prosecution in Cairo for his anti-regime views.

[61] PRO, FO371/104487-EL1013/4, 7 April 1953.

[62] *Summary of World Broadcasts*, No. 541, 8 February 1955, p 22.

[63] *al-Hayat*, Beirut, 30 July 1953.

[64] PRO, FO371/108349-JE1022/26, 23 November 1954. A report on Major Salah Salim's statement to Lebanese newspaper *al-Jarida*, which was conducted by Bassim al-Jisr. See also *Rose al-Yussuf*, Cairo, No. 1391, 7 February 1955, p 10: an essay written by Lebanese journalist, Wafiq al-'Alayli, owner of *Kul-Shay'* newspaper, on the Baghdad Pact.

[65] *al-Hayat*, Beirut, 23 June 1955. Five Lebanese newspapers were sued in front of the military court for launching staunch attacks against the Turkish president, Jalal Bayar, during his official visit to Lebanon. These papers were: *al-Sharq, Nida' al-Watan, al-Akhbar* (communist), *ila-al-Amam* (communist) and *al-Ahad*. In other words, none of these publications could have been considered as pro-Egyptian. In fact, they are classified as communist or pro-Saudi newspapers since both the Soviet Union and Saudi Arabia had opposed the Turco-Iraqi Pact.

[66] *al-Taqrir al-Iqtisadi al-'Arabi* (Beirut: The Union of Arab Chambers of Commerce, June 1962), pp 7, 12 and 32.

[67] *al-Hayat*, Beirut, 13 and 25 August, 8 September, 17 and 22 October 1953.

[68] *al-Taqrir al-Iqtisadi al-'Arabi*, p 29.

Chapter 2

[1] PRO, FO371/121230-V10345/5, 1 December 1956. See also Dwight D. Eisenhower, *The White House Years: Waging Peace 1956–1961* (London: Heinemann, 1966), pp 88–99.

[2] PRO, FO371/127758-V1076, 3 May 1957.

[3] Dawisha, *Egypt in the Arab World: The Elements of Foreign Policy*, pp 15–16. See also Haikal, *Malaffat al-Suways*. The author uses Nasser's notes and his own dialogue with him to explain Egyptian strategic thinking on the effects of the nationalization of the Suez Canal Company.

[4] PRO, FO371/127758-V1076, 3 May 1957. Dulles was quoted as saying that communism succeeded in converting one or two regimes in the Middle East, and he

was optimistic about isolating Egypt and Syria – King Saʿud had met the Crown Prince of Iraq in Washington in order to co-ordinate their efforts in this respect.

5 US Joint Chiefs of Staff/1957/CCS 381/EMMEA(11-19-47). A message to commanders about the situation in Jordan, the US interest in maintaining King Hussein in power, and an alert to the Sixth Fleet to intervene if necessary.

6 Dawisha, *Egypt in the Arab World: The Elements of Foreign Policy*, pp 18–19.

7 PRO, FO371/121607-VL1016/17A, 7 September 1956.

8 *al-Hayat*, Beirut, 17 and 27 November 1956.

9 *al-Hayat*, Beirut, 29 March, 3 April and 16 July 1957.

10 PRO, FO371/121609-VL10316/3, 11 July 1956.

11 *al-Hayat*, Beirut, 28 July 1956.

12 *al-Hayat*, Beirut, 7 August 1956.

13 *al-Hayat*, Beirut, 10, 12 and 14 August 1956.

14 PRO, FO371/121607-VL1016/17G, 5 September 1956. A letter from the British Foreign Secretary to President Shamʿun asking him 'to use his influence with Colonel Nasser to counsel restraint and to urge on him the wisdom of accepting proposals, which will satisfy the legitimate concern of the users of the Suez Canal as expressed at the London conference, while at the same time fully maintaining Egypt's rights'. See also VL1016/17A, 7 September 1956: a reply from the British ambassador in Beirut, George Middleton, in which he states that Shamʿun is sending a message to Nasser 'by hand of Saʿeb Salam urging him that Egypt should observe all moderation and seek agreement with the Western powers'.

15 *al-Hayat*, Beirut, 22 August 1956.

16 PRO, FO371/121607-VL1017, 4 September 1956. The British ambassador to Beirut said that the head of the Lebanese Security Service, Emir Farid Shihab, suggested some ideas to stiffen President Shamʿun's stance.

17 *al-Hayat*, Beirut, 2, 11, 13 and 22 September 1956.

18 *al-Hayat*, Beirut, 31 October, 3 November 1956.

19 *Foreign Relations of the United States, 1955–57*, Vol xiii, p 193.

20 *al-Hayat*, Beirut, 17 November 1956, 24 April, 11 May 1957.

21 *Foreign Relations of the United States, 1955–57*, p 194. The American Embassy in Beirut had characterized the formation of Sami al-Sulh's government in December 1956 as a pronounced defeat for Syria and for Nasser. The inclusion of Charles Malik as foreign minister and of other pro-Western political figures made it prone to 'possible subversive action by Syria and by Egypt'.

22 PRO, FO371/121609-VL10316/7, 21 November 1956.

23 *al-Hayat*, Beirut, 11 and 12 December 1956.

24 *Foreign Relations of the United States, 1955–57*, pp 196–7. Shamʿun was quoted as telling the US ambassador in Beirut, Donald Heath, that he supported the Eisenhower plan of 5 January 1957 'one hundred per cent'.

25 *al-Ahram*, Cairo, 9 January 1957.

26 *al-Hayat*, Beirut, 13 and 16 January 1957.

27 PRO, FO371/128014-VL10389/2, 24 January 1957.

28 PRO, FO371/127724/2, 14 January 1957.

29 *Foreign Relations of the United States, 1955–57*, pp 200–3.

[30] *Ibid.*, pp 210–11.

[31] *New York Herald Tribune*, 21 May 1957.

[32] *Summary of World Broadcasts*, No. 217, 8 April 1957, pp 4–5.

[33] *Summary of World Broadcasts*, No. 223, 15 April 1957, pp 6–7.

[34] *al- Hayat*, Beirut, 24 April 1957. See also *The Times*, London, 11 July 1957.

[35] *Summary of World Broadcasts*, No. 262, 3 June 1957, pp 10–12.

[36] *Summary of World Broadcasts*, No. 279, 24 June 1957, p 12.

[37] *al-Hayat*, Beirut, 17 and 30 July 1957. Lebanese Minister of Finance, Nasri al-Ma'luf, met Nasser while attending an Egyptian economic fair in Cairo.

[38] *al-Hayat*, Beirut, 18 July 1957.

[39] *al-Hayat*, Beirut, 30 and 31 July, 1 and 2 August 1957.

[40] *al-Hayat*, Beirut, 4 and 7 September 1957.

[41] *al-Hayat*, Beirut, 15 and 16 October 1957.

[42] *al-Hayat*, Beirut, 25 December 1957.

[43] PRO, FO371/121609-VL10316/4, 30 July 1956. See also *al-Hayat*, Beirut, 28 July 1956. Telegrams sent to Nasser from the conference of parties, committees and national personalities headed by Hussein 'Uwayni and the chairman of al-Maqasid Islamic Society.

[44] Mustafa Mahmud al-Hakim, *'Abd al-Nasser: Qadaya wa Mawaqif* [Nasser: Issues and Policies] (Beirut: Sawt al-'Uruba Publications, 1971). This book was written just after Nasser's death. 'Adnan al-Hakim wrote the introduction in which he presents his relationship with Nasser since he met him for the first time in Cairo on 16 August 1956. In return, he obtained material benefits to boost his popularity among the Sunni sub-proletariat in Beirut. See also Najla Wadih Atiyah, *The Attitude of the Lebanese Sunnis Towards the State of Lebanon*, Ph.D. thesis, University of London, 1973, pp 2, 296 and 320. Since 1920 the Sunni community always looked outside Lebanon's borders to affiliate itself with any Arab leader raising the unity banner. Hence, this community leapt to Nasser's support after the nationalization of the Suez Canal Company at a time when internal political rifts started to appear.

[45] *al-Hayat*, Beirut, 16 and 17 August 1956. The participants in Egypt Day included the Progressive Socialist Party, the Najjadah Party, al-Hay'a al-Watanya, the Arab Club and the Muslim Youth.

[46] PRO, FO371/121607-VL1016/16, 20 August 1956.

[47] *al-Hayat*, Beirut, 31 October, 2 and 4 November 1956.

[48] *al-Hayat*, Beirut, 3 November 1956. The all-party national conference which was called by Sham'un to debate the situation was split on two levels. The mainly Muslim side requested offering some support to Egypt such as banning all dealings with British and French ships which sought to obtain supplies from Lebanese ports, and the severing of relations with France and Britain. The mainly Christian side wanted to refrain from any real actions as it had enjoyed good relations with the West in general and France in particular.

[49] *al-Hayat*, Beirut, 18, 22 and 27 November 1956.

[50] *al-Hayat*, Beirut, 22 November 1956.

[51] *Ibid.*, See also *al-Hayat*, Beirut, 27 November 1956.

[52] *al-Hayat*, Beirut, 28 November 1956, 13 and 25 January 1957.

53 *al-Mussawar*, Cairo, No. 1684, 19 January 1957, pp 22–3. This magazine published an interview with Salam in which he refrained from spelling out the real reasons for his dispute with Sham'un for the sake of 'Arab unity's general interests'.

54 *Summary of World Broadcasts*, No. 182, 26 February 1957, pp 3–4.

55 *The Egyptian Gazette*, Cairo, 25 April 1957.

56 Interview with Dr Boutros Boutros-Ghali, Minister of State for Foreign Affairs, Cairo, 15 April 1989.

57 *al-Mussawar*, Cairo, No. 1685, 26 January 1957, p 40. See also No. 1700, 10 May 1957, pp 30–1.

58 *Summary of World Broadcasts*, No. 174, 16 February 1957, pp 4–5.

59 *Foreign Relations of the United States, 1955–57*, pp 201 and 209. Lebanon's foreign minister, Charles Malik, was obsessive in talking about Syrian–Egyptian and communist plots in front of US officials.

60 *Ibid.*, p 112. CIA boss, Allen Dulles, told the National Security Council on 11 April 1957 that 'news from the Lebanon is very encouraging, with the Egyptians apparently giving up hope of exercising much influence over the forthcoming Lebanese elections'.

61 *al-Hayat*, Beirut, 24 July 1957.

62 *al-Hayat*, Beirut, 17 July 1957. A Lebanese diplomatic source expresses his wonder over the Egyptian media publicizing Nasser's meeting with Hamid Franjieh, a Lebanese opposition figure, while ignoring completely Nasser's meeting with Lebanon's Minister of Economy, Nasri al-Ma'luf.

63 *Rose al-Yussuf*, Cairo, No. 1512, 3 June 1957, p 3. The editor-in-chief, Ihsan Abdel Quddus, charged that 'colonial publications' produced in Beirut by the Baghdad Pact propaganda agencies were reproducing Egyptian material after distorting the contents. Moreover, he specifically accused the American Embassy of reprinting his magazine, *Rose al-Yussuf*, and adding the anti-Islamic opinion of Soviet orientalists. The aim was to embarrass Nasser and charge him with being allied with communism.

64 PRO, FO371/121609-VL10316/6, 28 July 1956. A survey of 14 Lebanese newspapers revealed that all headlines were full of praise for Nasser, with reservations in a few newspapers, such as the pro-French *Le Jour*, on the legality of his action.

65 Atiyah, *The Attitude of the Lebanese Sunnis Towards the State of Lebanon*, pp 257–62. Two Sunni Muslim newspapers were described as expressing the wishes of the community in hailing Nasser, *Beirut* of 'Abdallah al-Mashnuq and *al-Siyassa* of 'Abdallah al-Yafi.

66 PRO, FO371/121609-VL10316/13, 24 November 1956. See also VL10316/15, 28 December 1956. The *al-Nahar* newspaper attacked the Egyptian destruction of the statue of Ferdinand de Lesseps, Suez Canal mastermind.

67 PRO, FO371/128034-VL1671/11, 23 March 1957. An article by journalist Bassim al-Jisi, published in *al Jarida*, praised Nasser's leadership and popularity among Middle Eastern peoples and asked the USA to take account of this when dealing with Middle Eastern affairs. See also VL1671/12. An editorial in *al-'Amal* said that Egypt's reliance on the Soviet Union had brought destruction to its people, while Iraq's reliance on the West had brought with it progress.

[68] *al-Hawadiss*, Beirut, No. 623, 18 October 1968, pp 4–5. An article commemorating the launch of the magazine through its 12 years of journalism.

[69] *Rose al-Yussuf*, Cairo, No. 1503, 11 April 1957, p 12. A report describes *al-Ahad* as being a struggler against the Baghdad Pact and foreign oil companies, refusing to receive any gifts from either side. It was claimed that this magazine had banned the advertising of French and British products since the attack on Suez – leaving no option but to rely on its readership as the sole basis for finance!

[70] *Rose al-Yussuf*, Cairo, No. 1498, 25 February 1957, p 10. An article written by Sa'id Frayha in which he asks Arab journalists to differentiate between the Lebanese people and their government.

[71] *al-Hayat*, Beirut, 28 June 1956, 26 May 1957. See also *Summary of World Broadcasts*, ME/W0218-A1/2, 18 February 1992. The Lebanese Foreign Minister, Salim Lahud, and the Egyptian ambassador, General Ghalib, signed the new agreement in Beirut on 27 June 1956.

[72] *al-Hayat*, Beirut, 13 and 18 July 1957.

[73] *al-Hayat*, Beirut, 25 July 1956.

[74] *al-Hayat*, Beirut, 20, 25 and 29 August 1956.

[75] *al-Hayat*, Beirut, 1 and 21 September, 1956.

[76] *al-Hayat*, Beirut, 28 April 1957.

[77] *al-Hayat*, Beirut, 21 September 1957.

[78] *al-Taqrir al-Iqtisadi al-'Arabi*, p 17.

Chapter 3

[1] A.S. Agwani, *The Lebanese Crisis, 1958. A Documentary Study* (Bombay: Asia Publishing House, 1965), p 103.

[2] Paul E. Zinner (ed), *Documents on American Foreign Relations 1958* (New York: Harper and Brothers, 1959), pp 296–300.

[3] PRO, FO371/131348-JE1072/1, May 1958.

[4] Zinner, *Documents on American Foreign Relations 1958*, pp 304–6.

[5] PRO, FO371/133795-V10338/10, 17 July 1958.

[6] PRO, FO371/133837-V1092/81, 3 November 1958.

[7] *al-Mussawar*, Cairo, No. 1740, 14 February 1958, pp 14–15.

[8] P.G. Vatikiotis, 'Dilemmas of Political Leadership in the Arab Middle East: The case of the UAR', *International Affairs* (London: Royal Institute of International Affairs), Vol 37, April 1961, p 197.

[9] *The Economist*, London, 1 March 1958, pp 770–1.

[10] PRO, FO371/134137-VL1022/5, 19 April 1958. The British ambassador to Baghdad mentions that the Iraqi foreign minister, Fadhil al-Jamali, made a request, but he thought that it was 'quite unrealistic'.

[11] PRO, FO371/134148-VL1041/4(D) and 7(B), 3 and 4 July 1958.

[12] Eisenhower, *The White House Years: Waging Peace 1956–1961*, p 270.

[13] PRO, FO371/133798-10349/4 and V10344/4G, 15 July 1958.

[14] Muhammad H. Haikal, *Sanawat al-Ghalayan* [The Years of Fury] (Cairo: al-Ahram Centre, 1988), p 343.

[15] *Ibid.*, pp 339–72.

[16] Fahim Qubain, *Crisis in Lebanon* (Washington: The Middle East Institute, 1961), p 28.

[17] Michael Hudson, *The Precarious Republic* (Washington: Westview Press, 1958), p 116. See also Walid Faris, *al-Ta'adudiah fi Lubnan* [Pluralism in Lebanon] (al-Kaslik, 1979), pp 261–4. Faris focuses exclusively on the religious and sectarian nature of the conflict. This was seen as a continuation of Muslim expansion as well as harassment of Christians in Mount Lebanon since the 'Abbasid's rule in the seventh century.

[18] Robert Murphy, *Diplomat Among Warriors* (London: Collins, 1964), pp 492– 6.

[19] Leila Meo, *Lebanon, Improbable Nation* (Connecticut: Greenwood Press, 1976), pp 182–5.

[20] *al-Ahram*, Cairo, 29 December 1957.

[21] *al-Ahram*, Cairo, 23 and 24 January 1958.

[22] *al-Hayat*, Beirut, 1 January 1958.

[23] PRO, FO371/133854-V1193/9, 8 January 1958.

[24] PRO, FO371/133791-V1022/1, 14 January 1958.

[25] *al-Mussawar*, Cairo, No. 1740, 14 February 1958, pp 6–7. An editorial by Fikri Abaza, editor-in-chief, calls on Lebanon, and all Arab states, to join the new entity immediately.

[26] *Ibid.*, p 18. See also *al-Hayat*, Beirut, 5, 7 and 12 February 1958.

[27] *New York Times*, New York, 11 February 1958.

[28] *al-Hayat*, Beirut, 7 February 1958. See also *al-Mussawar*, Cairo, No. 1740, 14 February 1958, p 18.

[29] *al-Hayat*, Beirut, 12 February 1958.

[30] *al-Hayat*, Beirut, 28 February 1958.

[31] *al-Hayat*, Beirut, 15 April 1958.

[32] *Summary of World Broadcasts*, Part ix, 27 March 1958, pp 9–10.

[33] *al-Hayat*, Beirut, 25 February, 11, 20 and 22 March 1958. There were reports of scuffles in Muslim cities between pro-Nasser demonstrators and Lebanese police over the removal of Nasser's and Sham'un's portraits from public places.

[34] *al-Ahram*, Cairo, 29 March 1958.

[35] *Dawn*, Damascus, 18 April 1958.

[36] *Ibid.*

[37] *al-Hayat*, Beirut, 6 April 1958.

[38] *Summary of World Broadcasts*, No. 524, 15 April 1958, p 4.

[39] *al-Hayat*, Beirut, 18 and 27 April 1958. Also an interview with Lebanese writer Munah al-Sulh, Oxford, 22 September 1989. Al-Sulh attributed the failure of 'Ussayran's mission to Nasser's reliance on Egyptian intelligence reports which branded 'Ussayran as an 'agent of Sham'un'.

[40] *al-Hayat*, Beirut, 9 May 1958.

[41] *Summary of World Broadcasts*, Part iv, 15 May 1958, pp 11–12.

[42] *al-Ahram*, Cairo, 15 May 1958.

[43] *al-Ahram*, Cairo, 16 May 1958. See also *al-Hayat*, Beirut, 17 May 1958.

[44] *al-Hayat*, Beirut, 15 May 1958.

[45] *Summary of World Broadcasts*, Part iv, 19 May 1958, pp 10–13.

[46] *Nasser's Speeches and Press Interviews, 1958* (Cairo: Information Department), pp 196–9.

[47] *al-Ahram*, Cairo, 22 May 1958.

[48] *al-Hayat*, Beirut, 22 and 27 May 1958.

[49] *al-Hayat*, Beirut, 28 July 1958. See also Tawfig Y. Hasou, *The Struggle for the Arab World, Egypt's Nasser and the Arab League* (London: KPI, 1985), p 93. Hasou analysed Nasser's endeavours to dominate the Arab League in the 1950s and 1960s. The author lists several examples to indicate Egyptian dominance in the League's hierarchy symbolized by the constant occupation of the post of Secretary General by an Egyptian national. In addition, the location of the League's headquarters in Cairo enshrined Egyptian hegemony over the League and its resolutions.

[50] *al-Hayat*, Beirut, 27 May 1958.

[51] *Current Intelligence Weekly Review* (Washington: Naval Historical Centre, CIA), 5 June 1958.

[52] *Rose al-Yussuf*, Cairo, No. 1565, 9 June 1958, pp 4, 5 and 36.

[53] *al-Ahram*, Cairo, 5 June 1958. See also Hasou, *The Struggle for the Arab World*, pp 94–5. The author says that the Sudanese foreign minister, Muhammad Ahmad Mahjub, a close ally of Egypt, collaborated with the Secretary General of the League in submitting this draft and claiming that it was accepted by the member states – except for the UAR and Lebanon.

[54] *al-Hayat*, Beirut, 6 and 7 June 1958.

[55] *Rose al-Yussuf*, Cairo, No. 1566, 16 June 1958, pp 8–9. An interview with Dr Murad Ghalib, head of President Nasser's political office.

[56] *al-Hayat*, Beirut, 22 and 23 May 1958. Lebanon's foreign minister, Charles Malik, tried to calm fears that this move might invite external military intervention by submitting 'a written undertaking' which stated that the Lebanese government would oppose any political or military intervention by foreign powers.

[57] Zinner, *Documents on American Foreign Relations 1958*, pp 298–9.

[58] *al-Hayat*, Beirut, 7 and 8 June 1958.

[59] Agwani, *The Lebanese Crisis 1958*, pp 122–47.

[60] *Ibid.*, pp 147–59.

[61] *Ibid.*

[62] *Ibid.*, pp 181–8 and 192–4.

[63] *Ibid.*, pp 188–92.

[64] *al-Hayat*, Beirut, 11 and 12 June 1958.

[65] *al-Hayat*, Beirut, 19, 22 and 26 June 1958.

[66] *al-Hayat*, Beirut, 29 and 30 June 1958. Charles Malik said 'some world politicians [i.e. the UN Secretary General] have allowed themselves to be paralysed and misguided by the troubled situation in Lebanon. But we are completely sure that they will wake up soon and will be able to see the real situation as it unfolds.'

[67] Agwani, *The Lebanese Crisis 1958*, pp 115–17.

[68] *al-Hayat*, Beirut, 6 July 1958. The head of the observation group, Senior Galo Plaza, said in Beirut that 'the arms that were seen [in the hands of the Lebanese opposition] consisted mostly of a varied assortment of rifles of British, French,

and Italian makes. Some hand-grenades were also seen at various places. Occasionally, opposition elements have been found armed with machine-guns.... It has not been possible to establish where these arms were acquired; ... nor was it possible to establish if any of the armed men observed had infiltrated from outside [i.e. the UAR]; there is little doubt, however, that the vast majority were in any case Lebanese.'

69 Agwani, *The Lebanese Crisis 1958*, pp 215–16.

70 PRO, FO371/134149-VL1042/1, 4 July 1958. The expellees were: Hanafi Muhammadien, Muhieddin Khafaja, Anwar al-Jamal (press counsellor and director of the Embassy Information Bureau), Muhammad Safieddin Fahmi, 'Abdel Aziz Hammam, 'Izzedin Hussayni and Fu'ad Qadri.

71 *al-Ahram*, Cairo, 5 July 1958.

72 PRO, FO371/134149-VL1042/2 and 2(a), 7 July 1958.

73 PRO, FO371/134149-VL 1042/2(b), 11 July 1958.

74 Hamdi al-Tahiri, *Siyasat al-Hukm fi Lubnan* [Politics in Lebanon] (Cairo: al-'Alamya Press, 1976), pp 372–3.

75 Agwani, *The Lebanese Crisis 1958*, pp 234–8.

76 *Rose al-Yussuf*, Cairo, No. 1569, 7 July 1958, pp 3–4. Kamal Rif'at, deputy minister for presidential affairs in the UAR, perceived the mere existence of Western troops in Lebanon a direct threat to the independence of the UAR. This, he claimed, would warrant the dispatch of the UAR army to Lebanon for the sake of self defence.

77 *Summary of World Broadcasts*, No. 604, 18 July 1958, p 1.

78 Agwani, *The Lebanese Crisis 1958*, pp 263–3.

79 *Summary of World Broadcasts*, No. 604, 18 July 1958, p 1.

80 Mahmud Riad, *Mudhakkirat Mahmud Riad* [The Memoirs of Mahmud Riad], Vol ii (Cairo: Dar al-Mustaqbal al-'Arabi, 1986), pp 190–1. See also Haikal, *Sanawat al-Ghalayan*, pp 325–8. Haikal agrees with Riad's account but adds that the date of the Nasser–Hare agreement was as early as 20 May 1958.

81 Agwani, *The Lebanese Crisis 1958*, pp 378–84.

82 *al-Hayat*, Beirut, 21 August 1958. See also Hasou, *The Struggle for the Arab World*, pp 101–7.

83 Agwani, *The Lebanese Crisis 1958*, pp 371–2. General Assembly Resolution 1237 (ES-III).

84 Muhammad H. Haikal, *'Abd an-Nasser wal 'Alam* [Nasser and the World] (Beirut: Dar al-Hilal, 1972), p 233.

85 *al-Ahram*, Cairo, 6 September 1958.

86 *al-Hayat*, Beirut, 18 September 1958.

87 *al-Ahram*, Cairo, 6 October 1958.

88 *The Egyptian Mail*, Cairo, 11 October 1958.

89 *al-Ahram*, Cairo, 1 November 1958.

90 *al-Hayat*, Beirut, 9 October 1958.

91 *Al-Ahram*, Cairo, 13 November 1958.

92 Agwani, *The Lebanese Crisis 1958*, pp 391–2.

93 *Ibid.*, p 393.

[94] PRO, FO371/133799-V10345/23, 11 December 1958.

[95] Desmond Stewart, *Orphan with a Hoop: The Life of Emile Bustani* (London: Chapman and Hall, 1967), p 165. The book is a biography of Emile Bustani, a Lebanese Christian politician. The author presents Bustani as an Arab nationalist who worked towards establishing better understanding with the West.

[96] *al-Hayat*, Beirut, 6 February 1958. It was estimated that 6000 cables of congratulations were sent to President Nasser. Although some of them came from political leaders across the board, it is noteworthy that the majority came from Sunni Muslim leaders, personalities and popular organizations.

[97] *Summary of World Broadcasts*, Part iv, 1 March 1958, p 1.

[98] *Nasser's Speeches and Press Interviews, 1958*, p 33. Nasser gave similar speeches to Lebanese delegations on 27 February (p 43) and three speeches on 2 March 1958 (pp 51–7).

[99] *al-Hayat*, Beirut, 25 February, 22 March, 11 and 18 April 1958.

[100] Michael Johnson, *Class and Client in Beirut: The Sunni Muslim Community and the Lebanese State 1840–1985* (London: Ithaca Press, 1986), pp 123–8.

[101] PRO, FO371/134183-VL1741/1, 20 February 1958. See also *al-Hayat*, Beirut, 7 February 1958.

[102] Johnson, *Class and Client in Beirut*, p 125.

[103] Interview with Amin Huwaidi, ex-head of Egyptian Intelligence, Cairo, 4 April 1989.

[104] *Summary of World Broadcasts*, Part iv, 19 May 1958, pp 15–16.

[105] PRO, FO371/133855-V1193/58, 29 May 1958.

[106] Salah Nasr, *'Abd al-Nasser wa Tajribat al-Wahdah* [Nasser and the Experience of the UAR] (Beirut: al-Watan al-'Arabi Publications, 1976), pp 158–9.

[107] Nawaf Salam, *L'Insurrection de 1958 au Liban* [The Insurgence of 1958 in Lebanon], Ph.D. thesis, Sorbonne University, Paris, 1979, Vol 4, pp 95–104.

[108] *Ibid.*, Vol 3, pp 697–8. See also *al-Mussawar*, Cairo, No. 1771, 19 September 1958, p 13.

[109] *The Economist*, London, 27 September 1958, pp 1032.

[110] al-Tahiri, *Siyasat al-Hukum fi Lubnan*, pp 380–1. The author, who served as a diplomat in the Egyptian Embassy in Beirut in the mid-1960s, claims that his book's publication was delayed several years due to 'sensible advice' given by Egyptian authorities, for fear of upsetting the Lebanese government or some other Lebanese figures. The book is descriptive of Lebanese politics with a bias against the right-wing Christian parties, and sympathetic towards Muslim grievances.

[111] *al-Ahram*, Cairo, 12 and 27 December 1958. See also *al-Mussawar*, Cairo, No. 1785, 26 December 1958, p 30.

[112] *al-Mussawar*, Cairo, No. 1740, 14 February 1958, pp 18–19. Maronite Patriarch, Bulus Ma'ushi, was bestowed with the title 'Patriarch of Arab nationalism'.

[113] *Rose al-Yussuf*, Cairo, No. 1565, 9 June 1958, pp 3–4. This magazine reported that the correspondent of Reuters news agency was a member in the Lebanese delegation. This was an implicit accusation of the Lebanese government's subservience to 'British imperialism'. Also, sarcasm was employed in noting that Bashir al-A'war, the head of Lebanon's delegation in the Arab League meeting in

Benghazi, was one-eyed, by playing on his family name which conveys the same meaning.
[114] *Summary of World Broadcasts*, No. 603, 17 July 1958, p 2.
[115] *al-Mussawar*, Cairo, No. 1765, 8 August 1958, pp 9–11. See also No. 1772, 26 September 1958, pp 12–15.
[116] Agwani, *The Lebanese Crisis 1958*, pp 48–9.
[117] Salam, *L'Insurrection de 1958 au Liban*, Vol 2, p 208. Salam enumerates all pro-Nasser publications during 1957–8, as follows: *al-Hawadiss, al-Sha'b, al-Sahafa, al-Hurriya, al-Anba', Sawt al-'Uruba, al-Sharq, al-Siyassa, Beirut al-Massa, al-Kifah* and the publications of *Dar al-Sayyad*.
[118] Interview with Lebanese journalist Sulaiman al-Firzili, London, 6 March 1991. Also an interview with Lebanese journalist Salim Nassar, who edited at some stage *al-Safa'* daily and *al-Hawadiss*, London, 13 March 1991.
[119] Interview with Anwar al-Jamal, Cairo, 1 April 1989.
[120] PRO, FO371/133888-V1742/2, 7 September 1958.
[121] PRO, FO371/142232-VL1121/1, 10 March 1959.
[122] *al-Hayat*, Beirut, 28 February 1958.
[123] *al-Hayat*, Beirut, 9 November 1958.
[124] *al-Hayat*, Beirut, 20 December 1958.
[125] *al-Hayat*, Beirut, 21 November 1958.
[126] *al-Ahram*, Cairo, 27 December 1958.

Chapter 4

[1] PRO, FO371/141836/V1071/43, 14 October 1959.
[2] PRO, FO371/141841-V1074/1, 4 February 1959.
[3] *Ibid.*
[4] PRO, F0371/141841/V1074/5, 29 April 1959.
[5] PRO, FO371/141836/V1071/43, 14 October 1959.
[6] Eisenhower, *The White House Years: Waging Peace 1956–1961*, pp 288–9.
[7] Malcolm Kerr, *The Arab Cold War: 1958–1964*, Chatham House Series (London: Oxford University Press, 1965), p 7.
[8] PRO, FO371/141835-V1071/2, 21 January 1959.
[9] Haikal, *Sanawat al-Ghalayan*, p 417. Haikal narrated the story of the Nasser–Qassim dispute from an Egyptian perspective, describing Qassim as 'half mad' and suspicious of any ideas of union or federation with the UAR. Thus, he imprisoned pro-UAR elements and attempted to suppress the pan-Arab movement with the help of the communists. This led the UAR to attack him as well as the Soviet leaders who rushed to strengthen Qassim as a possible substitute for Nasser as leader of the Arabs.
[10] PRO, FO371/150857-V1051/16, 1 October 1960.
[11] Faris, *al-Ta'adudiah fi Lubnan*, pp 266–7. Faris represented the views of the phalangist Christians who criticized Shihab for failing to give a special identity to Lebanon.

[12] Interview with Munah al-Sulh, Lebanese political essayist, London, 31 October 1990.

[13] PRO, FO371/151140-VL1015/13, 12 May 1960.

[14] PRO, FO371/151141-VL1015/22, 21 June 1960.

[15] Interview with Raymond Eddy, Paris, 10 July 1990.

[16] PRO, FO371/142217-VL10316/2, 30 March 1959. See also *al-Ahram*, Cairo, 30 March 1959.

[17] Interviews with Lebanese journalists Sulaiman al-Firzili and Salim Nassar, 6 and 13 March, 1991.

[18] Interview with Mahmud Riad, Nasser's adviser and foreign minister during the 1950s and 1960s, Cairo, 13 April 1989.

[19] *Dawn*, Damascus, 14 February 1959.

[20] PRO, FO371/142214-VL1022/1, 16 February 1959.

[21] *al-Hayat*, Beirut, 29 March 1959.

[22] PRO, FO371/141838-V1073/11, 22 April 1959.

[23] *Ibid.*

[24] *Ibid.*

[25] *al-Hayat*, Beirut, 16 and 23 January 1960.

[26] *Ibid.*

[27] *al-Hayat*, Beirut, 9 and 13 February 1960.

[28] PRO, FO371/150856-V1051/4, 16 March 1960.

[29] Arnon Medzini, *The River Jordan: The Struggle for Frontiers and Water: 1920–1967*, Ph.D. thesis, SOAS, London University, 1997, p 124.

[30] *al-Hayat*, Beirut, 30 June 1958.

[31] *al-Hayat*, Beirut, 10 August 1960.

[32] *al-Hayat*, Beirut, 25 and 30 August 1960.

[33] *al-Hayat*, Beirut, 1 and 11 September 1960.

[34] PRO, FO371/150857-V1051/16, 1 October 1960. A report from the British ambassador to the UN on the visits of Harold Macmillan to President Nasser and King Hussein in New York.

[35] *al-Hayat*, Beirut, 9 November 1960.

[36] *Christian Science Monitor*, New York, 6 December 1960.

[37] *al-Hayat*, Beirut, 26 November 1960.

[38] *Ibid.*

[39] PRO, FO371/151144-VL10316/6(c), 9 December 1960.

[40] *al-Ahram*, Cairo, 9 December 1960.

[41] *al-Hayat*, Beirut, 20 May 1959.

[42] *al-Hayat*, Beirut, 8 October 1959, 4 March 1960.

[43] Eisenhower, *The White House Years: Waging Peace 1956–1961*, p 286.

[44] *al-Hayat*, Beirut, 9 November 1960.

[45] *Ibid.*

[46] PRO, FO371/157580-EL103116/3, 11 March 1961. See also *al-Hayat*, Beirut, 24 February 1961.

[47] *al-Ahram*, Cairo, 25 and 27 February 1961.

[48] *Ibid.*, See also Haikal, *Sanawat al-Ghalayan*, pp 505–9.

49 *al-Ahram*, Cairo, 1 March 1961. See also *La Bourse Egyptienne*, Cairo, 13 March 1961.

50 *The Times*, London, 15 March 1961.

51 Hamdi al-Tahiri, *Syasat al-Hukum fi Lubnan* [Politics of Lebanon] (Cairo: al-Ahram Press, 1976), pp 500–1.

52 Interview with Bassim al-Jisr, Paris, 24 July 1990.

53 Interview with Hamdi al-Tahiri, Cairo, 20 April 1989.

54 Interview with Anwar al-Jamal, former Egyptian press attaché to Beirut 1957–78, Cairo, 1 April 1989.

55 Mustafa al-Hakim, *'Abdul Nasser* (Beirut: Sawt al-'Uruba Publications, 1971), pp 16–18.

56 *al-Ahram*, 1 June 1961. See also *al-Mussawar*, Cairo, No. 1823, 18 September 1959, pp 20–1. UAR agents were implicated in the killing of an 'Iraqi spy' at Beirut airport.

57 PRO, FO371/142221-VL10393/1, 17 February 1959. A press report stated that pro-Nasser elements attacked a delegation of Iraqi students in a Beirut school for showing their loyalty to Qassim by shouting 'no leader but one – he is Karim'. See also *al-Mussawar*, Cairo, No. 1825, 2 October 1959, pp 20–1. The magazine reported Lebanese demonstrators marching towards the Iraqi Embassy in Beirut to protest against the execution by Qassim of a pan-Arab Iraqi leader, Rif'at al-Haj Sirri.

58 *Daily Telegraph*, London, 14 January 1959.

59 *al-Hayat*, Beirut, 18 March 1959. A statement by Lebanese MP Ma'ruf Sa'ad.

60 *al-Hayat*, Beirut, 22 February 1959, 23 February 1960. See also *al-Ahram*, Cairo, 1 March 1961.

61 *al-Hayat*, Beirut, 18 January 1959.

62 *al-Ahram*, Cairo, 13 April 1959.

63 Interview with Raymond Eddy, leader of the National Bloc, Paris, 19 July 1990.

64 *al-Ahram*, Cairo, 24 and 25 February 1961.

65 PRO, FO 371-141843-V1076/4, 30 May 1959. See also *al-Hayat*, Beirut, 28 May 1959.

66 PRO, FO371-141833-V1053/1, 29 January 1959.

67 PRO, FO371/141833-V1053/6(a), 18 June 1959.

68 PRO, FO371/141833-V1053/7, 23 June 1959.

69 *Dawn*, Damascus, 13 May 1961. See also *The Sudan Daily*, Khartoum, 17 September 1961.

70 PRO, FO371/141843-V1076. Summary of daily newspapers in Beirut for 1959.

71 PRO, FO371/141899-VG1026/1. A weekly report on Syrian affairs was compiled in the British Embassy in Beirut during 1959.

72 PRO, FO371/142259-VL1672/1, 20 June 1959. A report from the British ambassador to Beirut on inaccuracies in stories published in London newspapers emanating from Beirut, such as the exile of the Crown Prince of Jordan.

73 PRO, FO371/150857-V1051/16, 1 October 1960.

[74] *al-Ahram*, Cairo, 28 March 1959.

[75] *al-Mussawar*, Cairo, No. 1810, 19 June 1959, p 35; No. 1824, 25 September 1959, pp 34–5.

[76] PRO, FO371/151142-VL1015/3, 9 August 1960.

[77] *Ibid.* See also *al-Hayat*, Beirut, 7 and 9 August 1960.

[78] *al-Mussawar*, Cairo, No. 1786, 3 January 1959, pp 24–5.

[79] *al-Mussawar*, Cairo, No. 1794, 27 February 1959, pp 14–15. See also Nos. 1791, 1793, 1803 and 1811 (1959) on interviews with Lebanese poet Michael Na'imah, former president Bishara al-Khuri, poet Elias Farhat, and a report on the Maronite patriarch's visit to Europe.

[80] *al-Mussawar*, Cairo, No. 1793, 20 February 1959, pp 30–1. See also PRO, FO371/141906-VG1022/12, 17 June 1959. A report on UAR propaganda in Brazil.

[81] *al-Ahram*, Cairo, 24, 25 and 27 February 1961.

[82] *La Bourse Egyptienne*, Cairo, 12 March 1961.

[83] *Rose al-Yussuf*, Cairo, 20 March 1961. See also PRO, FO371/157595. A file contains correspondence between the British Embassy in Beirut and the Foreign Office, concerning press attacks on MECAS.

[84] *Guardian*, Manchester, 23 March 1961.

[85] Interview with UAR press attaché to Beirut 1957–78, Anwar al-Jamal, Cairo, 1 April 1989.

[86] Interview with Lebanese journalist Salim Nassar, London, 13 March 1991.

[87] Interview with UAR press attaché to Beirut 1957–78, Anwar al-Jamal, Cairo, 1 April 1989.

[88] *al-Hayat*, Beirut, 7 June 1959. See also *al-Mussawar*, Cairo, No. 1809, 12 June 1959, pp 10–11.

[89] PRO, FO371/142221-VL10393/2, 17 June 1959.

[90] PRO, FO371/141898-VG1015/2, 10 January 1959.

[91] PRO, FO371/142215-VL1023/1, 19 March 1959. See also PRO, FO371/142060-VG1681/2, 21 March 1959.

[92] PRO, FO371/150869-V1075/13, 3 March 1960. A report on Lebanese reactions to an Arab League meeting held in Cairo, which included an analysis of Beirut newspapers which supported the UAR: *Beirut al-Massa, al-Syassah* and *Sawt al-'Uruba*.

[93] PRO, FO371/150870-V175/25, 11 April 1960.

[94] *al-Taqrir al-Iqtisadi al-'Arabi*, pp 8, 13 and 32.

[95] *al-Hayat*, Beirut, 4 January 1959.

[96] *al-Ahram*, Cairo, 27 December 1958.

[97] PRO, FO371/142235-VL11316/1, 24 January 1959. See also *al-Hayat*, Beirut, 18 January 1959.

[98] PRO, FO371/142235-VL11316/2, 7 February 1959.

[99] *La Bourse Egyptienne*, Cairo, 3 March and 23 April 1959.

[100] *al-Hayat*, Beirut, 18 March 1959. See also PRO, FO371/142232-VL1121/1, 14 April 1959.

[101] *al-Hayat*, Beirut, 25 and 26 March 1959, 1 June 1960.

102 *Le Commerce du Levant–Beyrouth Express*, 23 December 1961. See also *al-Hayat*, Beirut, 5 March and 26 November 1960.

103 *al-Taqrir al-Iqtisadi al-'Arabi*, pp 12–13.

104 PRO, FO371/142235-VL11316/5, 30 May 1959. See also *Financial Times*, London, 4 June 1959.

105 *al-Ahram*, Cairo, 25 June 1959, 26 May 1960.

106 *Le Commerce du Levant–Beyrouth Express*, Beirut, 23 December 1961. The following is a list of the size and value of some important Egyptian exports to Lebanon in 1960: potatoes, L£1. 531 million; rice, L£3.6 million; cotton, L£1 million.

107 PRO, FO371/142235-VL11316/1, 2 and 3. Reports on Lebanese–UAR commercial relations on 24 January, 7 and 21 February 1959. See also *al-Hayat*, Beirut, June 4, 1959.

108 *Financial Times*, London, 11 June 1959.

109 PRO, FO371/141899-VG1016/25, 12 June 1959.

110 PRO, FO371/141899-VG1016/27, 27 June 1959.

111 *al-Hayat*, Beirut, 5 July 1959.

112 PRO, FO371/142217-VL10316/4(a), 22 August 1959.

113 PRO, FO371/141899-VG1016/38, 10 October 1959. See also *Dawn*, Damascus, 10 October 1959.

114 PRO, FO371/141899-VG1016/45, 27 November 1959.

115 PRO, FO371/141850-V1123/1, 12 December 1959.

116 *al-Hayat*, Beirut, 5 March and 1 July 1960.

117 Khalid al-'Azm, *Mudhakkarat Khalid al-'Azm* [The Memoirs of Khalid al-'Azm] (Beirut: al-Dar al-Muttahidah lil-Nashr, 1973), Vol iii, p 350.

118 *al-Hayat*, Beirut, 30 May 1959. See also *Financial Times*, London, 11 June 1959.

119 *al-Hayat*, Beirut, 13 June 1959.

120 *al-Hayat*, Beirut, 27 June 1959.

121 *al-Hayat*, Beirut, 5 July 1959.

122 *al-Hayat*, Beirut, 1 and 6 July 1960.

Chapter 5

1 William B. Quandt, 'United States Policy in the Middle East: Constraints and Choices', in Paul Y. Hammond and Sidney S. Alexander (eds), *Political Dynamics in the Middle East* (New York: American Elsevier Publishing Co. 1972), p 513.

2 CIA Report, Reel 1, 25 February 1964, 'Storm warnings up for US–Arab relations', p 2.

3 Haikal, *Sanawat al-Ghalayan*, pp 675–82. Haikal narrates, in his flamboyant style, the events surrounding the fall of Qassim.

4 Quandt, 'United States Policy in the Middle East. Constraints and Choices', p 518

5 Kerr, *The Arab Cold War*, p 26.

6 *Ibid.*, pp 48–92. Kerr gives details of the encounters between Nasser and Iraqi and Syrian officials in which Nasser retained the moral high ground. See also Haikal, *Sanawat al-Ghalayan*, pp 675–99.

[7] Ali Abdel Rahman Rahmy, *The Egyptian Policy in the Arab World: Intervention in Yemen 1962–1967: Case Study* (University Press of America, 1983). The author accounts for the whole episode of Egyptian intervention in North Yemen.

[8] Adeed Dawisha, *Egypt's Foreign Policy* (London: Macmillan, 1976), p 43.

[9] CIA Report, Reel 2, 'Nasser's Arab Policy – The Latest Phase', 28 August 1964, p 10.

[10] *al-Hayat*, Beirut, 28 September 1966, 7 January 1967.

[11] Hrair Dekemejian, *Patterns of Political Leadership* (New York: State University of New York Press, 1975), pp 54–5.

[12] *Daily Telegraph*, London, 8 January 1962. See also Antun Sa'adah, *al-'Athar al-Kamilah*, Vol ii (Beirut: SSNP Publications, 1974), pp 39–42. Sa'adah's essays in the early 1940s were full of contempt for Egyptian designs for Greater Syria under a vague notion of Arabism. While his party sought to oppose Egyptian policies since Mustaha al-Nahha's government, he claimed that the Hashimite dynasty in Amman and Baghdad were forced by popular pressure to work on an agenda similar to his. Thus, Iraq's Fertile Crescent project meant co-opting Greater Syria into a scheme with Baghdad to ward off Egyptian hegemony.

[13] Bassim al-Jisr, *Le Pacte Nationale Libanais*, p 172.

[14] *al-Mustaqbal*, Paris, No. 623, 28 January 1989, p 30. A report by Nabil Khalifa entitled 'Syria and Lebanon from Faisal Ibn al-Hussein to Hafiz al-Assad'.

[15] *al-Ahram*, Cairo, 4 October 1961.

[16] *al-Hayat*, Beirut, 7 November 1961.

[17] *al-Hayat*, Beirut, 16 November 1961.

[18] *al-Hayat*, Beirut, 17 May 1962.

[19] Haikal, *Sanawat al-Ghalayan*, pp 596–7.

[20] *La Bourse Egyptiene*, Cairo, 6 January 1962.

[21] *Daily Telegraph*, London, 8 January 1962.

[22] *al-Hayat*, Beirut, 7 February 1962.

[23] *Dawn*, Damascus, 11 August 1962

[24] *La Bourse Egyptienne*, Cairo, 15 August 1962.

[25] *al-Hayat*, Beirut, 11, 20, 23 and 24 May 1962.

[26] *The Economist*, London, Vol 204, 28 July 1962, p 337. It was reported that the basis for Syrian suspicions of Egyptian activities was that 'when, as on two recent occasions, Syria's currency suddenly shoots up on the Beirut market, the Syrian authorities take it for granted that Cairo is paying its agents'.

[27] al-'Azm, *Mudhakkirat*, Vol 3, p 353.

[28] *Ibid.*

[29] *Ibid.*, pp 412–13.

[30] Interview with Anwar al-Jamal, Egyptian press attaché to Beirut 1957–78, Cairo, 1 April 1989.

[31] al-'Azm, *Mudhakkirat*, pp 415–16.

[32] Interview with Anwar al-Jamal, Egyptian press attaché to Beirut 1957–78, Cairo, 1 April 1989.

[33] al-'Azm, *Mudhakkirat*, pp 416–17. See also *The Economist*, London, Vol 204, 1 September 1962, p 761.

[34] *al-Ahram*, Cairo, 9 September 1962.

[35] *al-Ahram*, Cairo, 11 March 1963.

[36] *al-Hayat*, Beirut, 30 January 1963.

[37] al-'Azm, *Mudhakkirat*, pp 357–9.

[38] *al-Hayat*, Beirut, 30 January 1963. See also *Dawn*, Damascus, 2 May 1963.

[39] *al-Hayat*, Beirut, 7 January 1964. Pro-Sham'un MP, Habib al-Mutran, said that Lebanon should be represented in Cairo by the government and the opposition, but not the president, on the grounds that Shihab was not accountable. This manoeuvre helped to avoid subjecting Lebanon to embarrassment by other Arab countries, since Beirut was not capable of performing what was required.

[40] Charles Hilu, *Mudhakkirati: 1964–65* [My Memoirs] ('Araya, Lebanon: al-Matba'a al-Catholikia, 1984), p 46. See also *al-Hayat*, Beirut, 17 January 1964.

[41] *al-Hayat*, Beirut, 17 January 1964.

[42] CIA Report, Reel 2, 'Nasser's Arab Policy: The Latest Phase', 28 August 1964, p 5.

[43] *Financial Times*, 23 February 1966.

[44] Hilu, *Mudhakkirati*, pp 194–5.

[45] *al-Hayat*, Beirut, 27 August 1964.

[46] Hilu, *Mudhakkirati*, p 46.

[47] Haikal, *Sanawat al-Ghalayan*, pp 670–1.

[48] Hilu, *Mudhakkirati*, pp 54–5.

[49] *The Economist*, Vol 212, 12 September 1964, p 1004.

[50] Hilu, *Mudhakkirati*, pp 56–7.

[51] *The Economist*, Vol 212, 12 September 1964, p 1004.

[52] Hilu, *Mudhakkirati*, p 65.

[53] *Ibid.*

[54] *Ibid.*, pp 65–6.

[55] *al-Ahram*, September 25, 1964.

[56] *al-Hayat*, Beirut, 8–11 September 1964.

[57] *al-Hayat*, Beirut, 9 January 1965.

[58] *al-Hayat*, Beirut, 10 January 1965.

[59] *al-Hayat*, Beirut, 13 and 23 January 1965. The Lebanese delegation was headed by Prime Minister Hussein 'Uwayni, and included Foreign Minister Philip Taqla, and the Chief of Staff, Brigadier Joseph Shumayt.

[60] *al-Hayat*, Beirut, 16 January 1965.

[61] *al-Hayat*, Beirut, 22 January 1965.

[62] Hilu, *Mudhakkirati*, p 95.

[63] *al-Hayat*, Beirut, 17 January 1965.

[64] Hilu, *Mudhakkirati*, p 98. See also *al-Hayat*, 28 April 1965.

[65] *Ibid.*, pp 99–100. Hilu narrates, in a journalistic and somewhat sarcastic manner, how the Egyptian regime manipulated the 'masses' by welcoming foreign guests of the state in a very grand and public show. This was, in fact, an attempt to accrue prestige, internally and externally.

[66] *al-Hayat*, Beirut, 4 May 1965.

[67] Hilu, *Mudhakkirati*, pp 101–2.

[68] *Ibid.*, pp 102–3. See also *al-Hayat*, Beirut, 4 May 1965.

69 *al-Hayat*, Beirut, 17 September 1965.

70 Hilu, *Mudhakkirati*, pp 193–4.

71 Arnon Medzini, *The River Jordan: The Struggle for Frontiers and Water 1920–1967*, pp 136–51. The author gives a useful account of the whole issue of water in the context of Arab–Israeli conflict, but discounts the theory that the 1967 war was motivated by Israel's quest for water resources to cater for new immigrants.

72 *The Egyptian Gazette*, Cairo, 7 April 1966.

73 *al-Hayat*, Beirut, 21 January 1966.

74 *The Egyptian Gazette*, Cairo, 4 August 1966.

75 *al-Hayat*, Beirut, 9 September 1966.

76 *al-Hayat*, Beirut, 19 October 1966.

77 *Daily Telegraph*, London, 19 October 1966.

78 *al-Ahram*, Cairo, 23 October 1966.

79 *The Egyptian Gazette*, Cairo, 15 January 1967.

80 *al-Hayat*, Beirut, 21 January and 22 February 1967.

81 *al-Hayat*, Beirut, 2 March 1967.

82 *al-Hayat*, Beirut, 23 February, 29 March and 30 April 1967.

83 Hilu, *Mudhakkirati*, p 35.

84 *al-Hayat*, Beirut, 6 October 1961.

85 PRO, FO371/157579-EL1022/4, 25 November 1961.

86 PRO, FO371/157582-EL103200/1, 24 October 1961.

87 al-'Azm, *Mudhakkirat*, p 361.

88 *al-Hayat*, Beirut, 10 February 1963.

89 *al-Hayat*, Beirut, 12 March 1965.

90 *al-Hayat*, Beirut, 14 and 16 March, 14 May 1965.

91 *al-Hayat*, Beirut, 22 March 1965. See also Michael Johnson, *Class and Client in Beirut* (London: Ithaca Press, 1986), p 150.

92 *al-Hayat*, Beirut, 1, 22 and 30 March 1965.

93 *al-Hayat*, Beirut, 5 May 1965. See also Mustafa al-Hakim, *'Abdul-Nasser* (Beirut: Sawt al-'Uruba Publications, 1971), p 21.

94 Haikal, *Sanawat al-Ghalayan*, p 147.

95 *al-Hayat*, Beirut, 9 February 1966.

96 Interview with Lebanese journalist Salim Nassar, London, 13 March 1991. Nassar believes that Mruweh was killed because he was the only significant Muslim journalist who supported the Islamic Pact. Nassar also mentioned the names of some Christian journalists who propagated, paradoxically, the pact, such as Robert Abilla, Rushdi al-Ma'luf, Ilias al-Giriafi and Farid Abu-Shahla.

97 *al-Hawadiss*, Beirut, No. 593, 22 March 1968, p 5. See also Johnson, *Class and Client in Beirut*, p 84. Johnson argues that despite the acquittal of Qulailat, many people indicated that he masterminded the affair since he had been on the payroll of the Egyptian Embassy since 1958. Moreover, Qulailat had enjoyed political protection from some Lebanese political bosses who were backed in turn by the Lebanese intelligence service, the Deuxieme Bureau, namely the Mufti Hassan Khalid and 'Uthman al-Dana.

98 *The Egyptian Gazette*, 16 February 1967.

99 *The Egyptian Gazette*, 15 March 1967.

[100] *al-Ahram*, Cairo, 6 March 1967.

[101] *The Egyptian Gazette*, 6, 7, 12 and 17 March 1967. The Mufti's high profile visit to Cairo as the head of a delegation of religious scholars lasted more than two weeks, 3–18 March 1967. He met President Nasser and Prime Minister Sidqi Sulaiman and visited Port Said and the Gaza Strip at the invitation of the Egyptian government.

[102] *The Economist*, London, Vol 223, 15 April 1967, pp 241–2.

[103] al-'Azm, *Mudhakkirati*, pp 351–3 and 361.

[104] *al-Hawadiss*, Beirut, 11 May 1962.

[105] *al-Hayat*, Beirut, 27 and 30 June 1964.

[106] Interview with Raymond Eddy, Paris, 19 July 1990.

[107] *al-'Amal*, Beirut, 12 January 1965.

[108] *al-Hayat*, Beirut, 30 March 1965.

[109] *Dawn*, Damascus, 30 April 1965.

[110] Hilu, *Mudhakkirati*, pp 102–3. Hilu does not give many details over this episode, perhaps for fear of offending somebody. However, he claims that he communicated to Nasser, with diplomatic skill, the wisdom of avoiding visiting Lebanon because it would antagonize 'some people' and could lead to riots (among right-wing Christians).

[111] *al-Safa'*, Beirut, 6 May 1965.

[112] *al-Jumhuria*, Beirut, 7 May 1966.

[113] *al-Hayat*, Beirut, 15 May 1965.

[114] *al-Hayat*, Beirut, 29 March 1967.

[115] *The Economist*, London, Vol 223, 15 April 1967, p 242.

[116] Interview with Mahmud Riad, Egyptian foreign minister 1964–72, Cairo, 13 April 1989.

[117] *Ibid.*

[118] *al-Hayat*, Beirut, 9 and 10 October 1964.

[119] *al Taqrir al Iqtisadi al-'Arabi*, pp 300–1.

[120] *Ibid.*, pp 306–8. See also *al-Hayat*, Beirut, 5 and 15 May 1965.

[121] *La Bourse Egyptienne*, 12 June 1962.

[122] *Le Commerce du Levant–Beyrouth Express*, 14 December 1963.

[123] *al-Hayat*, Beirut, 25 December 1964.

[124] *al-Hayat*, Beirut, 25 December 1964, 6 May 1965.

[125] *al-Hayat*, Beirut, 5 May 1965.

[126] *al-Ahram*, Cairo, 1 January 1967.

[127] *The Egyptian Gazette*, 4 August 1969.

[128] Interview with Mahmud Riad, Cairo, 13 April 1989.

[129] Interview with Hamdi al-Tahiri, Cairo, 20 April 1989.

Chapter 6

[1] Oded Eran, 'Soviet Middle East Policy, 1967–1973', in Itamar Rabinovich and Haim Shaked (eds), *From June to October: The Middle East Between 1967 and 1973* (New

Jersey: Transactions Books, 1978), p 30. See also Karen Dawisha, *Soviet Foreign Policy Towards Egypt* (London: Macmillan Press, 1979), pp 42–3.

[2] Quandt, 'United States Policy in the Middle East: Constraints and Choices', pp 524–5. See also Mahmud Riad, *The Struggle for Peace in the Middle East* (London: Quartet Books, 1981), pp 68–9.

[3] Quandt, 'United States Policy in the Middle East: Constraints and Choices', p 526.

[4] Sir Anthony Nutting, *Nasser* (London: Constable and Company, 1972), pp 395–401. See also Kerr, *The Arab Cold War*, pp 126–8.

[5] Ali al-Din Hillal and Jamil Matar, *al-Nizam al-Iqlimi al-'Arabi* [The Arab Regional Order] (Cairo: Dar-al-Mustaqbal al-'Arabi, 1983), pp 80–5.

[6] Kerr, *The Arab Cold War*, p 129.

[7] *Ibid.*, pp 130–2.

[8] Dawisha, *Egypt in the Arab World: The Elements of Foreign Policy*, pp 54–9.

[9] *The Economist*, London, Vol 225 (ii), 7 October 1967, p 39.

[10] *al-Hayat*, Beirut, 29 December 1968. See also Wadi Goria, *Sovereignty and Leadership in Lebanon 1943–76* (London: Ithaca Press, 1985), pp 95–104.

[11] *The Economist*, London, Vol 231, 3 May 1969, pp 35–6.

[12] *al-Hayat*, Beirut, 18 May 1967.

[13] *al-Hayat*, Beirut, 25 May 1967.

[14] *al-Hayat*, Beirut, 28 May 1967.

[15] *al-Hayat*, Beirut, 3 June 1967.

[16] *Summary of World Broadcasts*, ME/A7, 7 June 1967.

[17] Bassim al-Jisr, *Le Pacte Nationale Libanais*, p 175.

[18] *al-Hayat*, Beirut, 10 June 1967.

[19] *al-Hayat*, Beirut, 11 June 1967.

[20] Riad, *The Struggle for Peace in the Middle East*, p 56.

[21] *al-Hayat*, Beirut, 7 and 8 September 1967.

[22] *al-Mussawar*, Cairo, No. 2247, 3 November 1967, p 27. A press interview with Lebanese prime minister, Rashid Karami.

[23] *al-Ahram*, Cairo, 3 January 1969.

[24] Riad, *The Struggle for Peace in the Middle East*, pp 95–6.

[25] *al-Hayat*, Beirut, 8 May 1969.

[26] *al-Hawadiss*, Beirut, No. 658, 20 June 1969, p 4.

[27] *al-Hawadiss*, Beirut, No. 653, 16 May 1969, pp 3–4.

[28] *al-Hayat*, Beirut, 12 April 1969.

[29] *al-Hayat*, Beirut, 8 May 1969.

[30] *al-Hawadiss*, Beirut, No. 653, 16 May 1969, p 4.

[31] *al-Hayat*, Beirut, 10 and 11 May 1969.

[32] *al-Hayat*, Beirut, 24 May 1969.

[33] *al-Hawadiss*, Beirut, No. 658, 20 June 1969, pp 4–5.

[34] *The Economist*, Vol 232, 2 August 1969, p 3.

[35] *al-Hawadiss*, Beirut, No. 669, 5 September 1969, p 3.

[36] *al-Ahram*, Cairo, 23 October 1969.

[37] *al-Hayat*, Beirut, 24 October 1969.

[38] *al-Ahram*, Cairo, 26 and 29 October 1969.

39 *The Economist*, Vol 233, 22 November 1969, p 37.
40 *al-Hawadiss*, Beirut, No. 678, 7 November 1969, pp 4–7.
41 *al-Hawadiss*, Beirut, No. 684, 19 December 1969, p 9.
42 *al-Hayat*, Beirut, 7 and 20 February, 24 May 1970.
43 *al-Hayat*, Beirut, 25 July, 4 August 1970.
44 *al-Hawadiss*, Beirut, No. 717, 7 August 1970, pp 6–7.
45 *al-Hayat*, Beirut, 2 June 1967.
46 *al-Hayat*, Beirut, 11 June 1967. Other leaders adopting similar positions included the Sunni Mufti, Sheikh Hassan Khalid; the Shi'a Mufti, Sheikh Hussein al-Husseyni; the Druze Mufti, Sheikh Muhammad Abu Shaqra; the Syriac Patriarch and the leader of the Najjadah Party, 'Adnan al-Hakim.
47 *Ibid.*
48 *The Economist*, Vol 231, 3 May 1969, p 35.
49 *al-Hayat*, Beirut, 11 May 1969. See also *al-Hawadiss*, Beirut, No. 658, 20 June 1969, p 4.
50 *al-Hayat*, Beirut, 25 July, 2 November 1969.
51 *al-Hayat*, Beirut, 8 November, 9 December 1969. See also *al-Mussawar*, Cairo, No. 2355, 28 November 1969, p 24.
52 *al-Hayat*, Beirut, 20 November 1969.
53 *al-Hawadiss*, Beirut, No. 678, 7 November 1969, pp 4–5, No. 679, 14 November 1969, pp 7 and 11.
54 *al-Hawadiss*, Beirut, No. 717, 7 August 1970, pp 6–7.
55 *al-Hayat*, Beirut, 9 November 1970. A commemoration rally was held in Beirut attended by Sa'ib Salam, Rashid Karami, Kamal Jumblatt and the Egyptian ambassador to Beirut.
56 *al-Hayat*, Beirut, 28 May 1967.
57 *al-Hayat*, Beirut, 5 July 1967. See also Faris, *al-Ta'adudiah fi Lubnan*, pp 274–6.
58 *al-Mussawar*, Cairo, No. 2269, 5 April 1968, pp 16–17.
59 *al-Ahram*, Cairo, 13 January 1969.
60 *al-Hayat*, Beirut, 16 February 1969.
61 *al-Hawadiss*, Beirut, No. 646, 28 March 1969, p 4.
62 *al-Hawadiss*, Beirut, No. 653, 16 May 1969, p 4.
63 *al-Hawadiss*, Beirut, No. 664, 1 August 1969, p 5.
64 Faris, *al-Ta'adudiah fi Lubnan*, pp 281–2. See also *al-Hawadiss*, Beirut, No. 678, 7 November 1969, pp 4–5, No. 679, 14 November 1969, p 9.
65 *al-Mussawar*, Cairo, No. 2362, 16 January 1970, pp 22–3.
66 *Rose al-Yussuf*, No. 2202, 24 August 1970, pp 2–3 and 49. See also al-*Mussawar*, Cairo, No. 2394, 28 August 1970, pp 7–8.
67 Dawisha, *Egypt and the Arab World*, pp 51–2.
68 *al-Mussawar*, Cairo, No. 2240, 15 September 1967, pp 2–3.
69 *al-Mussawar*, Cairo, No. 2241, 22 September 1967, pp 23–4.
70 *al-Mussawar*, Cairo, No. 2269, 5 April 1968, pp 16–17.
71 *al-Ahram*, Cairo, 13 January 1969.

[72] *al-Mussawar*, Cairo, No. 2312, 31 January 1969, pp 1–4. An interview with the moderate minister Sheikh Khalil al-Khuri and his wife, who expressed their loyalty to Lebanon and the Palestinian and Arab causes.

[73] *al-Mussawar*, Cairo, Nos. 2325 and 2326, 2 and 9 May 1969. See also *Rose al-Yussuf*, Cairo, Nos. 2134 and 2136, 5 and 19 May 1969. Interviews with right-wing leaders such as Pierre Jumayyil and Raymond Eddy, who expressed their views frankly, while ex-President Camille Sham'un was ignored completely.

[74] *Rose al-Yussuf*, Cairo, No. 2159, 27 October 1969, pp 3–7.

[75] *al-Mussawar*, Cairo, No. 2351, 31 October 1969, pp 16–17.

[76] *al-Mussawar*, Cairo, No. 2348, 10 October 1969, pp 32–3.

[77] *al-Mussawar*, Cairo, No. 2369, 6 March 1970, pp 18–19. See also *Rose al-Yussuf*, Cairo, No. 2191, 8 June 1970, pp 25–32.

[78] *The Times*, London, 7 October 1968.

[79] *al-Hayat*, Beirut, 9 July 1967.

[80] *al-Hawadiss*, Beirut, No. 581, 29 December 1967, pp 16–17.

[81] *al-Hayat*, Beirut, 1 March, 28 November 1968.

[82] *al-Hawadiss*, Beirut, No. 599, 3 May 1968, p 3.

[83] *al-Hayat*, Beirut, 29 September 1968.

[84] *al-Hawadiss*, Beirut, No. 612, 2 August 1968, p 7; No. 625, 1 November 1968, p 3; No. 630, 13 December 1968, p 14.

[85] Interview with Lebanese journalist Sulaiman al-Firzili, London, 6 March 1991.

[86] *al-Hawadiss*, Beirut, No. 716, 31 July 1970, p 12. See also Munah al-Sulh, *Misr wal-'Uruba* (Beirut: al-Mu'assassa al-'Arabia lil Dirasat wal Nashr, 1979), p 37.

[87] Interview with Lebanese journalist Salim Nassar, London, 13 March 1991. Nassar noted that the Egyptian press attaché in Beirut, Anwar al-Jamal, had few visitors after 1967, as a sign of a lack of financial prowess.

[88] *al-Hawadiss*, Beirut, No. 673, 3 October 1969.

[89] *al-Hayat*, Beirut, 9 and 14 October 1967.

[90] *al-Hayat*, Beirut, 24 February and 12 March 1968.

[91] *al-Ahram*, Cairo, 19 January 1970.

[92] *al-Taqrir al-Iqtisadi al-'Arabi* [The Arab Economic Report] (Beirut: Matba'at al-Bayan, January 1971), pp 564–7.

Chapter 7

[1] Anthony McDermott and Kjell Skjelsbaek, *The Multinational Force in Beirut 1982–1984* (Miami: Florida International University Press, 1991), pp 109–10.

[2] Alasdair Drysdale and Raymond Hinnebusch, *Syria and the Middle East Process* (New York: Council on Foreign Relations Press, 1991), pp 160–3 and 210–15.

[3] Naomi J. Weinberger, *Syrian Intervention in Lebanon: The 1975–1976 Civil War* (Oxford: Oxford University Press, 1986), pp 250–61.

[4] *Arab Palestinian Documents for 1971* (Beirut: The Institute for Palestine Studies, 1974), pp 247–8, 540–1 and 906–7.

[5] *Ibid.* Statement by the Lebanese Foreign Minister, Fuad Naffa', in parliament on 15 November 1973.

[6] *al-Mussawar*, Cairo, No. 2561, 9 November 1973, p 27.

7 *New York Times*, 20 September 1972.

8 *al-Ahram*, Cairo, 11 December 1972.

9 *New York Times*, 4 May 1973.

10 *New York Times*, 16 May 1974.

11 *New York Times*, 16 April 1975.

12 *New York Times*, 9, 15 and 16 October 1975.

13 *International Documents on Palestine for 1975* (Beirut: The Institute for Palestine Studies, 1977), pp 521–2.

14 *Ibid.*, 1976, pp 362–3.

15 *Ibid.*, pp 426–8.

16 *al-Mussawar*, Cairo, No. 2699, 2 July 1976, pp 21–3.

17 *al-Wasat*, London, No. 114, 4 April 1994.

18 *International Documents on Palestine for 1976* (Beirut: The Institute for Palestine Studies, 1978), pp 497–9.

19 *al- Wasat*, London, No. 114, 4 April 1994, pp 12–13.

20 *International Documents on Palestine for 1978* (Beirut: The Institute for Palestine Studies, 1980), pp 439–41.

21 *New York Times*, 28–9 March 1978.

22 *International Documents on Palestine for 1978*, pp 580–1 and 599–601.

23 *New York Times*, 31 March and 26 April 1979.

24 *The Middle East Journal*, Vol 38, No. 1, Winter 1984, p 88.

25 *New York Times*, Summer 1982–Spring 1983.

26 *Rose al-Yussuf*, Cairo, No. 2893, 21 November 1983, pp 8–9. The leader bore the headline 'What does Syria really want?', and was highly critical of Syrian policies.

27 *Arab News*, Jeddah, 8 May 1986.

28 *New York Times*, 11 November 1987. See also *Washington Post*, 13 May, 24 and 29 June 1989.

29 *al-Hayat*, London, 11 March and 27 April 1994. Statements by the Egyptian ambassador to Beirut, Sayyid abu Zaid Umar, on Lebanon and the peace process.

30 *As-Sharq al-Awsat*, London, 19 August 1994.

31 *al-Hayat*, London, 15, 16 and 18 March 1996.

32 *al-Hayat*, London, 22 April 1998. See also *al-Mussawar*, Cairo, No. 3838, 1 May 1998, pp 4–7. A lengthy interview with Premier Hariri conducted by the magazine's editor, Makram Muhammad Ahmad.

33 Weinberger, *Syrian Intervention in Lebanon*, pp 250–1.

34 *al-Mussawar*, Cairo, No. 2654, 22 August 1975, p 21.

35 *Rose al-Yussuf*, Cairo, No. 2841, 29 December 1975, pp 24–9.

36 *New York Times*, 12 September 1975.

37 *International Documents on Palestine for 1976*, pp 426–8.

38 *International Documents on Palestine for 1979* (Beirut: The Institute for Palestine Studies, 1981), pp 144–5.

39 *al-Hayat*, London, 5 March 1994.

40 *As-Sharq al-Awsat*, London, 3 May 1994.

[41] *As-Shiraa*, Beirut, 22 February 1997, pp 15–17.

[42] *al-Hayat*, London, 3, 4 and 5 July 1995.

[43] *al-Wasat*, London, No. 226, 27 May 1996. See also *as-Sharq al-Awsat*, London, 5 May 1996. Both publications ran favourable reports on the first visit by an Egyptian Speaker of Parliament to Beirut for 15 years. He offered the Egyptian people's sympathy to their Lebanese brethren in the aftermath of the Qana massacre committed by Israeli forces.

[44] *al-Hayat*, London, 12 April 1994. A statement by the Egyptian Chancellor of the Arab University of Beirut, Dr Muhammad Abdul Rahim.

[45] *al-Hayat*, London, 26 October 1998. A press interview with new Vice Chancellor Dr Fathy Ahu 'Ayanah.

[46] *al-Hayat*, London, 17 March 1996. See also *al-Wasat*, London, No. 133, 15 August 1994.

[47] *As-Sharq al-Awsat*, London, 26 August 1994.

[48] *al-Hayat*, London, 19 March 1996.

[49] *al-Mustaqilla*, London, 25 March 1996.

[50] *As-Sharq al-Awsat*, London, 11 and 21 March 1997.

[51] *As-Sharq al Awsat*, London, 21 March 1997.

[52] *al-Hayat*, London, 22 March 1997. See also *al-Wasat*, London, No. 95, 22 December 1993, p 46. In the 1993–4 season, Lebanon produced 500,000 tons of apples. While the local consumption reached 60,000 tons, it was necessary to export the rest. Due to the inability to compete with Turkish and US apples in the Arab Gulf markets, the Lebanese government sought, and obtained, a pledge from Cairo to import 20–30,000 tons of apples as part of a barter.

[53] *al-Hayat*, London, 9 August 1997.

[54] *al-Hayat*, London, 7 September 1998, 12 February 1999. See also *al-Afkar*, Beirut, 21 September 1998, pp 17–18.

Conclusion

[1] Interview with Raymond Eddy, a respected Maronite Christian leader and head of *al-Kutlah al-Watania* (the National Bloc), Paris, 19 July 1990. Eddy spelled out that Syria represented the real threat to Lebanese independence and sovereignty. Therefore any alliance Lebanon was able to make with Syria's Arab rivals was bound to check its ambitions. A case in point was the continuous tension in relations between Syria and Lebanon from 1961 until 1973, while Egypt enjoyed a balancing power in this respect.

Tables

Table 1a

Lebanese imports from Egypt 1951–55

	1951	1952	1953	1954	1955
Total trade*	320.77	347.05	361.68	484.40	527.32
Egypt	4.60	2.31	2.99	5.12	7.33
As % of total Lebanese imports	1.43	0.66	0.82	1.00	1.39

Table 1b

Lebanese exports to Egypt 1951-55

	1951	1952	1953	1954	1955
Total trade*	97.66	77.43	87.71	105.58	120.53
Egypt	9.42	7.08	5.96	8.76	6.83
As % of total Lebanese exports	9.64	9.14	6.79	8.29	5.66

* Includes gold bullion specie
Value in LL million
Source: United Nations, Yearbook of International Trade Statistics, 1955,
New York, 1956
Percentages calculated by the author

Table 2

Lebanese imports and exports with Egypt and Syria 1956–57

	IMPORTS		EXPORTS	
	1956	1957	1956	1957
Egypt	10.26	12.78	6.05	5.18
As % of total trade	1.82	2.00	4.14	3.40
Syria	111.08	92.16	16.25	18.23
As % of total trade	19.79	14.62	11.14	11.97
Total trade*	561.08	629.99	145.80	**152.23

* Includes gold bullion and specie
** Revised total in LL million: 152.18
Value in LL million
Source: United Nations, Yearbook of International Trade Statistics, 1958, New York, 1959
Percentages calculated by the author

Table 3

Lebanese imports and exports with the UAR 1958

	IMPORTS	EXPORTS
Egypt (UAR)	8.71	1.89
As % of total trade	1.68	1.71
Syria (UAR)	54.01	19.32
As % of total trade	10.42	17.48
Total trade*	518.34	110.50

* Includes gold bullion and specie
Value in LL million
Source: United Nations, Yearbook of International Trade Statistics, 1958, New York, 1959
Percentages calculated by the author

Table 4a

Lebanese imports from the UAR 1959–61

	1959	1960	1961
Egypt	12.07	32.15	51.68
As % of total			
Lebanese imports	1.72	3.76	4.86
Syria	62.76	52.57	43.50
As % of total			
Lebanese imports	8.96	6.15	4.0
Total trade	699.83	854.60	1 061.36

Table 4b

Lebanese exports to the UAR 1959–61

	1959	1960	1961
Egypt	2.21	1.67	2.19
As % of total			
Lebanese exports	1.58	0.76	0.55
Syria	20.66	18.60	20.78
As % of total			
Lebanese exports	14.58	8.53	5.23
Total trade	139.10	218.04	397.27

Value in LL million
Source: United Nations, Yearbook of International Trade Statistics, 1962, New York, 1964
All percentages calculated by the author

Table 5a

Lebanese imports from Egypt (UAR) 1962–66

	1962	1963	1964	1965	1966
UAR (Egypt)	9.55	12.32	13.63	20.12	14.18
As % of total Lebanese imports	0.90	1.23	1.14	1.12	0.72
Total trade	1,049.56	996.59	1,194.88	1,791.87	1,958.79

Table 5b

Lebanese exports to Egypt (UAR) 1962–66

	1962	1963	1964	1965	1966
UAR (Egypt)	2.98	2.01	3.25	3.44	4.04
As % of total Lebanese exports	1.55	1.00	1.50	1.00	1.10
Total trade	192.04	196.33	216.04	324.06	369.46

Value in LL million
Source: United Nations, Yearbook of International Trade Statistics, 1967, New York, 1969
Percentages calculated by the author

Table 6a

Lebanese imports from Egypt 1967–71

	1967	1968	1969	1970	1971
Egypt (UAR)	12.91	13.74	18.80	3490.00	4156.00
As % of total Lebanese imports	0.88	0.85	1.14	0.61	0.61
Total trade*	1,450.76	1,605.12	1,638.51	567,489.00	677,173.00

Table 6b

Lebanese exports to Egypt 1967-71

	1967	1968	1969	1970	1971
Egypt (UAR)	2.97	5.13	6.71	3983.00	7052.00
As % of total Lebanese exports	0.80	1.14	1.27	0.20	0.27
Total trade*	367.34	449.83	525.07	197,833.00	256,058.00

* Prior to 1967, includes gold bullion, specie and bank notes
Value 1967–69 in LL million, 1970–71 in US$ million
Source: United Nations, Yearbook of International Trade Statistics, 1969 and 1970-71, New York, 1971 and 1973
Percentages calculated by the author

Bibliography

Primary sources

Official documents and archives
CIA Reports, Reels 1 and 2, 1951–1967
Current Intelligence Weekly Review (Washington: Naval Historical Centre, CIA, 1957–1978)
Glennon, John P. (editor-in-chief), *Foreign Relations of the United States 1952–1957* (Washington: US Government Printing Office 1986 and 1988)
Kesaris, Paul (ed), *OSS/US State Department Intelligence and Research Reports: The Middle East 1950–1961* (Washington, 1979)
Nasser's Speeches and Press Interviews, 1957–1963 (Cairo: Information Department)
Public Record Office, London, FO371: 1952–1961
UN Yearbook of International Trade Statistics 1951–1971, Statistical Office of the United Nations (New York: Department of Economic and Social Affairs)
US/NARA, IR-SM, R-SM and C-WDC: US State Department Correspondence 1949–1954
Zinner, Paul E. (ed), *Documents on American Foreign Relations 1958* (New York: Harper and Brothers, 1959)

Unpublished theses
Atiyah, Najla Wadih, *The Attitude of the Lebanese Sunnis Towards the State of Lebanon*, Ph.D. thesis, University of London, 1973
Haddad, William, *Le Liban Entre la Politique de Neutralité et la Politique Arabe* [Lebanon between Neutrality and Arab Politics], Ph.D. thesis, University of Paris, 1967
al-Jisr, Bassim, *Le Pacte Nationale Libanais* [The Lebanese National Pact], Ph.D. thesis, University of Paris, 1978
Medzini, Arnon, *The River Jordan: The Struggle for Frontiers and Water: 1920–1967*, Ph.D. thesis, University of London, 1997
Salam, Nawaf, *L'Insurrection de 1958 au Liban* [The Insurgence of 1958 in Lebanon], Ph.D. thesis, Sorbonne University, Paris, 1979

Interviews conducted by the author
Muhammad 'Awdah, pan-Arab Egyptian writer, Cairo, 20 March 1989
Dr Boutros Boutros-Ghali, Egyptian Minister of State for Foreign Affairs in the 1970s and 1980s, Cairo, 15 April 1989
Nadim Dimashqieh, Lebanese chargé d'affaires in Cairo in the 1950s, London, 19

March 1990

Raymond Eddy, leader of *al-Kutlah al-Watania* Party (the National Bloc) in Lebanon, Paris, 19 July 1990

Sulaiman al-Firzili, Lebanese journalist, London, 6 March 1991

Amin Huwaydi, Egyptian head of Intelligence and Minister of National Guidance and Defence during the 1960s, Cairo, 14 April 1989

Anwar al-Jamal, Egyptian press attaché to Beirut 1957–78, Cairo, 1 April 1989

Bassim al-Jisr, Lebanese writer and journalist, Paris, 24 July 1990

'Addul Majid Farid, Egyptian ambassador in the 1950s and 1960s and head of President Nasser's office, London, 26 September 1988

Salim Nassar, Lebanese journalist and editor of *al-Safa'* daily, London, 13 March 1991

Mahmud Riad, Egyptian ambassador to Syria in the 1950s, adviser to President Nasser and the foreign minister of Egypt 1964–72, Cairo, 13 April 1989

Munah al-Sulh, Lebanese pan-Arab writer and journalist, London, 31 October 1990

Hamdi al-Tahiri, Egyptian diplomat who served in Beirut in the mid-1960s, Cairo, 20 April 1989

Secondary sources

Published books

Agwani, A.S., *The Lebanese Crisis, 1958: A Documentary Study* (Bombay: Asia Publishing House, 1965)

'Ajami, Fu'ad, *The Arab Predicament* (Cambridge: Cambridge University Press, 1981)

al-'Azm, Khalid, *Mudakkarat Khalid al-'Azm* [The Memoirs of Khalid al-'Azm], Vol. iii (Beirut: al-Dar al-Muttahidah lil-Nashr, 1973)

Dawisha, Adeed, *Egypt in the Arab World: The Elements of Foreign Policy* (London: Macmillan, 1976)

Dawisha, Karen, *Soviet Foreign Policy Towards Egypt* (London: Macmillan Press, 1979)

Dekemejian, Hrair, *Patterns of Political Leadership* (New York: State University of New York Press, 1975)

Diab, Mohammed, *Inter-Arab Economic Cooperation 1951–60* (Beirut: American University of Beirut, 1963)

Drysdale, Alasdair and Raymond Hinnebusch, *Syria and the Middle East Process* (New York, Council on Foreign Relations Press, 1991)

Eisenhower, Dwight D., *The White House Years: Waging Peace 1956–1961* (London: Heinemann, 1966)

Eran, Oded, 'Soviet Middle East Policy, 1967–1973', in Itamar Rabinovich, Itamar and Haim Shaked (eds), *From June to October: The Middle East Between 1967 and 1973* (New Jersey: Transactions Books, 1978)

Faris, Walid, *al-Ta'adudiah fi Lubnan* [Pluralism in Lebanon] (al-Kaslik, 1979)

Goria, Wade R., *Sovereignty and Leadership in Lebanon 1943–1976* (London: Ithaca Press, 1985)

Haikal, Muhammad H., *'Abd an-Nasser wal 'Alam* [Nasser and the World] (Beirut: Dar al-Hilal, 1972)

— *Malaffat al-Suways* [The Suez Files] (Cairo: al-Ahram Centre, 1986)

— *Sanawat al-Ghalayan* [The Years of Fury] (Cairo: al-Ahram Centre, 1988) al-Hakim, Mustafa Mahmud, *'Abd al-Nasser: Qadaya wa Mawaqif* [Nasser: Issues and Policies] (Beirut: Sawt al-'Uruba Publications, 1971)

Hammond, Paul Y. and Sidney Alexander (eds), *Political Dynamics in the Middle East* (New York: American Elsevier Publishing Co. 1972)

Hamrush, Ahmad, *'Abdel-Nasser wal-'Arab* [Nasser and the Arabs], Vol. iii (Beirut: al-Mu'assasa al-'Arabia lil-Dirasat wal-Nashr, 1976)

— *Shuhud Thawrat Yulyu* [The July Revolution's Witnesses] (Beirut: al-Mu'assasa al-'Arabia lil-Dirasat wal-Nashr, 1977)

Hasou, Tawfig Y., *The Struggle for the Arab World, Egypt's Nasser and the Arab League* (London: KPI, 1985)

Hilu, Charles, *Mudhakkirati: 1964–65* [My Memoirs] ('Araya: al-Matba'a al-Catholikia, 1984)

Hudson, Michael, *The Precarious Republic* (Washington: Westview Press, 1958)

Johnson, Michael, *Class and Client in Beirut: The Sunni Muslim Community and the Lebanese State 1840–1985* (London: Ithaca Press, 1986)

Kerr, Malcolm, *The Arab Cold War: 1958–1964*, Chatham House Series (Oxford: Oxford University Press, 1965 and 1975)

Korany, Bahgat and Ali E. Hillal Dessouki, *The Foreign Policies of Arab States: The Challenge of Change* (Washington: Westview Press, 1991)

Matar, Fu'ad, *Bisaraha 'an 'Abd al-Nasser* [A Frank Talk about Nasser] (Beirut: Dar al-Qadaya, 1975)

Matar, Jamil and Ali E. Hillal Dessouki, *al-Nizam al-Iqlimi al-'Arabi* [The Arab Regional System] (Beirut: Dar al-Mustaqbal al-'Arabi, 1979)

McDermott, Anthony and Kjell Skjelsbaek, *The Multinational Force in Beirut 1982–1984* (Miami: Florida International University Press, 1991)

McDonald, Robert W., *The League of Arab States: A Study in the Dynamics of Regional Organisation* (New Jersey: Princeton University Press, 1965)

Meo, Leila, *Lebanon, Improbable Nation* (Connecticut: Greenwood Press, 1976)

Murphy, Robert, *Diplomat Among Warriors* (London: Collins, 1964)

Nasr, Salah, *'Abd al-Nasser wa Tajribat al-Wahdah* [Nasser and the Experience of the UAR] (Beirut: al-Watan al-'Arabi Publications, 1976)

Nutting, Anthony, *Nasser* (London: Constable and Company, 1972)

Qubain, Fahim, *Crisis in Lebanon* (Washington: The Middle East Institute, 1961)

Rahmy, Ali Abdel Rahman, *The Egyptian Policy in the Arab World: Intervention in Yemen 1962–1967: Case Study* (University Press of America, 1983)

Riad, Mahmud, *The Struggle for Peace in the Middle East* (London: Quartet Books, 1981)

— *Mudhakkirat Mahmud Riad* [The Memoirs of Mahmud Riad], Vol. ii (Cairo: Dar al-Mustaqbal al-'Arabi, 1986)

Sa'adah, Antun, *al-'Athar al-Kamilah* [Complete Collection] (Beirut: SSNP Press, 1974)

Stebbins, Richard, *The United States in World Affairs, 1958* (New York: Harper and Brothers, 1959)

Stewart, Desmond, *Orphan with a Hoop: The Life of Emile Bustani* (London: Chapman and Hall, 1967)

al-Tahiri, Hamdi, *Siyasat al-Hukum fi Lubnan* [Politics in Lebanon] (Cairo: al-'Alamya

Press, 1976)
Weinberger, Naomi J., *Syrian Intervention in Lebanon: The 1975–1976 Civil War* (Oxford: Oxford University Press, 1986)

Selected newspapers
al-Ahram, Cairo
al-Akhbar, Cairo
al-'Amal, Beirut
Arab News, Jeddah
As-Sharq al-Awsat, London
La Bourse Egyptienne, Cairo
Le Commerce du Levant-Beyrouth Express, Beirut
Daily Telegraph, London
Dawn, Damascus
The Egyptian Gazette, Cairo
The Egyptian Mail, Cairo
Guardian, Manchester and London
al-Hayat, Beirut
al-Hayat, London
al-Jumhuria, Beirut
al-Jumhuria, Cairo
al-Mustaqilla, London
New York Herald Tribune, New York
New York Times, New York
Observer, London
al-Safa', Beirut
Scotsman, Edinburgh
The Sudan Daily, Khartoum
Sunday Times, London
al-Syiassah, Beirut
The Times, London

Selected magazines and periodicals
al-Afkar, Beirut
Akhir Sa'ah, Cairo
Arab Palestine Documents then re-titled *International Documents on Palestine 1971–1979* (Beirut: The Institute for Palestine Studies)
Ash-Shiraa, Beirut
Economic Review (The Central Bank of Egypt, CBE Printing Press, Cairo, 1969)
The Economist, London
al-Hawadiss, Beirut
al-Mussawar, Cairo
al-Mustaqbal, Paris
Rose al-Yussuf, Cairo
Summary of World Broadcasts, British Broadcasting Corporation, Caversham
al-Taqrir al-Iqtisadi al-'Arabi [The Arab Economic Report] (Beirut: The Union of

Arab Chambers of Commerce, June 1962)
al-Wasat, London

Articles in periodicals
Kerr, Malcolm, 'Lebanese views on the 1958 Crisis', *Middle East Journal*, Vol. 15, 1961
Vatikiotis, P.G., 'Dilemmas of Political Leadership in the Arab Middle East: The Case of the UAR', *International Affairs* (London: Royal Institute of International Affairs, London), Vol. 37, April 1961

Index